U.S. Multinationals and Worker Participation in Management

New Titles from
QUORUM BOOKS

The Uses of Psychiatry in the Law: A Clinical View of Forensic Psychiatry
Walter Bromberg

Abuse on Wall Street: Conflicts of Interest in the Securities Markets
Twentieth Century Fund

The Politics of Taxation
Thomas J. Reese

Modern Products Liability Law
Richard A. Epstein

U.S. Multinationals and Worker Participation in Management

THE AMERICAN EXPERIENCE IN THE EUROPEAN COMMUNITY

Ton DeVos

Q

Quorum Books WESTPORT, CONNECTICUT

Library of Congress Cataloging in Publication Data

DeVos, Ton, 1926-
    US multinationals and worker participation in management.

    Bibliography: p.
    Includes index.
    1. Collective bargaining—International business
enterprises—European Economic Community countries.
2. Employees' representation in management—Europe-
an Economic Community countries. 3. Corporations,
American—European Economic Community countries—
Personnel management. I. Title.
HD6660.5.D48   658.3'152'094   80-23597
ISBN 0-89930-004-9 (lib. bdg.)

Library of Congress Catalog Card Number: 80-23597
ISBN: 0-89930-004-9

First published in 1981 by Quorum Books

Greenwood Press
A division of Congressional Information Service, Inc.
88 Post Road West, Westport, Connecticut 06881

Printed in the United States of America

10   9   8   7   6   5   4   3   2   1

For permission to reproduce materials, we are indebted to the following:

Table 5 from John H. Dunning, *U.S. Industry in Britain*, Gower Publishing Co., Ltd., Hampshire,
England, 1976, p. 50. Used with the permission of the publisher.

Figure 6 is reprinted by permission of the *Harvard Business Review*. Exhibit from "Changing
Employee Values: Deepening Discontent?" by Michael R. Cooper, Brian S. Morgan, Patricia
Mortenson Foley and Leon B. Kaplan (January-February 1979). Copyright © 1979 by the
President and Fellows of Harvard College; all rights reserved.

To Vaughn
with love and admiration

CONTENTS

FIGURES

TABLES

PREFACE

This book represents the convergence of several interests. It evolved, first of all, from my interest in the role multinational corporations play in the transmission of values across national boundaries. Almost all the literature on this topic has focused on the way MNCs have impacted on host-country cultures. This volume pays more attention to the inverse impact. The key question dealt with here is: has the experience of American business managers in Europe had any effect on the way they conduct labor relations in the United States?

This study was also stimulated by my interest in one of the less obvious, yet very crucial, problems facing persons living and working in democratic societies. The answer to this problem must have a very important effect on the overall success of such societies. That problem is: how can a person who is constantly being socialized to participate democratically in the politics of society be content to spend most of his energy and waking hours within the context of the hierarchical, authoritarian politics that characterizes so many industrial enterprises? Or posing the question from a different angle: how realistic is it to expect workers to be content and constructive in a non-democratic work process if they have been socialized to think of themselves as individuals whose ideas have value for society as well as for themselves?

My considerable appreciation of and preference for the academic style of work life, in which faculties have traditionally been given extensive opportunities to participate in the determination of certain university policies, have left me with the gnawing question of why others could not similarly experience dignity and individuality within their work environments. All arguments against the expansion of participatory opportunities given by either autocratic university administrators or by those who defend the sacred rights of property have never satisfied me. I, therefore, became understandably fascinated by what seemed to be happening in the workplaces of different West European countries. The experience there with worker participation did not necessarily provide me with the perfect solution to the dissonance problem or to the question of individuality and personal dignity. It did, nevertheless, indicate that governments, employers, and trade unionists were making an interesting attempt that was distinctly different from that pursued on this side of the Atlantic.

My two interests converged as American business investments in Europe increased dramatically and as an increasing number of Stateside newspapers, business periodicals, and academic journals began to speculate whether worker-participation practices might be imported to the United States. I decided that what was needed at this point was a study of the American experience in Europe that placed the subject in a broader context and that would particularly emphasize the relationship of that experience to American values and workplace-reform experiments.

This monograph is the product of original research as well as of a review of the existing literature. The original information was obtained by direct observation, personal interviews, and the examination of primary sources. This was done in various locations in Western Europe and at the International Labour Organisation headquarters in Geneva. Approximately sixty interviews were conducted with managerial personnel of American multinational companies in Europe, with U.S. Chamber of Commerce officials, with national and international trade unionists, with officials of national and international employer organizations, with high-ranking personnel of the European Commission, with national government officials, and with academicians. Some of these interviews were with delegates to the 1976 World Employment Conference of the International Labour Organisation.

No conscious attempt has been made to separate the information obtained through original research from that acquired from a review of the literature and public sources. This style of presentation was selected for two reasons. First, much of the original research was done to double-check for possible biases in the published materials. This seemed to be a necessary research strategy since a certain amount of the literature came from sources that had, rightly or wrongly, been accused of entertaining institutional or ideological loyalty to the interest groups that were contenders in this issue area. The second reason for writing in this manner was that the study was not designed to reach only academicians who specialize either in worker participation or in industrial relations. I am frankly much more interested in informing generalists and, even more particularly, those who have or expect to have managerial responsibilities in American industrial corporations. It is they who need to discover that the experiments with democracy in the workplace in Western Europe have not been as disastrous and irrelevant to American business interests as some people would suggest.

The structure of this book is rather simple. The first four chapters describe the American business community in Western Europe, its value commitments, its reputation, and its experiences with worker participation in the United States. The next two chapters deal with the West European trade-union movement and its responses to American multinationals, as well as with the general picture of worker participation in the various European Community countries. Subsequent chapters review how U.S. multinationals have responded to the European laws and practices and how much impact their experience seems to have already had, and will probably have, on the Stateside practices of these companies.

I would be distinctly amiss if no acknowledgment were made of the different kinds of support given me in this project. The Faculty Research and Development Council of Trinity University provided a large part of the necessary financial support. Extremely valuable logistical support was extended by many people from the ranks of employers and of labor. Special mention should be made, however, of the courtesies extended by Wilhelm E. Stoermann of the International Labour Office and by Albert Tévoédjrè and Hans Günter of the International Institute of Labour Studies. These three gentlemen and their staffs deserve considerable thanks. Numerous other persons graciously granted me interviews, made referrals, and provided me with materials, all of which has given me ample opportunity to present as accurate and complete an account as is humanly possible. My close friend and colleague Philip Detweiler, Willyn Cobb, Dorothea Grigsby, and a series of student assistants have made their own particular contributions. Each of them deserves my heartfelt thanks. The greatest contribution certainly was made by my wife, who not only endured all the extensive traveling and interviewing, but who was also most particularly helpful in getting me to express myself more clearly and directly.

The ultimate responsibility for what has been written here is, as usual, totally and irrevocably mine.

U.S. Multinationals and Worker Participation in Management

1

AMERICAN INVESTMENT IN EUROPE

In 1967, Jean-Jacques Servan-Schreiber wrote: "Fifteen years from now it is quite possible that the world's largest industrial power, just after the United States and Russia, will not be Europe, but American industry in Europe.[1] With these words, he opened his stimulating discussion of what he perceived to be *The American Challenge (Le défi américain)*, a book that became a best-seller. It seemed that finally someone had taken the bold, analytical look that "Americanization," or the "American takeover of Europe," deserved.

What Servan-Schreiber projected for the 1980s, however, had been described numerous times before, most particularly at the turn of the century and again around 1930.[2] Thus, what to many lay persons in the sixties appeared to be a totally new phenomenon—that is, extensive direct investment by American multinational corporations in Western Europe—was really nothing new.

Already in 1801, American traders in cotton and other products had organized an American Chamber of Commerce in Liverpool, England, and manufacturing operations apparently began as early as 1810. In that year, Joseph Dyer and associates became involved in the manufacture of cotton spinners and other textile machinery in Manchester, an operation that was expanded into France some fifteen years later.

The most significant acceleration occurred after the Civil War, when the same men who had been successful at home began to apply their ingenuity to production and marketing overseas. They eagerly sought to capitalize on existing demand and to awaken the spirit of consumerism that has always been the prime stimulant of business expansion. While Isaac Singer peddled and manufactured his sewing machines, Alexander Graham Bell and Thomas Edison competed and merged—as opportunity and necessity required—to acquire a major share of the European telephone-equipment business. Edison made his light bulbs; Eastman, his photographic plates; Westinghouse, his brakes. Meanwhile, Rockefeller sold his oil products, and J. P. Morgan extended his banking business.

European outcries about American "commercial aggression" are also ironic because the accelerated growth of direct investment by American multinational corporations can be explained to a considerable degree as having resulted from European initiatives. Direct investment by American businesses became almost inevitable after national governments raised their tariffs and began to practice preferential purchasing of homeland products and local patent laws began to require the "working" of registered inventions. Given the imaginative and buoyant spirit of the American business community, the inevitable happened. Their reactive strategies were just as important as were the other motivations for direct investment: a desire to cut transportation costs, to warehouse materials and products closer to the market so that demand could be met more speedily and consistently, to develop products lines and designs more particularly suited for markets of different culture and language, and last but not least, to attack local competitors in their own backyards.

Table 1 shows the nature and location of some of the American firms that had built or bought controlling interests in manufacturing plants in Western Europe by 1914. Most striking is the preponderance of Great Britain and Germany as locations for these subsidiaries, a fact that undoubtedly reflects their more advanced stage of industrialization, the size of their markets, as well as a certain amount of cultural affinity. Both countries have continued to be prime investment areas. The list of firms also indicates the wide range of products involved.

Regardless of the degree of American business expansion into Europe, for most of the period from 1860 to 1914, the United States was mainly an importer rather than an exporter of capital; its total pre-World War I worldwide investments only amounted to some $3.5 billion.[3] Most of these investments were direct — that is, investments by multinational corporations in subsidiaries rather than purchases of noncontrolling segments of foreign corporate stocks (so-called portfolio investment). Also, only about one-fifth of total U.S. direct investment was in Europe, a figure that includes such countries as Russia and Austria, which are not members of the current European Communities.[4]

In contrast, in 1914, British investments overseas amounted to a book value of $8.3 billion; French, $8.7 billion; and German, $5.6 billion. In that year, even the foreign holdings of Belgian, Dutch, and Swiss investors exceeded those of American individuals and corporations.[5] The bulk of the European overseas investments tended to be more portfolio-oriented. Being more clearly designed for short-term profit, they were less visible and thus caused less turmoil and political backlash than the American presence, which, not only brought American products, but also American managers and American ways of merchandising.

Business expansion at home generally stimulates overseas expansion. Such was also the case in the twenties, when American direct investment in Europe virtually doubled; it increased from a book value of $694 million in 1919 to $1,353 million in 1929. (See Table 2.) This growth rate was essentially the same for all U.S. overseas investments, yet it was significantly lower than

Name of Firm	GREAT BRITAIN	GERMANY	FRANCE	ITALY	BELGIUM	NETHERLANDS
Alcoa			x			
American Bicycle		x				
American Chicle	x					
American Cotton Oil						x
American Gramophone	x	x	x			
American Radiator	x	x	x	x		
American Tobacco	x	x				
Carborundum	x	x				
Chicago Pneumatic Tool	x	x				
Colt	x					
Diamond Match	x	x				
Eastman Kodak	x		x			
Ford	x		x			
General Electric*	x	x	x			
Gillette	x	x	x			
Heinz	x					
International Harvester		x	x			
International Steam Pump	x	x	x			
International Telephone and Telegraph**	x	x	x	x	x	
Mergenthaler Linotype	x	x				
National Cash Register		x				
Norton		x				
Otis Elevator	x	x	x			
Parke, Davis	x					
Quaker Oats		x				
Sherwin-Williams	x					
Singer	x	x				
United Shoe Machinery	x	x	x			
Westinghouse Air Brake	x	x	x			
Westinghouse Electric	x		x			

Sources: Mira Wilkins, *The Emergence of Multinational Enterprise,* and Raymond Vernon, *Sovereignty at Bay*, who added some data to the Wilkins table. (Wilkins, pp. 212-13; Vernon, pp. 72-73.)

*General Electric in Germany, France, and Italy contracted with (and did not control) local manufacturing firms.

**ITT operated under a different name in that time period.

TABLE 2   U.S. Direct Investment in Europe, 1897-1940

	Total	Manu-facturing		Sales		Petroleum		Utilities		Mining	
	mil. $	mil. $	%	mil. $	%	mil. $	%	mil. $	%	mil. $	%
1897	131	35	(26.7)	25	(19.1)	55	(42.0)	10	(7.8)	—	
1908	369	100	(27.1)	30	(8.1)	99	(26.8)	13	(3.5)	3	(0.8)
1914	573	200	(37.7)	85	(14.8)	138	(24.1)	11	(19.2)	5	(0.9)
1919	694	280	(40.3)	95	(13.7)	158	(22.8)	5	(0.7)	—	
1929	1,353	637	(47.1)	133	(9.8)	239	(17.7)	138	(10.2)	37	(2.7)
1940	1,420	639	(45.0)	245	(17.3)	306	(21.5)	74	(5.2)	53	(3.7)

Source: Wilkins, Emergence, p. 110.

Note: The percentages do not total 100. Direct investments of insurance companies are not broken down, and Ms. Wilkins suggests that they may make up a large part of the difference.

those for South and Central America, which were 158.6 percent and 124.1 percent, respectively. Thus, the American presence in Europe remained substantially smaller than in Latin America ($3,706 billion) and not even as large as that in Canada ($1,657 billion).[6]

The Great Depression not only called for retrenchment or a holding pattern, it also brought a whole new array of government regulations in national economies in Europe as well as in the United States. Investigations into the causes of the depression as well as of World War I prompted a large number of questions about the free-enterprise system and business combinations, not least of all about business combinations that were international in operation.

Very few American firms were willing to run the financial and political risks that would flow from purchasing or establishing new subsidiaries in such a hostile climate. In addition, many felt that it would be much more patriotic to contribute to economic recovery at home than to become embroiled in European power politics. And, more importantly and practically, Europeans did not have the capability to purchase many American products. The only significant expansions in the thirties came in the area of sales and petroleum, the latter clearly reflecting the continuing growth of the automobile culture.

The most spectacular growth in American direct investment in Western Europe came in the late fifties and especially in the sixties. From a value of $6.7 billion in 1960, its book value had risen to $24.8 billion by the end of the decade. For the first time in the history of U.S. overseas investment, the total interests in Europe exceeded those in Canada and even those in Latin America. The bulk of this postwar investment again occurred in Great Britain. By 1960, the United Kingdom had in fact become the second most popular country for Americans to invest in, with a book value of

$3.194 billion which was still considerably below the $11,198 billion invested in Canada, its Commonwealth partner.[7]

However, the pattern of investments by American multinationals began to change during the sixties. When it became clear that Britain would not enter the Common Market, American multinationals began to jump the tariff wall. By 1970, American subsidiaries in the six Common Market countries had assets valued at $11,695 billion, an increase of $2,644 billion since the beginning of the decade, a growth of 342.3 percent. Direct investments in Britain increased only 150.9 percent; nevertheless, they remained a very significant element in the total American investment pattern in Europe. The book value of U.S. investments in the United Kingdom in 1970 was still $8,015 billion, an amount that almost equaled the investments in all Common Market countries combined.[8]

West Germany remained the most attractive investment target within the Common Market, a pattern that was undoubtedly related to the German people's reputation for industriousness as well as to the country's past technological accomplishments. However, other factors were as persuasive to investors: the size of the market; the comparative prosperity of its consumers; the stability of its labor relations system; and its commitment to free enterprise. By 1970, U.S. direct investment in the Federal Republic had a book value of $4,579 billion, almost twice the amount invested by American multinationals in France, and three times the amount for Italy, Belgium-Luxembourg, and the Netherlands.

THE AMERICAN PRESENCE IN THE LATE SEVENTIES

By the beginning of 1979, American direct investment in the then-expanded Common Market amounted to $55,283 billion, which was almost a third of worldwide total U.S. investment of $168.081 billion. This made Europe substantially more important to American multinationals than either Canada ($37.280 billion) or the combined Latin American countries ($37.509 billion).[9] Within the European Communities (as the Common Market had become known), direct investments were distributed as shown in Figure 1.

The United Kingdom remained the prime investment area in the European Communities, with Germany a somewhat distant second and France continuing to have a much smaller share than its relative size of population and per-capita GNP seemed to warrant. Even more disproportionate was Italy's share. The relative significance of these latter two countries to American multinationals stands out especially when direct investments there are compared with those in Belgium-Luxembourg and the Netherlands. Figure 2 traces this distribution pattern over time.

The pattern in which American multinationals have become distributed over the different European Community countries can be explained in a

FIGURE 1 U.S. Direct Investment in EEC Countries, Year-End 1978

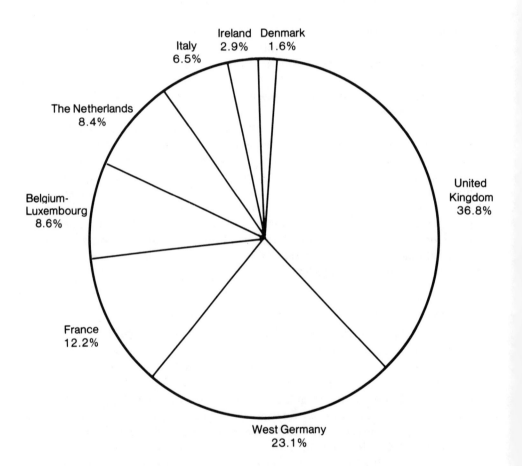

Source: Based on data from *Survey of Current Business*, August 1979, p. 27.

FIGURE 2 Country Shares of
U.S. Direct Investment in the EEC, 1950-1979
(by percentages)

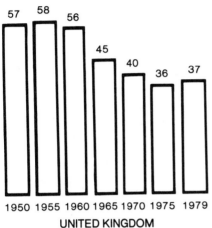

UNITED KINGDOM

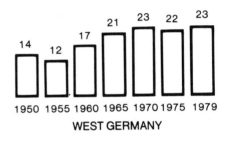

WEST GERMANY

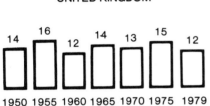

FRANCE

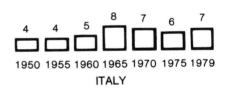

ITALY

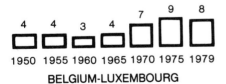

BELGIUM-LUXEMBOURG

THE NETHERLANDS

Source: Based on *Survey of Current Business* data.

variety of ways. It is partly the result of the postures and policies of the various countries. Also quite important are the social and economic characteristics of different locations. The third independent variable is the way in which the potential investors view the situation. For example, most countries obviously tend to welcome the creation of new jobs and, therefore, offer a variety of tax incentives and occasionally grants to attract new investors, whether domestic or foreign. However, while such countries as Germany, Britain, and the Netherlands have been particularly open to foreign investments, France and Italy have generally been more restrictive. National governments have also differed in the manner in which they have channeled funds available through European Communities organs and programs. Some of these differences result from the social and economic features of the particular countries. European Coal and Steel Community grants and loan guarantees are clearly available only for projects in areas where the coal and steel industries predominate. Similar limitations apply to moneys available through the European Regional Fund; only those countries that have distinctly underdeveloped regions qualify for these.

Having an attractive incentive program and having access to European Communities funds do not themselves guarantee investor interest. Individual investors may still be hesitant to take risks, whether that hesitancy flows from their evaluation of the situation or whether it is based on purely economic considerations such as a limited market or a poor transportation system.

At certain times—especially when a country is in dire need of new jobs—another factor can become extremely important. Under such circumstances, a multinational corporation that projects a particularly large investment and that is shrewd in the art of negotiation can obtain some very attractive, directly tailored investment packages from a government that is more needy and resourceful than its competitors. Such direct-assistance arrangements not only include sizable grants, they may well involve several additional perquisites, which could include free industrial land, free construction of transportation terminals, as well as reduced utility rates for the initial period of operation of the facility. There have been numerous cases in which very attractive bargains have been struck, and where one national government has outbid another.

A typical case of a multinational bargaining with national governments was that of the Ford Motor Company in early 1979. Having obtained a very attractive incentive package from the British government two years before, the company began to contact West European governments a year and a half later to determine their interest in the construction of a new automobile-assembly plant. The company preferred to build in Spain, and the Spanish government was asked to grant a cash subsidy equal to 35 percent of the cost of plant, subsidies to defray the costs of training programs, tax reductions, exemptions from import duties for needed machinery (that could not be obtained locally), and loans from state banks. The Spanish turned down the opportunity—at least under such conditions. Other governments indicated their interest, however. The Belgian, French, German, and British put in their bids. An intense effort was made by Chancellor Bruno Kreisky of Austria, who was facing elections in May and who had already negotiated unsuccessfully for car plants with Porsche, Mitsubishi, Chrysler, Fiat, and the Soviet government. In the end, nobody got the projected $750 to 900-million plant. The company decided, instead, to expand existing facilities, at a combined outlay that was later in the year projected to total about $5.8 billion by 1985. Chancellor Kreisky finally did succeed, though. He obtained an engine-assembly plant project from General Motors, which also announced plans in the summer of 1979 to build a new parts-making plant in Spain, both components of its $2-billion expansion program for Europe.[10]

One of the most striking features of the way American multinationals have distributed their investments over the various EC countries is the relatively small investment total for France and Italy. In both cases, the main reason appears to be related to the perceptions of the investors, whether such perceptions conform to reality or not. Not only do potential investors see ideological and confrontationist trade unions, they also have been more concerned about the politics within these countries: Communist parties have obtained sizable voter support there, and the ability of the French and Italian governments to manage their nations' affairs consistently and predictably has been sincerely questioned. There is also uncertainty about their commitments to private property. In addition, the leftist commitment of these governments made it extremely difficult for plant managers who felt compelled to lay off large numbers of workers (something that is especially true in France), and has significantly increased local labor costs through the imposition of rather high social-insurance charges.

The situation in France was unique. When General de Gaulle came to power in 1958, it appeared that the country's politics would become much more stable and that governmental policies would become more pragmatic. However, French pragmatism did not last long. Governmental attitudes toward foreign investment soon became apprehensive, distinctly less inviting, and, finally, quite hostile. The government's apprehensions did not result only from irrational nationalism. It is true that many nationalist politicians began to express concern about American acquisitions of well-known local firms. However, a considerable amount of aversion was also caused by the way the Frigidaire Division of General Motors and the Remington Company handled massive layoffs in 1963. The breaking point was reached in 1966 when the United States government prohibited Control Data Corporation from selling two large computers to the French Atomic Energy Commission.

The French government responded to this sequence of events with its so-called Frenchification program legislated in December 1966. This program sought to prevent further foreign, and particularly American, takeovers of key French industries, and planned to shift decision-making powers from foreign to French boards of directors. In the future, foreign acquisitions exceeding 20 percent of equity were to be approved by the government if such investments were projected for nuclear power, data processing, telecommunications, machine tool, and aerospace industries.[11] In appropriate cases, American companies were bought out.

French restrictions eased by the second half of 1969. As soon as the Frenchification program was initiated, the European Commission alerted the French government to the fact that the program violated its Treaty of Rome commitments to the free flow of investments. These commission protestations and consequent legal actions did not provide as much relief, however, as did the political demise of President de Gaulle and the evolution of the more pragmatic Pompidou and Giscard d'Estaing regimes.

Matters changed even more strikingly when the French Left failed to gain control of the National Assembly in the spring of 1978. France, more than ever before, was becoming very attractive to American investors. Two months after the election, General Motors divulged plans to build a plant for automobile heater cores and assemblies; six months later, they announced plans to build a new Delco Remy battery plant in the Lorraine. Quaker Oats, Caterpillar, Chrysler, and Merck had already expanded their investments in the preceding year, a year in which American investment in France grew by some 25 percent. It is thus quite possible that the French share of American MNC investments in Europe will become proportionally much larger than it has been, particularly if French politics remain stable, if labor remains relatively cheap, and, of course, as long as French consumers continue to prosper.

Italy's secondary position as an American investment target, which is even smaller than that of France, is of relatively long standing. Even the Italian government's liberal investment incentives have not been able to attract American firms in very meaningful numbers and with large enough stakes. Nor is the low cost of Italian labor attractive. As long as the country's politics are perceived by investors as being very risky and as long as antibusiness terrorism continues, American multinationals will probably prefer to make their contribution to Italy's welfare indirectly. They seem to prefer hiring Italians as guest workers in their plants in other European countries, such as Germany, rather than opening plants or offices in Italy itself.

The relative attractiveness of the Netherlands, Belgium, and Luxembourg is partly the reverse of the French and Italian cases: their politics have been generally stable, labor productivity has been good, and the governments of these Low Countries have generally been very hospitable to foreign investment. Probably equally important is the role played by Rotterdam and Antwerp. Both port cities handle a large volume of transit trade into Germany and into the industrial areas of northern France. Not to be ignored either is Brussels, which serves as host city to the European Commission and as the headquarters of the North Atlantic Treaty Organization. Holland's attractiveness is, to some extent, due to its being the home base of several very aggressive, powerful multinational enterprises, and to the extensive international experience of its business community. Not only do these factors make Holland an attractive source of personnel recruitment, they also make it a logical battleground for meeting one's competitors' challenges in the home market, a strategy that is widely used by international business enterprises.

The Low Countries did not fare very well in the middle and late seventies. Belgium not only had considerable difficulty in holding on to established American investments (Chevron Oil and Control Data were only two of more than one hundred firms that pulled out in 1975 and 1976 alone), but it became even less effective in attracting new money. By 1977, American firms had dropped from a 1959 share of nearly two-thirds of all foreign investment in Belgium to a comparatively meager 28 percent share. New foreign investment in manufacturing dropped 86 percent during that same period.[12] These trends have been duplicated to some extent in Holland.

For years, American companies showed little interest in investing in the Irish Republic. All that began to change, however, when that country entered the European Economic Community and started to make concerted efforts to attract multinationals. Undoubtedly, investing in Ireland became more attractive as it became clear that good profits could be made there. For example, while American manufacturing firms earned an average pretax return on investment of 12 percent in the entire European Community (and only 5.4 percent in Britain), their profits in Ireland amounted to 29.5 percent. The impact of such earnings was magnified even more because of the country's tax policies. Apparently, Ireland is the only European Communities country that exempts from taxation all profits made on exports, and most of the products of American multinationals are exported.[13] The only problem that foreign investors have to cope with in Ireland is its occasionally unstable labor relations.

The attractiveness of Britain is generally based on cultural affinity and on its early commercial ties with the United States. Not only were the first American plants in Europe generally built in the United Kingdom, but these operations also frequently served as initial bases (rather than from Stateside headquarters) for the further internationalization of American marketing and manufacturing. Early American investors needed British international trade experience and made good use of such supportive service industries as banking and insurance, which were widely available there.

Britain proved attractive for other reasons as well. Free enterprise prevailed there. The British entrepreneurial class has always been as strongly committed to the market system as has its American counterpart. In addition, British labor relations were unregulated for most of the nation's history, even though its trade unions were more political than American unions, and the Labour party became increasingly important in the country's politics.

One other consideration must have played its part, although hardly anyone mentions it: labor costs in Britain have been very low compared to those in the other European countries. In 1977, for example, the hourly labor cost in British manufacturing was less than $4.00, compared to Germany, Belgium, Holland, and Denmark, where it was more than twice that amount. Even French and Italian workers earned significantly more at that time.[14]

The British share of American investments should improve as firms continue to withdraw from continental locations, where expenses have become higher and higher. Also, more and more corporations are centralizing their operations, both administratively as well as in terms of production, on the early bases they had developed in the United Kingdom.

It is not only important to consider how American multinationals have distributed their direct investments over the various countries in Europe; it is equally important to look at how they are apportioned by industrial sectors (see Figure 3). In general, American investments are made predominantly in manufacturing, even though that sector's share of the total investment is gradually diminishing.[15] Almost one-fourth of all dollars are in petroleum, with the trade sector and the finance-insurance sector coming behind but showing steady growth.

When the totals for American investment in manufacturing are broken out into the more specialized subsectors, it becomes evident how large a share of U.S. investment is involved in the manufacturing of machinery (34.2 percent), with chemicals and allied products (22.4 percent) and transportation equipment (14.7 percent) following behind. Investments in the manufacture of food products and metals are definitely less significant (7.6 percent and 4.1 percent, respectively). These book-value figures do not indicate the volume and value of the sales of the various product lines nor the number of persons employed by American firms in the several subsectors. The employment figures are most distinctly affected by the comparative capital and labor intensity of the subsectors—that is, the manufacture of some products requires a heavier investment in production or processing machinery and/or a larger number of workers than does the production of other goods.

Figure 4 shows the distribution of U.S. investments in manufacturing from 1955 to the beginning of 1979 in several European Community countries. As a general category, they have basically been distributed in the same pattern as has the total of American direct investments. However, there are some interesting variations both over countries and time. For example, the United Kingdom has generally had a larger share of the manufacturing dollar than any other country; nevertheless, it has found its importance halved since the fifties, losing much of its relative standing to Germany, the Netherlands,

FIGURE 3 U.S. Direct Investment in the EEC by Industrial Sectors, Year-End 1978

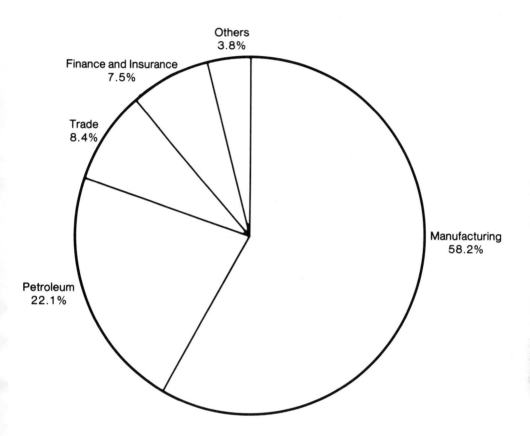

Source: Based on Data from the *Survey of Current Business*, August 1979, p. 27.

TABLE 3 U.S. Direct Investment in Manufacturing by Countries and by Industrial Subsectors, Year-End 1978 (in millions of dollars and in percentages)

	Total	Country Share (%)	Machinery Total	Machinery Country Share (%)	Chemicals and Allied Prod. Total	Chemicals and Allied Prod. Country Share (%)	Transportation Equipment Total	Transportation Equipment Country Share (%)	Food Products Total	Food Products Country Share (%)	Metals Total	Metals Country Share (%)	Country's Share of Total Investment in EC Countries (%)
United Kingdom	$10,070	31.3	$3,121	28.3	$2,060	28.5	$1,472	31.0	$908	37.3	$377	28.5	36.8
Germany	8,324	25.9	3,098	28.1	1,370	19.0	*	‡	388	16.0	*	‡	23.1
France	4,629	14.4	1,782	16.2	772	10.7	*	‡	325	13.4	110	8.3	12.2
Italy	2,389	7.4	1,181	10.7	543	7.5	*	‡	200	8.2	*	‡	6.5
Belgium-Luxembourg	2,812	8.7	1,064	9.7	817	11.3	258	5.4	*	‡	104	7.9	8.6
The Netherlands	2,523	7.8	637	5.8	847	11.7	87	1.8	334	13.7	203	15.4	8.4
Denmark	159	0.5	49	0.4	*	‡	†	—	*	‡	11	0.8	2.9
Ireland	1,276	4.0	84	0.8	*	‡	†	—	*	‡	31	2.3	1.6
TOTAL in EC	$32,182		$11,016		$7,219		$4,741		$2,433		$1,321		
The subsector's share of U.S. investment in EC manufacturing			(34.22%)		(22.4%)		(14.7%)		(7.6%)		(4.1%)		

Source: Survey of Current Business, August 1979, p. 27.

*Data suppressed to avoid disclosure of data of individual companies.
†Investments are very small.
‡Data not available.

FIGURE 4 Country Shares
of
U.S. Direct Investment in EEC Manufacturing
1955-1979
(by percentages)

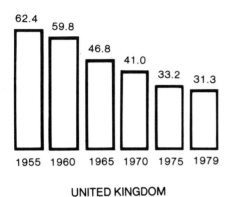

UNITED KINGDOM

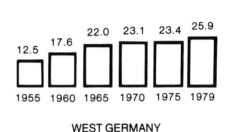

WEST GERMANY

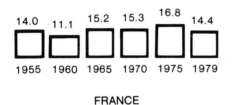

FRANCE

ITALY

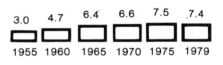

BELGIUM-LUXEMBOURG

THE NETHERLANDS

Source: Based on (Survey of Current Business data.

and Italy. Table 3 completes the information given in Figure 4 by identifying Ireland's 1978 share to be 4.0 percent and Denmark's 0.5 percent; it also shows the particular pattern in which manufacturing investments are distributed over subsectors as well as over countries.

Even though the United Kingdom has had a large number of dollars invested in the manufacture of machinery, the proportional shares of American money in this subsector for Germany, France, Italy, and Belgium-Luxembourg are greater. While the machinery subsector in the total EC attracted only slightly more than one-third of the total American investment in manufacturing, the percentages for Italy and France were 49.4 and 38.4. In fact, machinery production in Italy and France has attracted more dollar investments than any other industrial sector or subsector. Germany's share of U.S. investments in the machinery subsector (in addition to that in the manufacturing of transportation equipment, about which more will be said later) comes closer to Britain's share than in any other area. Also striking is the comparatively small U.S. stake in machinery production in Ireland and the Netherlands.

In chemicals and allied products, Great Britain clearly dominates, with Germany and France proportionately far behind. The relatively heavier American investments in this subsector are located in Belgium, the Netherlands, and Ireland.[16] In the first two countries, in fact, American investments in the chemical industry amounted to 29.1 percent and 33.6 percent of total U.S. investment in manufacturing, as compared to 22.4 percent for the entire European Community.

West Germany and the United Kingdom clearly have been the favorite locations for American investments in the manufacture of transportation equipment—primarily, the production of automobiles. Published data for earlier years bear this out. In fact, at year-end 1975, Germany very definitely had the largest share (40.5 percent) of all American dollars invested in EC transportation-equipment manufacturing); Britain trailed with a 32.9-percent share. At that time, France and Italy, for whom no year-end 1978 figures have been released either, had only 9.7-percent and 4.3-percent shares.[17] Table 3 figures do not suggest any drastic changes in that earlier picture.

Even though American investments in food processing are not very significant in the context of the total U.S. presence in any of the countries, it is quite clear that Britain is very attractive in this subsector also. So is the Netherlands. However, some striking changes have been taking place in the food-industry investment patterns. At the beginning of 1976, Holland's share of American investments was only 8.8 percent; three years later, it had grown to 13.7 percent. In that same period, Britain's share fell from 41.2 percent to 37.3 percent.

Great Britain, the Netherlands, and Denmark have also been able to attract a larger-than-proportionate share of the American investment in petroleum, which should not be surprising considering the recent exploitation of oil and natural gas in the North Sea. What is important, however, is how rapidly the United Kingdom's share of this sort of investment grew in recent years. (See Figure 5.) At year-end 1975, it amounted to an already healthy 40.4 percent (considerably above Britain's overall investment share of 35.6 percent); three years later, it had grown to 48.6 percent.

Impressive also is the picture for Denmark. Here, American investments in petroleum (a 49.7-percent share in 1978) have tended to dominate all other American investments, although that dominance is not as great as it was three years earlier, when they made up 60.3 percent of the total investment there. The petroleum investments in Holland, nevertheless, are still three times as large and almost as much as all American investments in Denmark combined.

American investments in trade operations are distributed in a somewhat different way. In this particular sector, France has been especially attractive. Its trade-dollar share compares well with its overall investment share. Not noticeable from the published figures for year-end 1978, however, was the role played by Belgium-Luxembourg. The data for 1975 indicated that their share then was 15.6 percent, which was almost double their general investment share at that time. Holland also appears to be an important center for American trade activity.

What stands out about the investments in the banking and insurance industry is the obvious importance Americans in this industry attach to London. The United Kingdom attracted almost half of this sort of investment in the EC (almost as disproportionate a share as the British role in the petroleum industry and probably also related to that). Equally outstanding is the significance of Belgium-Luxembourg. Third-ranking in this sector has been Germany, at least in terms of the proportionality of its share of the American banking- and insurance-investment dollar.

THE IMPACT OF THE AMERICAN PRESENCE

There are several ways to determine the significance of the American presence to the economy of the European Communities. One way is to consider the number of subsidiaries and the number of people employed by them. One conservative estimate suggests there are about seven thousand firms, with a combined payroll of more than two million persons. Some of these firms are genuine giants. Several years ago, The Economist reported that ITT alone employed more than two hundred thousand; Ford, more than one hundred forty thousand; General Motors, more than one hundred ten thousand; and IBM, close to one hundred thousand.[18]

The magnitude of some of these subsidiaries becomes evident also when one realizes that forty-four of the five hundred largest European-based

FIGURE 5 Country Shares
of
U.S. Direct Investment in EEC Petroleum, 1955-1979
(by percentages)

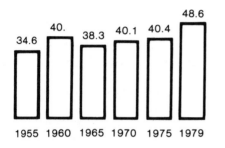

UNITED KINGDOM

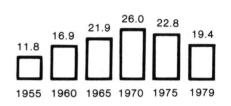

WEST GERMANY

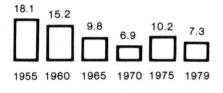

FRANCE

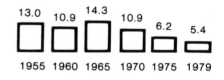

ITALY

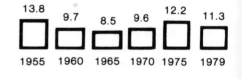

BELGIUM-LUXEMBOURG

THE NETHERLANDS

Source: Based on *Survey of Current Business* data.

companies are American-owned, and that two-thirds of the total American investment in Western Europe has been held by only twenty firms! Esso Deutschland (an Exxon subsidiary), Adam Opel (a General Motors property), Ford Werke, and IBM-Deutschland have rather consistently ranked within Germany's top twenty-five companies. In France, the local Exxon and IBM affiliates generally have been among the top twenty. The British operations of Exxon and Ford and American Tobacco are of similar proportional significance.[19]

The Ford Motor Company has some seventy thousand employees in the United Kingdom alone and more than fifty thousand in Germany. Even more awesome in this context are the sizes of the ITT work forces in EC countries: some sixty thousand in Germany, forty-two thousand in Britain, twenty-one thousand in France, and twenty thousand in Italy. Undoubtedly, the wage scale and the total industrial-relations systems of such large firms will have their impact on the labor-relations configurations of the host countries.

In its most extensive analysis of American foreign investments, published in 1973, the Senate Finance Committee looked at the impact of the American presence in Europe in another way.[20] It not only compiled the sales and employment figures for U.S.-owned affiliates, it also computed what share these subsidiaries had of the total sales and employment of the major manufacturing sectors of several European Community countries. (See Table 4.) Even though the picture has changed somewhat, the report at least represented the reality at the beginning of the seventies and, at minimum, makes a significant impression of the contemporary situation.

The Finance Committee study, for example, showed how important the American presence has been to Belgium and Luxembourg. When American-owned affiliates obtain 82 percent of the sales and employ more than half the workers in one subsector (rubber products), when they employ two-thirds of the workers in another (instruments), and come close to obtaining half the sales in three sectors (chemicals, machinery, and instruments), one could say that American firms must have a great impact on that nation's economy, if not also on its social and political system. It certainly makes the appointment of Harvey Firestone as U.S. ambassador to Belgium a much more interesting story.

American rubber companies are not only dominant in Belgium, but in Britain as well. Their 1970 share of that sector's employment was rather impressive, and those figures become even more interesting when it is pointed out that the share increased threefold since 1966.

The one manufacturing sector that apparently has been dominated most widely by U.S.-owned affiliates is the instruments industry. The American share of that sector's 1970 employment ranged from a low of 7 percent to a high of 27 percent (in Britain), and its share of sales was even larger. While U.S. subsidiaries in France made one-fifth of the 1970 sales in that country, their share in Britain was a most impressive 56 percent.

TABLE 4   U.S. MNC Share of Sales and Employment in Major Manufacturing Sectors, 1970 (in percentages)

Sector	United Kingdom		West Germany		France		Belgium–Luxembourg	
	Sales	Employment	Sales	Employment	Sales	Employment	Sales	Employment
Chemicals	21	14	7	4	12	7	48	21
Transport equipment	27	14	25	17	8	6	18	6
Machinery								
nonelectrical	21	12	11	6	14	6	41	28
electrical	18	10	6	5	8	8	43	32
Primary and								
fabricated metals	10	8	7	4	2	2	6	6
Food products	10	5	4	4	3	3	5	6
Paper and allied products	5	3	2	2	8	6	19	18
Instruments	56	27	25	13	20	7	45	67
Textiles and apparel	1	*	1	1	*	*	10	7
Rubber	31	26	11	4	6	4	82	56
All manufacturing	16	8	8	5	6	4	16	13

Source: U.S., Congress, Senate, Committee on Finance. Implications of Multinational Firms for World Trade and Investment and for U.S. Trade and Labor. (Washington, D.C.: Government Printing Office, 1973). The percentages for employment were extracted from pp. 709-23; sales, from pp. 733-47.

*Negligible.

This rather general picture becomes even more vivid when the figures are broken out for particular countries and for narrower product lines. (Table 5 does this for Great Britain.) Although the data are several years old, the table gives rather valid impressions, even if only for the early seventies.

The impact of American multinationals on the French economy was not much different from that on the United Kingdom in the early and middle sixties. One OECD report indicated that American subsidiaries in France produced 95 percent of the carbon black; 90 percent of the synthetic rubber; 87 percent of the razor blades; 70 percent each of the computers, sewing machines, confectionary, and biscuits; 60 percent each of the agricultural machinery, elevators, photographic products, equipment for telecommunications, telegraphs, and telephones, electric razors, and semiconductors. These figures represent only those product lines in which American firms clearly dominated. Circumstances in Germany were not quite the same: the computer industry was apparently the only one in which Americans were particularly powerful in the sixties. The American share of that industry in 1964 was reported to be 75 to 77 percent.[21]

The most publicized case of dominance of a product market by a singular company throughout the European Community has been the IBM story. In the early sixties, this company not only monopolized the computer business in Great Britain, France, and Germany, and the other EC countries, but by 1968, it still owned 57.1 percent of the computers installed in Germany, 30.4 percent in Great Britain, 65.7 percent in France, 68.8 percent in Italy, and 51.8 percent in Belgium, the Netherlands, and Luxembourg.[22] The company operates seven research and development laboratories, scientific centers in six countries, fourteen manufacturing plants, twenty-six support centers, over one hundred fifty computer centers, and more than three hundred sales locations in Europe.

A second market in which American firms play an extremely significant role is the European car and commercial-vehicle market. Some observers even call Ford and General Motors the only truly European car manufacturers, because they are, in terms of their production and merchandising organizations, more oriented to the European market than are their home-grown competitors. Such firms as Fiat, Volkswagen, and Renault have remained much more national in their orientation.

U.S. car subsidiaries have consistently produced more than one-fourth the total number of cars and trucks manufactured in the European Community. Even though that share must be smaller now since Chrysler sold all its European operations to Peugeot-Citroën, Ford and General Motors are European industrial powers to be reckoned with, even if only because they have a worldwide production organization to support them. The figures for the United Kingdom and Germany are most striking. For example, since

TABLE 5   U.S. MNC Share of Particular Products Produced in the United Kingdom, 1973

It has been possible to compile a list from a number of sources of the approximate share in 1971 of the total production of all British enterprises of various products accounted for by American-financed companies. In some cases, their share of the total goods bought by British consumers will be less because of the contribution of imports.

Percentage:

80 or more	Boot and shoe machinery, cameras, photocopying equipment, carbon black, cash registers, color films, starch, canned baby foods, typewriters.
69-79	Aluminum semimanufactures, breakfast cereals, calculating machines, cigarette lighters, domestic boilers, sewing machines, spark plugs.
50-59	Cake mixes, commercial vehicles, computers, cosmetics and toilet preparations, crawlers and tractors, dog and cat foods, electric shavers, electric switches, pens and pencils, cars, petroleum refinery construction equipment, synthetic detergents, canned milk, vacuum cleaners.
40-49	Abrasives, agricultural implements, electronic and measuring and testing instruments, ethical proprietaries (drugs sold to National Health Service), locks and keys, printing and typesetting machinery, razor blades and safety razors, refined petroleum products, rubber tires, safes, locks, latches, etc., watches and clocks.
30-39	Agricultural tractors, commercial vehicles, contractors plant (graders), excavators, dumpers, etc., floor polishers, foundation garments, instant coffee, potato chips, elevators and escalators, portable electric tools, polystyrene plastics, refrigerators, washing machines.
15-29	Greeting cards, materials handling equipment, medicinal preparations, machine tools, paperback books, petrochemicals, polyethylene plastics, man-made fibers, telephones and telecommunications equipment, tobacco products, toilet tissues.

U.S. firms are also important producers of specialized automatic transmission equipment, copper tubing and nickel alloys, cork products, electric blankets, chocolates and sweets, kitchen apparatus, laundry machinery, ophthalmic products, plastic semimanufactures, refined platinum, polishes, canned soup and vegetables, processed cheese products, caravans and trailers, mining machinery, distilled whisky. Outside the manufacturing industry, they are especially strongly represented in advertising, credit and financial reporting, market research, and the production and distribution of films. American firms account for more than 15 percent of the bank deposits in Britain. Three of the leading car rental companies are U.S.-owned, as are several publishing companies, hotels, and supermarkets.

Source: John H. Dunning, *U.S. Industry in Britain* (Hampshire, England: Gower Publishing Co. Ltd., 1976), p. 50. Used with the permission of the publisher.

the middle fifties, Ford alone has been manufacturing more than a fourth of both the cars and the trucks in Britain. Combined with General Motors, its share of British commercial-vehicle production has been close to 40 percent. Ford UK has even been its host country's third largest exporter. In Germany, Ford and Opel (the GM affiliate) have been doing about 40 percent of the car and truck manufacturing.[23]

American multinationals have not only been playing a key role in the manufacture of entire automobiles, they have been equally powerful in the production of car components. This line of manufacturing has involved more than just the established automobile companies. Typical of the not-so-easily-recognizable participants in this sector is Rockwell International, which is already the biggest Stateside manufacturer of heavy truck axles. Rockwell recently bought up and joined into ventures in the United Kingdom and elsewhere in the EC with a combined capacity that promises it will also become the biggest axlemaker in Europe.[24]

PUBLIC AND ELITE OPINIONS ABOUT AMERICAN INVESTMENT

A foreign business presence of the magnitude just described, not only can be expected to have a distinct impact on its host countries, logically, it may well arouse considerable apprehension among public leaders as well as the general public. A series of studies bears this out.

One distinct problem seems to be the tendency of many people to over-estimate the size and impact of the investments by American multinationals. In 1969, for example, a British research organization found that 51 percent of the civil servants and 67 percent of the businessmen in their sample of middle- and senior-management personnel definitely exaggerated the percentage of British industry owned by American firms.[25] One in four business executives even estimated Americans to own more than half of their country's industrial establishment. When asked whether they thought the extent of American ownership was likely to change, 93 percent of the civil servants and 88 percent of the business people said they expected it to increase.

Five years later, samples of the general public in Great Britain, France, West Germany, and the Netherlands were asked what they considered to be the most serious disadvantage or criticism of multinational companies.[26] Twenty percent of the public in these four countries thought it was their capability to "get a stranglehold on whole sectors of the economy and, as a consequence, [to] threaten the existence of local national companies." In Germany, 25 percent of the public selected this to be most serious. When respondents were asked which multinationals—European, Japanese, American, or other origin—they considered to be most powerful in their own countries and in Europe, American companies were predominantly selected. One in three also considered them to be the most uncontrollable, the less socially concerned, and the most dishonest. More recent polls of elite opinion reflect other kinds of apprehensions.

A 1975 private poll of a stratified sample of 2,449 senior executives in business, the professions, and government, conducted for ITT-Europe, found that in Germany, France, Italy, and Spain, from 78 to 94 percent of the respondents were either critical or very critical of multinational companies.[27] Their critical attitudes were reflected in their agreement with such statements as "MNCs are not sufficiently concerned with the interests of the countries in which they operate," "The power of MNCs often means that they behave as if they were above the law," "Most MNCs take out more than they put into the countries where they operate," and "The growth of international companies tends to lead to price fixing and monopolies."

The following year, the Euro-Baromètre, an EEC-wide survey conducted for the European Commission, found that 45 percent of the "leaders" among the respondents considered controlling the activities of multinational corporations a very important problem. Granted, this issue was not rated as important as unemployment, rising prices, environmental protection, consumer protection, housing construction, and education reform. Nevertheless, they judged it to be significantly more vital than defense of the countries' interests against the superpowers and the strengthening of military defense. It is particularly noteworthy that this same issue ranked first among the problems that were of greater concern to leaders than to nonleaders.[28]

Even though opinions about the general phenomenon of multinational corporations cannot automatically be read as opinions about American-owned firms, they do serve as rough indicators. This is particularly so since people, when asked to name some multinationals, tend to name American firms even more than those multinationals headquartered in their own country.[29]

PROSPECTS FOR THE FUTURE

Several things have happened recently in relation to American investment in the European Community. First, a number of American firms have divested themselves of all or part of their European holdings. Typical of this phenomenon is Chrysler Corporation's selling out to Peugeot-Citroën. While some firms found themselves in trouble at home and were therefore compelled to pull back from overseas, they and others also made some drastic mistakes and could not avoid adjusting. Whatever the reasons, American divestments have increased significantly.

Second, the general rate of U.S. direct investment has slowed down. The recession of the seventies—Stateside as well as in Europe—took its toll. Neither the divestments nor the slowed rate of investment suggests that all American firms will withdraw. The European market is far from saturated. Nor will the community cancel the kind of external tariffs that help make direct foreign investment not only advisable but even imperative. The odds are that the tariffs will become higher rather than lower.

The third phenomenon, and possibly the most interesting one, is the extent to which European-based firms have moved into the home territory of the American multinationals. Not only has direct foreign investment in the United States generally skyrocketed during the seventies (from a total book value of $13 billion in 1970 to more than $40 billion by year-end 1978), but a number of European-based multinationals are deeply anchored in the American economy. For example, one of the earliest foreign-owned companies in the United States, Shell Oil, a subsidiary of the Royal Dutch Petroleum Company and the British Shell Transport and Trading Company, is clearly one of the nation's major oil companies. Equally awesome and established is the Nestlé Corporation, which does more business in the States than such well-known American firms as Heinz, Standard Brands, and Campbell Soup do in the entire world! This type of sales record has resulted partly from some significant Nestlé acquisitions, not least of which were Stouffer Foods; Libby, McNeill and Libby; and Crosse & Blackwell.[30] The mention of these household names as being European-owned opens a virtual Pandora's box of subsidiary names and European acquisitions. It certainly requires mention of such names as Lever Brothers, Norelco, Lipton, Keebler, Beecham, Brown & Williamson, American Petrofina, Grand Union, Fed Mart, W. R. Grace, Miles Laboratories, Foster Grant, Bantam Books, U.S. Borax, Ohrbach's, Gimbel's, Saks Fifth Avenue, Travelodge, Coats & Clark, Cutter Laboratories, and Copperweld—all of them owned and controlled by European multinationals.

With the dollar weak, foreign investors have been able to make the kind of generous offers that few American businessmen could turn down. And, even as the dollar improves its standing and the stockmarket recovers, European multinationals are in the United States to stay. They, like the American companies in Europe, must cut transportation costs, must provide for a consistent supply, and must tailor their goods to the peculiarities of the local market. In other words, there are an increasing number of European firms that have reached the stage of development in which foreign direct investment is an imperative if they want to continue growing, if not merely to survive.

This European invasion of their home economy presents the American multinational corporations with a new set of circumstances and challenges. They clearly are no longer the dominant force in the world of international business. At home, they are faced with overseas competitors who are as knowledgeable, as shrewd, and, now, also as experienced as they have been known to be. Overseas, their operations may still be impressive and of considerable consequence to many host-country economies; however, they can be outflanked at any time by aggressive competitors. If there was ever a time not to take things for granted and not to be too casual about American business overseas, it is now. Only those who take their affairs seriously and who are willing and able to take some risks will survive in the days to come. The days of high profits and chauvinistic posturing may well be gone forever. These are the times of an increasingly interdependent global economy and of governments that are less submissive and less tolerant of the ethnocentric behavior of foreign investors. American businessmen can no longer insist on doing things the American way. When in Europe, they will increasingly have to do as the Europeans do. In fact, there may be a number of lessons to learn from one's competitors, including new ways of distributing authority in the workplace and in the boardroom.

NOTES

1. J.-J. Servan-Schreiber, *The American Challenge* (New York: Atheneum, 1968), p. 3.

2. Mira Wilkins's two-volume history, *The Emergence of Multinational Enterprise* and *The Maturing of Multinational Enterprise* (Cambridge: Harvard University Press, 1974), gives an excellent review. Most of the historical data in this section are based on her work. She also reports that the phrase "the American invasion of Europe," which was first used by an Austrian minister of foreign affairs in the 1890s, soon came to be used regularly in titles and texts of commentaries, for example, B. H. Thwaite's *The American Invasion* (London, 1902) and Fred A. McKenzie's *The American Invaders* (London, 1901). (*Emergence*, p. 71).

3. Wilkins, *Emergence*, p. 201.

4. Ibid., p. 110.

5. Ibid., p. 201.

6. Ibid., p. 55.

7. *Survey of Current Business*, vol. 41, August 1961, p. 22.

8. *Survey of Current Business*, vol. 51, October 1971, p. 32.

9. *Survey of Current Business*, vol. 59, August 1979, p. 27. Rainier Hellman's *The Challenge to U.S. Dominance of the International Corporation* (Cambridge, Mass.: Dunellen, 1970) contains an analysis similar to that presented here. It is more detailed; however, its statistics have become rather dated.

10. *The Economist*, January 20, 1979, pp. 72-73, and *The Wall Street Journal*, June 6 and 8, 1979.

11. See "The Institutionalization of Interdependence: Elements of British, French, and West German Economic Foreign Policy," Norman A. Graham and Carl F. Lankowski. Paper presented at the 1977 Annual Meeting of the International Studies Association, St. Louis, Mo.

12. *The Economist*, November 11, 1978.

13. *The Economist*, February 4, 1978.

14. Ibid.

15. These figures, and those cited in the following discussion, are again taken from the *Survey of Current Business*, vol. 59, August 1979.

16. Even though the year-end 1978 figures have deleted the specific figures for Ireland, *Survey of Current Business* reports of previous years (and other sources)

had already established the relative significance of Ireland's role in the chemical subsector.

17. *Survey of Current Business*, vol. 56, August 1976, p. 39.

18. *The Economist*, September 10, 1977.

19. *The Economist*, October 21, 1978, and *Restrictive Business Practices of Multinational Enterprises* (Paris: Organization for Economic Cooperation and Development, 1977), p. 11.

20. U.S. Congress, Senate, Committee on Finance, *Implications of Multinational Firms for World Trade and Investment and for U.S. Trade and Labor* (Washington, D.C.: Government Printing Office, 1973), pp. 709-23 and 733-47.

21. *Gaps in Technology* (Paris: Organization for Economic Cooperation and Development, 1970), p. 29.

22. *Fortune* 80 (August 15, 1969): 88.

23. Y. S. Hu, *The Impact of U.S. Investment in Europe: A Case Study of the Automotive and Computer Industries* (New York: Praeger Publishers, 1973), pp. 23 and 26.

24. *The Economist*, July 7, 1979.

25. Published in Michael Hodges, *Multinational Corporations and National Government: A Case Study of the United Kingdom's Experience, 1964-1970* (Lexington, Mass.: Lexington Books, D. C. Heath, 1974), p. 141.

26. George Peninou, Manfred Holtus, Dietrich Kebschull, and Jacques Attali, *Multinational Corporations and European Public Opinion* (New York: Praeger Publishers, 1978), pp. 62, 70, and 69.

27. *European Attitudes to Multinationals* (Brussels: ITT Europe, 1976).

28. *Euro-Baromètre No. 5* (Brussels: Commission of the European Commission, July 1976), p. 6. The ITT survey showed 66 percent of the German, 66 percent of the French, 73 percent of the Italian, and 80 percent of the Spanish elite agreeing with the statement that "International companies should be more strictly controlled in their operations than they are at present."

29. *The Economist*, June 17, 1978, p. 91.

30. An interesting account of the Nestlé initiatives is Robert Ball's "Nestlé Revs up Its U.S. Campaign," *Fortune* 8 (February 13, 1978): 80-90. A more complete analysis of European direct investment is contained in the U.S. Department of Commerce's *Report to Congress on Foreign Direct Investment in the U.S.* (Washington, D.C.: Government Printing Office, 1976). Several more recent studies are contained in Hugh D. Menzies, "It Pays to Brave the New World," *Fortune* 90 (July 30, 1979): 86-91.

2

THE AMERICAN PERSPECTIVE ON
INDUSTRIAL DEMOCRACY

Several years ago, a number of people were predicting that worker representatives would soon not only be sitting on company boards in Britain but that this practice would then also be introduced in Canada and the United States. The probability of such a thing happening and of its becoming common practice in the States obviously hinges on a variety of factors. Not least of these is the way in which relevant elements in the American community perceive the nature and extent of management prerogatives and workers' rights. This chapter focuses, therefore, on some of the general mindsets of Americans, on the perspectives on industrial democracy of the American business and labor communities; on the ways these may be changing; and on some of the reasons such changes may be occurring.

GENERAL AMERICAN MINDSETS

Committing generalizations about how a certain people perceive reality is admittedly risky business. Any such propositions certainly deserve to be subjected to the most rigorous scrutiny. Nevertheless, some generalizations will be introduced here. What we must do is examine them in the light of three distinct understandings. One is that all national cultures contain subcultures—either regional, socioeconomic, ethnic, or occupational. It should also be understood that individuals will clearly differ from one another even though they may all be part of the same general socialization process. The third caveat is to remember that there are considerable ambivalences and contradictions in perceptual screens. Not only do individuals and peoples see things differently over varied points in time, they also tend to hold contradictory views.

The general mindset that is most uniquely American is optimism. This optimism is the product of a variety of cultural traits. It is, in the first place, an integral part of the Judeo-Christian heritage within which the Messiah is expected to deliver the nation and the benevolent God is known to provide for the needs of his children. American civic religion is permeated with a gospel of hope, with a faith in the inevitable victory of good over evil,

31

and with the knowledge that progress is inevitable. This kind of civic-religious faith dovetails with the optimistic assumptions underlying the democratic philosophy. Even though the latter does not project man and human institutions to be perfectable, it certainly contains the tenet that if men reason for themselves as well as together, they can improve their lot and their institutions. The true believer in democracy "knows" that democratic politics and government are man's ultimate, if not divinely ordained, destiny, even if merely because it allows individuals to reason for themselves and to achieve their life goals to the best of their abilities and motivation. Americans continue to believe that anyone can become president, anyone can succeed; all it takes is determination.

Inversely, many Americans have tended to consider the absence of success, including the experience of poverty, as a product of laziness, irresponsibility, or stupidity. A large percentage of those who have succeeded in life have been inclined to view manual laborers either as people who were on their way up the success ladder or as undermotivated failures who were satisfied with their six-pack and their Monday-night football. In fact, many manual workers themselves have been convinced that they could rise out of their less desirable circumstances if they worked harder, played their cards better, or got the right break. Others have made it; so can they. The result of all this is that, generally, little patience has been felt for those who did not seem to strive for success. Some people even came to see underachievers as parasites and predators who were, not only "feeding on the public trough," but who were, above all, hell-bent on taking away (through taxation, transfer payments, and collective bargaining) that little amount of wealth for which the ambitious worked so hard and made so many sacrifices. Many of these attitudes are still very prevalent today.

Another manifestation of American optimism is the denial by many people that the nation has had or is having any problems, whether these problems would be social, economic, or political. In this vein, many an American corporate manager's rosecolored glasses keep him from fully knowing or understanding the private lives of his employees. He certainly tends to have little awareness of the fate of the unemployed, virtually all of whom he has never personally known and who live in the parts of town that he rarely, if ever, frequents. On the other side of the fence, optimistic and naive employees (and people outside the business world) do not have the slightest idea or understanding of the physical, mental, and emotional stresses experienced by most managers and entrepreneurs.

In optimistic America, critics of the nation's way of life are called "doom-sayers." At times, these "radicals" have even been given the suggestion to leave it if they don't love it. Reformers are readily labeled "ivory tower dreamers" or "social tinkerers," whose bent to planning is judged to be more related to communism and totalitarian politics than to American freedom. All the while, if problems are not expected to solve themselves, the American optimist knows that they *can* be solved if the nation were only determined to commit itself.

This American optimism is not without its ambivalence; even the most optimistic person has his pessimistic moments. Some would even suspect that those people who are so strongly optimistic may well be manic-depressives, swinging from moods of extreme optimism to moods of extreme pessimism. This can certainly be the case sometimes with the American people.

While they are generally optimistic about how things will turn out, Americans can also be very pessimistic about specific dimensions of the human reality. For example, many Americans are very pessimistic about the nature of man. A widespread belief in the ennobling and enriching quality of competition is frequently accompanied by an almost-compulsive inclination to distrust others. Many assume that it is a dog-eat-dog world, in which everyone seeks to overtake you, if not to rob you of all you have and are. Accordingly, many workers are convinced that their employers are trying to get by with paying them as little as possible. They also "know" that management constantly opposes public policies that are in the interests of the workers while at the same time seeking to maintain their tax loop-holes, their government subsidies, and their government contracts (with their liberal cost-overrun provisions). From their vantage point, employers are convinced that inflation is mainly caused by unreasonable wage demands by the unions, by cost-of-living clauses in labor contracts, and by excessive public (that is, welfare) spending.

American optimism is distinctly coupled with a second mindset: individualism. When Martin and Lodge (for the purpose of surveying the ideological perceptions and expectations of *Harvard Business Review* readers) sought to summarize the individualist philosophy, they did it succinctly. They suggested the value system of the traditional "American way" to read something like this:[1]

The community is no more than the sum of the individuals in it. Self-respect and fulfillment result from an essentially lonely struggle in which initiative and hard work pay off. The fit survive and if you don't survive, you are probably unfit. Property rights are a guarantor of individual rights and the uses of property are best controlled by competition to satisfy consumer desires in an open market. The least government is the best. Reality is perceived and understood through the specialized activities of experts who dissect and analyze in objective study.

This sort of mixture of optimism and individualism can readily lead to the axiom that "if everyone would just take care of himself and his dear ones, no one would be experiencing injustice." With man's responsibility defined as primarily to himself and to his own self-interest, adversary relationships (another term for competition) are seen not only as natural but as the foundation stones for economic, social, and political justice. From such a perspective, the marketplace appears to be the most sublime form of human interaction, a format that frequently appears to be judged best for all social systems, including the workplace.

When this compulsive appreciation for the adversary process becomes coupled with the American propensity toward moralism, talk about consensus-building and common good become very suspicious. Negotiation, a basic road to consensus, becomes identified as betrayal because everyone knows that persons of moral integrity do not compromise their principles. A true believer does not sit down with the devil; he certainly does not sell out to him. To the dichotomizing moralist, consensus procedures like collaboration, consultation, and codetermination easily appear to be immoral and unnatural. Such practices appear to be "un-American" and more indicative of collectivism than individualism.

When individualism is fused with a belief in the inevitability of conflict, it is difficult to generate a national sense of social consciousness and conscience. Even though contemporary European elites may not be as convinced that "noblesse oblige," as were their countries' earlier, more established elites, many European "haves" still do feel a sense of obligation toward those who have been less fortunate. As such, they do not tend to shy away from engaging in socioeconomic policies that are designed to deal with such problems as poverty and unemployment. In contrast, many prosperous Americans—most of whom are "nouveaux riches"—exhibit the paranoia of the recently arrived. To many of them, what has been gained through hard work and struggle can also be quickly lost and should therefore be carefully preserved. Thus, American acts of reconciliation are frequently limited to voluntary gestures of benevolence through such institutions as the United Fund, the service club, the church, or the telethon, or through individual, personal acts of assistance rather than through public policy. Rarely is it contemplated that the causes for the hurt and agony of the poor may lie in some of the nation's basic institutions and policies.

Americans frequently portray themselves as pragmatic and practical, in the sense that they consider themselves not to be ideologues. This characteristic is then linked to an apparently widespread dislike for abstract philosophies, utopian doctrines, and monolithic ideologies, and to a general hesitation to embrace social schemes that seem to be built upon idealistic, unrealistic "pipedreaming." It is said that most Americans will certainly accept radically new arrangements and institutions but that they will only do so if and when they can see their payoff. When they are convinced that these proposals will work, it is argued, they will embrace "responsible" sociopolitical innovations as readily as they have embraced innovations in science and technology.

One could as easily argue almost the exact opposite. It could be asserted that most Americans are politically very conservative. To begin with, the basic Madisonian formula of American government is designed to be incrementalist—that is, it seeks to produce stability through very gradual change rather than to represent the multiple nuances and changes in opinion and attitudes. The same is true about the nation's social and economic institutions. Thus, most Americans are quite doctrinaire in the way they wave off and ridicule those who challenge the social, economic, and political status quo.

Any characterization of the general American perspective on life would be incomplete if mention were not made also of the prevailing propensity toward materialism. It is accepted practice in the States to equate success with material achievement and to assume, as suggested in the Martin-Lodge formulation quoted above, that when a person experiences material rewards, he or she will know personal fulfillment. Accordingly, "everybody knows" that stockholders are predominantly interested in bigger dividends; managers, in bigger salaries and more liberal stock options; and workers, in more pay. Justice, therefore, has frequently been defined in terms of attaining material awards that are comparable to those of others. Not only are all persons expected to be given equal opportunity, but such equal opportunity is frequently assumed to bring about equal material success for all those who apply themselves. Thus, the motivating force of life is broadly perceived to be the desire to get as big a slice of the pie as one's neighbor—to keep up with the Joneses.

There may be some problems with assuming that the only goal is more material wealth, particularly when one considers some of the findings of the Opinion Research Center.[2] Its analysts have found, for instance, that increasingly workers expect more from their jobs than just good pay. Hourly and clerical workers, particularly, have indicated increased dissatisfaction with their companies' failure to show respect for them as individuals. They also have been very critical about the limited degree to which companies have been "doing something about" the workers' problems and complaints. These attitudes are especially striking when they are examined alongside the higher ratings workers have been giving company pay rates. (See Figure 6.) Pay is clearly not the sole key to making a worker happy.

A second manifestation of the materialistic mindset is the apparent inclination to see labor as just another factor of production, as a commodity of an economic status not much above that of raw materials or capital funds and certainly of a lesser genre than entrepreneurial spirit and skill. Particularly in times of recession and unemployment, many workers find themselves con-

FIGURE 6 Changing Employee Attitudes

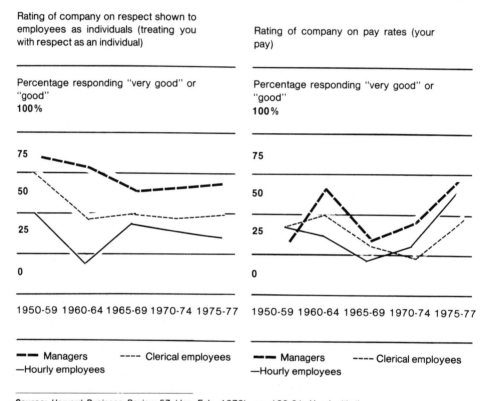

Rating of company on respect shown to employees as individuals (treating you with respect as an individual)

Rating of company on pay rates (your pay)

Percentage responding "very good" or "good"
100%

Percentage responding "very good" or "good"
100%

75
50
25
0

1950-59 1960-64 1965-69 1970-74 1975-77

75
50
25
0

1950-59 1960-64 1965-69 1970-74 1975-77

━━ Managers   ---- Clerical employees
—Hourly employees

━━ Managers   ---- Clerical employees
—Hourly employees

Source: *Harvard Business Review* 57 (Jan.-Feb. 1979), pp. 120-21. Used with the permission of the publisher.

sidered to be mere commodities, "whose human qualities," as Richard Pfeffer suggested, "are irrelevant to their disposition." In such times, they perceive themselves to be mere objects of decisions made in the marketplace, decisions that are transmitted to them by impersonal corporate bureaucracies.[3]

The impression that workers have become mere factors of production may well have been magnified by the introduction of the corporate form of business organization and by the increasing size of the business firm. In such a context, the manager's first responsibility is to maximize profits for the stockholders rather than to champion economic, social, and political justice for the members of his corporate household. In addition, the ever-larger physical and social distances between the people in the shop and the ultimate decision makers at corporate headquarters have made workers see management as heartless, calculating automatons who only read balance sheets and draw exhorbitant salaries. Many workers see the corporate manager as incessantly driven to achieve the ultimate pinnacle of corporate success—the chairmanship of the board—even if that requires stepping over the dead bodies of workers and colleagues.

Curiously enough, many Americans appear to be so sold on the inevitable merits of the market mechanism, and so absorbed in the assumption that justice and goodness will prevail in the hearts of men, that they have basically ignored the cynicism that these points of view represent, or they simply have accepted them as natural, inevitable dimensions of the struggle for the survival of the fittest.

While there may appear to be considerable consensus in the American community on the merits of the free-enterprise system, business has not fared well recently in the public's esteem. Public-opinion pollsters such as Harris, Gallup, and Yankelovitch have all reported how little confidence the public appears to have in the management of the large corporations, in the fairness of the balance between corporate profits and the public interest, and in the "honesty, dependability and integrity" of businessmen.[4] In the spring of 1979, 28 percent of Gallup Poll respondents even judged "big business" to be the greatest threat to the country in the future.[5]

THE VALUE SYSTEM OF AMERICAN CORPORATE MANAGERS

There is one thing on which most observers of American business readily agree: most of them are convinced that the prime concern of corporate managers is profit maximization. A manager's career obviously hinges on his ability to deliver an optimum and, if at all possible, an increasing return on investment. Such an achievement, not only makes stockholders happy and benefits most managers directly because of their stock options, but it also provides an objective, easily quantifiable gauge of the manager's effectiveness. A person may be a good manager of corporate human resources, but if the optimizing of human talents does not also produce greater efficiency—more production for each dollar invested—any other definition of "good human resource management" will easily be regarded as a corporate luxury.

The supremacy of the profit-maximization objective is borne out by various systematic studies. Seider, for example, analyzed the content of some five hundred speeches delivered by top officers of American industrial corporations between 1934 and 1970. He found business oratory to be dominated by such classical ideological themes as the necessity of profit as a bulwark of the free-enterprise system and the necessity of the market as its regulatory mechanism. Those particular creeds were used more frequently in the executives' speeches than any other themes, which included nationalism, a perception of management as trustees of all the firm's interests, and the need for management to do its professional job well.[6]

In a more specifically related research piece by Abouzeid and Weaver in which corporation executives were asked to list the four goals their companies judged to be most important, "financial" goals were listed by 97.7 percent of the respondents. Following at some distance were: "growth and expansion" 79.1 percent; "efficient utilization of resources" 54.1 percent; and "company stability" 51.8 percent. And when the same 220 respondents were asked which goal their corporations considered the dominant goal, to which all other goals were subordinate, 144 (or 63.6 percent) identified the "financial goal."[7]

A second prime goal of American corporate executives is the maximization of entrepreneurial freedom, which Vogel suggests has certainly been the case since the Civil War. Rather than make a blanket condemnation of governmental intervention in the economic life of the society, corporate management has judged that practice mainly on the intervention's effect on management's autonomy. The key concern has been: will this governmental action strengthen or weaken the entrepreneur's discretion to invest, produce, and market? Thus, governmental subsidies, loan guarantees, and legal protection of the right of property have been welcomed and even solicited, provided, of course, that the cost, in terms of the loss of managerial autonomy, would not be too great. Autonomy-minimizing interference has only been acceptable to corporate management when patriotism and national security made it imperative or inevitable, and such acceptance generally has waned rapidly as the imminent danger passed and the passion of collective commitment wore off.[8]

Since governmental infringements in the United States have not been the working of totalitarian or authoritarian regimes, management's fear of government has not simply been a fear of nondemocratic government and its propensity to interfere in the freedoms of persons. Vogel suggests that the opposite is the case: it is the relatively democratic nature of their political system that has made the fears of American management so vehement. It has been the government's openness to the political clout of such nonbusiness, anticorporate elements as the small farmers, organized labor, welfare-rights advocates, the consumer movement, environmental protectionists, and the welfare- and government-regulatory bureaucrats that has led, in management's understanding, to the imposition of the highly despised curtailments on management's autonomy.[9]

It is not surprising, therefore, to find some of the nation's leading business managers utter such antidemocratic statements as:

We are dinosaurs at the end of an era. There is a shift of power from industry and commerce to masses who cannot cope with the complexities of the modern world. Dolts have taken over the power structure and the capacity of the nation in the U.S. as well as in Western Europe.

One man, one vote will result in the eventual failure of democracy as we know it.

The normal end of the democratic process gives unequal people equal rights to pursue happiness in their own terms.

A representative democracy has never worked in the history of the world and we are seeing that here. Autocracy has always followed democracy.[10]

Statements like these make American businessmen sound ominously undemocratic and elitist. Nevertheless, studies like the now-somewhat-dated international survey of managerial thinking by Haire, Ghiselli, and Porter show that American managers have considerably more confidence in the capacity of the average human being than do the corporate managers in thirteen other industrialized countries. What American managers say on questionnaires, however, is not necessarily what their organizational behavior indicates. As these University of California psychologists concluded: "The fact remains that the tremendous majority of American businesses are still run on a tight rein—highly centralized and supervised."[11] This sort of discrepancy between the values pronounced and the values lived is similar to the paradox between what some have called the public ideology of the American people and their stances on specific policy questions. Most Americans passionately declare themselves in favor of such long-honored principles as freedom of speech and of association. However, when it comes down to allowing anti-American overseas students to demonstrate in a public square, or to tolerating persons who belong to and support the Socialist Workers party, many Americans immediately draw the line. The nation of Thomas Paine and Thomas Jefferson also has within its legacy the Alien and Sedition Acts, McCarthyism and the Red Scare, and the Ku Klux Klan. It is possible, therefore, that when management says it places confidence in the worker, such a statement does not automatically mean that worker representatives will be considered to be persons of equal corporate governance rights or that they would be welcomed as members of the corporate board of directors.

The business community's hostility toward governmental interference and the democratic process, Vogel suggests, really reflects a possible broader intolerance directed toward all nonbusiness institutions and nonmarket roles.[12] He hypothesizes that, in fact, American big business was never seriously challenged until the New Deal days. It was then that the trade unions obtained their magna charta, the federal bureaucracy blossomed and reached its maturity, and the brain trust introduced the use of academics in government. The Great Depression also seemed to change the minds of many who were previously enthusiastic supporters of big business, a change of heart that increasingly became reflected in a variety of governmental regulatory policies. Many members of the business community have not felt comfortable about majority rule since.

There is a curious contradiction between what is generally expected to be the businessman's pragmatic perspective on life and his frequently ideological, antagonistic posture toward trade unionists, bureaucrats, and "eggheads." It would be assumed that a practically oriented, calculating manager would make a complete and accurate assessment of situations. Vogel suggests, however, that managers, in contrast to entrepreneurs, tend to be of a bureaucratic mentality, preoccupied with survival and success and thus blind to the nature of the world outside the business firm, and unable to understand it so that they might shape it.[13] Whether or not this characterization is accurate, it is a fact that many corporate managers have become ideologues—that is, they appear to make large numbers of a priori judgments, especially concerning management's autonomy.

The prime example of management theories that are based on hasty judgments, and specifically those about the creativity and independence of mind of the worker, was Taylorism. This management philosophy has dominated the larger American workplaces for much of this century. Frederick W. Taylor's theory of scientific management views the worker strictly mechanistically. It claims that by scientifically developing the best way of doing each work task and by thoroughly analyzing the character and capabilities of each worker, the productive efficiency of each worker and of the total workplace could be so increased that earnings would be maximized for workers and employers alike. Accordingly, through the receipt of higher wages, the worker would be more satisfied, and such disturbers of traditional workplace harmony as trade unions would no longer be necessary.[14] The following anecdote illustrates rather well the sort of mechanistic view of the industrial worker held by Taylor and many of his followers. Reportedly, while Taylor was doing an efficiency study of a steelplant, he was confronted by a skilled worker who made a suggestion about the plant's production process. Enraged and in utter frustration, Taylor cried out: "You're not supposed to think. There are other people paid to do your thinking for you."[15]

One ironical thing about Taylorism and the way it came to be practiced in many American firms is the fact that managers were not to be excluded from the scrutiny of scientific management. Yet, in many businesses, the techniques of scientific management became applied very conscientiously in the offices and factories, but were rarely, if ever, imposed on the executive suite.

As could be expected, skeptics and humanists soon protested the excesses of scientific management. To begin with, questions were being raised about the efficacy of vocational psychology and of psychological testing. Not only were they suggested by some to be lacking as exact vehicles of science, they also became less and less accepted as reliable evaluators of the total person. Consequently, management theories began to move away from their pre-occupation with behaviorist psychology, with its tendencies to focus only on directly observable behavior and its inclination to see the human being as a stimulus-response mechanism.

A growing number of management theorists began to call for the analysis and consideration of the worker's unobservable inner needs and desires.[16] One of the earliest scholars to do so in the late twenties and early thirties was Elton Mayo and his coworkers at the Harvard Business School. They suggested that we needed to build a society in which the individual could feel that his labor was socially significant. It seemed to Mayo that one way to achieve this objective was through the creation of work environments in which employees could fulfill their innate human desire for cooperative activity. In the workplace so organized, motivation rather than coercion would become the driving force. Management theories clearly had entered a new phase: the human-relations approach.

Others who contributed to this movement in the forties were Douglas McGregor, Kurt Lewin, and some of their colleagues at M.I.T. They projected an alternative model of management, a model that has become known as the Theory Y style of management. Under this model, the satisfaction of the worker's inner needs would become central to a more democratic style of workplace and office management. At Brandeis University, Abraham Maslow developed the inner-need theory to the point where he suggested that there was a hierarchy of human needs. He projected the apex of this pyramid as the need for a sense of personal worth. Bennis, Schein, Argyris, Herzberg, Davis, and Likert carried the torch even further. They expanded human-need theory and designed organizational forms most suitable to the fulfillment of these needs.[17] This whole school of human-relations management theories has generated a variety of workplace experiments, some of which will be described in a later chapter.

One point should be made here about these experiments: their number is small. Actual human-relations management is rather rare in practice, much rarer than the amount of human-relations rhetoric being spoken. Many managers who were willing to participate in human-relations experiments several years ago have quit them in disgust, blaming social scientists for making them look too easy and for promising, but not delivering, immediate worker happiness and tranquility.[18] It is almost as if these managers were expecting a people that has experienced generations of dictatorial rule to be immediately successful in operating a system of representative democracy. People just do not shed old roles and learn new values that easily and quickly.

Another problem that has presumably plagued Stateside worker-participation experiments is the fact that some people become accustomed to a paternalistic, law-and-order regime and prefer it over a system that demands many personal responsibilities. Accordingly, a great number of workers have learned to take their jobs and their working conditions in stride, knowing that their personal freedom and fulfillment do not lie in the workplace but in their private lives and in their days and hours away from the job. This type of labor mentality hardly holds much promise for labor productivity and quality work. Even though many workers may have reached such a state of resignation, the bulk of them still place the importance of their work and the feeling of accomplishment that results from it far above their desire for high income, and distinctly above their desire for shorter working hours and abundant free time.[19]

It is unfortunate that so many managers persist in perceiving their workers in a negative light. For example, a recent Katzell and Yankelovitch study found that 79 percent of their manager respondents felt that "the nation's productivity is suffering because the traditional American work ethic has eroded." One-fourth of them felt that "workers don't care what they produce or how they produce it as long as they are well paid," and that "the average unskilled worker is interested in doing as little as possible."[20] Managers who have such a negative image of workers can hardly be expected to create increased opportunities for the expression of worker creativity and judgment. It is even possible that their negative imagery has created and is perpetuating a self-fulfilling prophecy.

It is time to repeat an earlier admonition: generalizations can be a problem. Not only do they need to be stated and read carefully, but statistical generalizations should never be interpreted to be universal generalizations. Thus, what has been said before about managers and their perceptions, either in generalized or in percentage form, does not purport to be valid for all managers. There are, for example, a variety of differences among groups and categories of managers. One of these relates to company cultures. Johnson & Johnson, for example, has a company credo and a way of doing business that entails five main realms of corporate responsibility. After an opening paragraph in which the company's obligations to the customers are reiterated, the credo states:

Our second responsibility is to those who work with us, the men and women in our factories and offices.

They must have a sense of security in their jobs.

Wages must be fair and adequate, management just, hours short, and working conditions clean and orderly.

Workers should have an organized system for suggestions and complaints.

Foremen and department heads must be qualified and fair-minded.

There must be an opportunity for advancement—for those qualified and each person must be considered an individual standing on his own dignity and merit.[21]

Another example of a company's commitment to its employees is that of Harmon International Industries, whose philosophy of human-resource management contains the following five tenets:

The worker must feel secure about his job, health, safety, income and future.

He must feel he is fairly treated.

He must feel his needs are respected and that he can develop his capacities to the full.

He must have a say in the decisions that affect him, starting with the job itself.

He must be able to work in an atmosphere of respect and mutual trust.[22]

The cynic will immediately suggest that many companies undoubtedly have noble statements of corporate principles, but he will tend to doubt that the companies practice what they preach. There is no question that not all persons and organizations who have professed noble intentions have also put these into practice. It is questionable, though, to assume that all professors of good intention are liars or self-deceivers. A number of firms live up to their credos. And, a number of these are very large, complicated organizations rather than the smaller, somewhat paternalistic workplaces where participative management could logically be expected to occur more easily.

Many differences in the cultures of companies, and the value systems of their managers, appear to be related to the pattern of ownership of the company and to the manner in which its decision making is organized. Thus, most of the generalizations presented above—about the manner in which American corporate managers tend to see their roles, the role of government in the economy, and the capabilities of the worker—are particularly valid for American multinational corporations that can be classified as ethnocentric. Ethnocentric companies, according to Perlmutter, are business firms that wholly own their subsidiaries and where the decision making is concentrated in the home-country headquarters.[23] This sort of firm most distinctly reflects the values of the company's home culture. The exact opposite of this sort of organization is the geocentric firm, which is more of a well-integrated cluster of sister companies that have amalgamated to such an extent that the company has a culture all its own. The geocentric company, thus, does not exhibit any particular national culture, nor does it reflect a mozaic of varied national cultures.

The ethnocentricity of some multinational firms does not result only from its being highly centralized; it can also be related to the fact that the firm's decision center has been and is dominated by one person or family. The Ford Motor Company, for example, has reflected the predominant American management culture much more distinctly than has a firm like Exxon. The latter is much less identifiable as a family-oriented corporation than is Ford, and it has increasingly become an aggregate of previously independent firms, many of which were foreign-owned and thus reflected their local national cultures.

Two other variables that appear to coincide with the degree of ethnocentricity of a company's culture are the firm's size and its product lines. There seems to be a greater propensity to maintain home-country values in firms that handle a product line that is not very visible and thus has little need to appear native to the host-country consumers. The same tendency is true for a firm of limited size. In such a context, there just are not enough plants and employees for a company culture to develop that is distinctly separate from any particular national culture.

Our conclusion has to be that even though there are predominant patterns in the value commitments of American corporate managers, there are some significant differences among individual firms as well as among categories of firms.

AMERICAN MANAGEMENT AND THE EMPLOYEE-RIGHTS MOVEMENT

American managerial attitudes and prerogatives underwent a new form of challenge in the seventies—this time, in the form of the employee-rights movement.[24] This semiorganized drive to obtain for workers greater freedom of expression, privacy, due process, access to information, and opportunities to participate was a logical outgrowth of the civil-rights movement of the sixties.

The origins of the employee-rights movement undoubtedly lie in either the human-relations school of business management or in the passage of the 1935 National Labor Relations Act, or Wagner Act. Its short-term catalyst, however, was the civil-rights movement. After the armed services, defense plants, and public schools were ordered to desegregate, the right to vote was extended, and discrimination in employment and housing was confronted, a redefinition of the rights of the American worker had to follow.

Also important to the emergence of the employee-rights movement were the demands for open records and open meetings, which were an outgrowth of the widespread abuses of person and privacy experienced during the cold war, the Vietnam War, and the Watergate scandals. And last, but certainly not least, was the impetus provided by the ratification drive for the Equal Rights Amendment and by the consumer movement.

Alan Westin has included several additional stimuli. He rightly suggests that the various statutes and court decisions involved in the general civil-rights movement created widespread "expectations of constitutional regularity." Also, courts were confronted with an increasing number of employee lawsuits and consequently recognized the right of workers to assume postures other than that of unquestioning obedience to the employer. Demands for more regulation of management prerogatives were also stimulated by the increased popularity of investigative reporting and by the discovery of corporate wrongdoings through freedom-of-information actions.

The interesting thing about all this is the distinct change that appears to have come about in management attitudes. At earlier points in time, business leaders could be expected to have received proposals for increased employee rights with great animosity. Some surveys have shown, however, that opinions and attitudes on the questions are definitely changing.[25] In 1971, a sample of *Harvard Business Review* subscribers and a group of MBA students at Harvard Business School and at an unidentified well-known midwestern university were asked their opinions about a whole array of employee-rights propositions. Six years later, a second sample was asked some of the same questions.

The most significant attitudinal changes apparently occurred with regard to the rights of employees to be able to "express their preferences, by some suitable voting means" on the following issues:[26]

	In favor	
	1971	1977
Whether all employees in the company should be subject to relocation by management as new plants and offices are opened, regardless of their desire to move.	29%	43%
Whether retirement should be mandatory for all company employees at age 65 or some other age.	29%	44%

Even though the 1977 data have not been published in cross-tabulated form, it seems valid to assume that the change in response is primarily the result of the fact that the older 1971 respondents (age 60-65), who were also most reluctant to recognize the right of expression (27 percent), had retired, and that the ranks of HBR subscribers, and business management generally, had increasingly absorbed those who were under thirty years of age in 1971. Fifty-three percent of the latter group approved of workers voting on these issues. Those respondents who were MBA students in 1971 were even more strongly in favor: HBS students, 60 percent; the midwestern university's MBA day students, 71.5 percent, and the evening students, 62 percent.

Most important to our main topic—the reaction of U.S. MNCs to European worker-participation practices—are the opinions of executives in manufacturing enterprises and the opinions of executives of the larger firms. Only 27 percent (the lowest percentage of any industry category) of the respondents working in the manufacturing of consumer goods in 1971 favored the projected employee voting. Individuals in the sector that manufactures industrial goods did not feel much more favorable (29 percent). Those whose corporate payroll counted over twenty thousand employees were not very supportive either (30 percent), with managerial personnel in the category of five hundred to twenty thousand employees falling closely behind (34 percent). Respondents working for companies that were either "one of the largest" or "larger than most" in the industry were also distinctly more reluctant (33 percent and 26 percent, respectively) than were those associated with companies that were "one of the smallest" (52 percent).[27]

Management consultants seem almost as favorably inclined (54 percent) toward employee voting on these issues as respondents working in educational and social services (57 percent), and slightly more than those in government (52 percent). Thus, even though respondents in the categories that most logically relate to the management of industrial multinationals seem to be the ones who are most reluctant to accept the projected forms of employee consultation, the attitudes of their management consultants and the coming to power of the more participatory younger generations may offset that trend. We should realize, though, that the questions upon which worker consultation was projected were of much lesser magnitude than the sort of questions worker representatives on corporate boards would be concerned with. On the other hand, consulting workers on such an important issue as plant relocation is considerably more substantive than the kind of decisions many European works councils deal with (for example, decisions on such shop-floor matters as work assignments, vacation schedules, and certain social services). If a large number of managers would be willing to let workers participate in the former decision, they certainly might be willing to let them participate in decisions about issues of much less substance.

Somewhat related issues that were raised in both the 1971 and the 1977 surveys were those dealing with the treatment of dissident employees and the grievance procedures used by firms. For example, when asked whether an accountant who was fired for refusing to follow her superior's instructions to falsify the company's profit-and-loss statement should be put back on the payroll, respondents almost unanimously said yes: 1971, 94 percent; 1977, 98 percent. However, when the respondents were asked whether the accountant would be rehired if such an incident had occurred in their own company, significantly smaller percentages (76 percent and 78 percent) of the respondents said they thought she would be.[28]

The picture becomes somewhat clearer when we look at it in terms of the grievance procedures companies use. There has been some increase in respondents who report the existence of such "tough-on-management" procedures as management grievance committees (1971: 7 percent, 1977: 14 percent), corporate ombudsmen (8 percent and 11 percent), and hearings with the use of third parties or legal counsel (6 percent and 11 percent). Nevertheless, grievance procedures, which are generally much less automatically responsive, such as an open-door policy by senior executives or the handling of grievances by the personnel department staff, seem to predominate.[29]

	In favor	
	1971	1977
open-door policy	68%	63%
personnel staff	43%	42%

Thus, while changes in the appreciation for employee rights are visible, management will have to undergo a much more significant change of heart before it will be ready to delimit clearly the autonomy of the employer-manager and define a greater number of viable opportunities for employees to participate in corporate decision making.[30]

One issue should not be left unmentioned. Respondents were asked whether employees should be directly involved in the selection of corporate chief executive officers. In 1971, only 17 percent of executives felt that directors should never select a new CEO "without accurate knowledge first of his acceptability or lack of acceptability to key employee groups," and only 12 percent felt that directors should "make sure a candidate actually meets with the approval of such key groups before giving him the nod."[31] Such an overwhelming rejection of direct democratic selection is certainly not surprising; after all, business organizations traditionally have been hierarchically structured. Before the corporate structure of business organization ever became popular, the owner of productive property (land, machines, and/or the capital for the purchase of raw materials and the hiring of needed personnel) was universally recognized as the firm's ultimate authority. The professional managers of today apparently have been delegated the royal cloak, even if only because they are "selected" (ratified) by today's corporate owners (the stockholders).

This continued, although somewhat ebbing, reluctance to share the absolute powers of management is not just a product of a historically evolved pattern of succession, however. Nor is it a mere extension of the predominant right of private property. It can also be seen as a function of industrialization, in that it brought with it the division of labor, specialization, and professionalism. Today, many members of the American managerial class tend to perceive of themselves as part of a meritocracy—that is, as people who have earned their place at the top by hard work, sharpness of mind, and risk taking. Their right to authority, they feel, can in no way be equal to that of the plant or office worker, who only works forty (or fewer) hours a week and whose job security is protected by his union and by established grievance procedures. It is the person at the top, the managers say, who deals with the big stakes and who delivers such goods as the jobs for the rank-and-file workers and the money that will allow these workers to receive better wages and benefits.

A number of American managers do not primarily justify their authority on the basis of their having been delegated authority, their having achieved, or even on the claim that their hearts are filled with paternalistic benevolence toward the other employees. They base their appeal for legitimacy on the superiority of their training and their skills. They see themselves as deserving of dominant authority because they were trained for corporate governance. They believe that their professional preparation gives them superior capability to deliver the greatest good for the greatest number.

AMERICAN MANAGEMENT AND CORPORATE-GOVERNANCE REFORM

The challenges to the autonomy of corporate management have come, not only in the form of government regulations and of demands for employee rights, they have also emerged through the recent attention to the issue of management's responsibility toward the company's stockholders and to the general public. Questions about this dimension of corporate governance were a logical aftermath of a chain of well-publicized events of the seventies that severely tarnished the public image of corporate America.

The denouement began with the collapse of a number of what appeared to be sound and well-managed giant corporations, for example, the demise of the Penn Central Railroad. Then, firms like International Telephone and Telegraph were found to have intervened extensively in the politics of nations such as Chile. With the Watergate scandal came public awareness of the magnitude and the ingeniousness of widespread corporate political contributions at home and abroad. At the same time, Lockheed and other stalwart enterprises became identified with their widespread bribes and payoffs. And, finally, the public-interest lobbies became increasingly determined that existing patterns of corporate accountability needed to be reviewed and reformed.[32]

After the Corporate Accountability Research Group in 1976 called for federal, rather than state, chartering of the nation's giant corporations, a variety of other groups also entered the public debate on corporate-governance reform. In April 1977, a "new constitution for corporations" was suggested by the 62nd American Assembly, which has a large number of leading businessmen among its leaders. The Business Roundtable, which is generally considered to be the most powerful business organization in the United States, initiated its own study and presented that report to the Congress and to the nation. Joining in the public discourse were congressional committees, the American Bar Association, the Securities and Exchange Commission, and many other concerned governmental, professional, and business organizations.[33] A clear consensus soon emerged: internal corporate management needed to be counterweighted by more independent boards of directors. The major questions seemed to be: What exact changes should be made? Should they be made by governmental or by corporate initiative?

To the student of European worker participation, this whole movement for corporate-governance reform is extremely significant. If corporate managers were no longer allowed to be virtually autonomous (vis-à-vis shareholders, employees, and the general public), a definite start would be made toward sharing management authority. And, if authority were not going to be shared immediately, the question would easily be raised of whether management should be held as accountable to the firm's employees as they would be to stockholders and/or the general public. And, if these responsibility relationships should not be equal, how should they be ranked with regard to one another?

Most Americans believe that there is considerable difference between the contributions made to the business firm by the stockholders and those made by the employees, especially the nonmanagerial employees. Not only is capital more directly identifiable as property than are an employee's time, energy, and talent, but many people have also considered it to be more important. Apparently, the fact that capital is more scarce than labor has contributed to the tendency to rate it and those who make it available to the firm as superior in ranking. As long as that is the prevailing judgment, therefore, managerial accountability to stockholders can be expected to be rated much higher than accountability to employees.

As far as managerial accountability to the general public is concerned, several prevailing values come into play here. Many firms find it very difficult to accept that they should be made accountable to constituencies that are not directly involved in the economic activity of the enterprise. They consider the market system to be the instrument of accountability toward outsiders. They argue that if the public does not like the behavior of a corporation, it does not have to buy its products or services. The American business community, as has been pointed out several times before, has been very reluctant to welcome governmental infringements upon management's authority. Rarely have businessmen seen governmental interventions in their autonomy as linked to the public interest. It appears, thus, extremely unlikely that the managerial community will consent to the selection of "public" directors, whether that be done by the government, consumer groups, or other entities that are projected to represent the general public and the public interest.

There is one constituency that could be called both internal and external and that therefore could be a natural compromise base for the selection or appointment of one or more external directors: the labor union that has been recognized by the firm's employees as their bargaining representative. However, neither management nor labor-union leadership appears very eager to agree to such an arrangement; the American system of labor relations is adversarial in its outlook. To management, it would be like inviting the wolf into the hen house; to labor, it would be like selling out to the enemy.

In the light of all these observations, it is probable that if any legal stipulations are made about the composition and independence of corporate boards, such requirements will be stated in negative terms — that is, in terms of the kind of connections with a firm and its management that external directors are *not* allowed to have. The day appears far off when it will be legally prescribed that specific internal (other than management) and external constituencies shall have a certain percentage of directly elected representatives on corporate boards. The only constituency that should be expected to be given such a right in the near future will undoubtedly be the corporation's stockholders.

Whatever the degree of corporate governance reform that occurs, the erosion of management's authority may be closer at hand than has been generally recognized. The validity of this assertion is borne out by the amount of interest shown in the reform issue by such organizations as the Business Roundtable, the National Association of Manufacturers, the American Bar Association, and the American Assembly.

AMERICAN MANAGEMENT'S PERSPECTIVE ON TRADE UNIONISM

Although worker-participation schemes do not necessarily involve trade unions, many American and European corporate managers perceive these two to be inextricably linked. In several European countries (the Federal Republic of Germany, for example), the trade unions do in fact dominate worker participation both on the works councils as well as on the companies' supervisory boards (see Chapter 6). Industrial democracy, or worker participation, is also seen by many to be a logical by-product of social-democratic ideology, the predominant value commitment of international trade unionists. It is, therefore, not so strange to predict that the way many corporate managers react to suggestions of worker participation will be very similar to the way they react to trade unionism.[34] A short look at the American management perspective on trade unions should thus be helpful.

Historically, trade unions have not been held in high regard by the American business community. In fact, when they first became a significant factor in the American economy, they were widely regarded as infusions of radical foreign practices. Many considered them to be sores on the body social and economic (to paraphrase Mr. Jefferson's earlier judgment about the cities and, presumably, their artisan-workmen populations). Bendix, for example, reports that in 1910, the president of Harvard University declared trade unionism to be degrading to the human character since it encouraged restriction in output.[35] Other eminent citizens of that era made equally condemnatory judgments.

American labor relations in the late nineteenth century did not present a pretty picture: sweatshops, child-labor abuses, the Molly Maguires, the Pinkerton detectives, the application of the Sherman Anti-Trust Act on national trade unions rather than on business combinations, the Haymarket Square riot, blacklisting, the Gospel of Wealth. This was the Gilded Age, and such was the background against which the trade-union movement emerged. Its challenge against entrepreneurial and managerial autonomy—logical as it was, considering the events and phenomena just listed—has only been hesitantly accepted and, then, mostly only by those who knew some history. In addition, a number of managers continue to believe in the inherent rights of the fittest. Others resent the effect that trade-union bargaining has tended to have on their businesses' competitive position and on their profitability.[36] As long as these attitudes prevail, managers cannot help perceiving trade unions as their enemy.

It is true that a majority of the general public in the last thirty years has appeared to be supportive of the principle of labor unions. When, in the spring of 1979, for example, pollsters asked a representative sample of the American people whether they approved or disapproved of labor unions, 55 percent expressed their approval, and only 33 percent disapproved. As Figure 7 shows, the public approval rate even reached as high as 76 percent in January 1957 and did not begin to dip below the 60-percent level until 1972.[37] When people are asked whether they approve of a worker's right to join a

FIGURE 7 Approval of Trade Unions
by
General Public
and by
Professional and Business People, 1953-1979

Source: Compiled by the author from information provided by the *Gallup Public Opinion Index*.

FIGURE 8 Public Confidence
in
Organized Labor and in Major Companies, 1966-1979

Source: Based on data gathered from Everett Carl Ladd, Jr., "The Polls: The Question of Confidence," *Public Opinion Quarterly* 40 (Winter 1976-1977): 545, and the *Gallup Public Opinion Index*, May 1979, pp. 9 and 11.

union of his choice, with the purpose of bargaining collectively with his employer, an even greater number say they do.[38] Both questions, though, are rhetorical. Asking them is almost like asking whether the respondent believes in freedom of speech and in the right of free association. Very few members of a democratic society are apt to vote against such moral propositions.

Figure 7 also indicates that professional and business people have categorically been more disapproving of trade unions than has the general public. What should be noted, though, is that respondents in the category to which most multinational corporation managers belong—the college educated—generally have been less disapproving than has the public.[39]

Approving, in principle, of trade unionism and of the right of workers to bargain collectively is one thing; having confidence in trade unions, their practices, and their leadership is a different question. The American public certainly has not been as generous in its confidence in labor leaders as it traditionally has been in the clergy and the medical profession. It has also approved more of business than of labor. Figure 8 shows the degree to which public-opinion poll respondents have expressed "a great deal of confidence" in big labor and big business. The graph clearly shows that the American public has generally placed much less confidence in labor than in business. One striking thing about Figure 8 is the considerable slippage in public confidence experienced by business since 1966 and how most of that depletion occurred in the late sixties.

The response to organized labor has been a little more positive when people are asked which they consider to be the biggest threat to the country in the future—big business, big labor, or big government. Even though 41 percent of the respondents in 1959 said "big labor" (compared with 15 percent who picked "big business" and 14 percent "big government"), twenty years later, the percentage that particularly feared big labor dropped to 17 percent. In 1979, big government was perceived to be the dominant threat (43 percent). Big business did not fare well at that time either: 28 percent of the public feared it most.[40]

Public skepticism about organized labor has been particularly pronounced when respondents were asked to rate the honesty and ethical standards of trade-union leaders and people in other socioprofessional groups. For example, in July 1977, some 79 percent of the public rated business executives from average to high in honesty and ethics. Only 52 percent gave this same rating to labor leaders, a rating that was only slightly better than that given to used-car salesmen! Professional and business leaders were distinctly more critical; only 39 percent of them rated trade-union leaders to be honest and ethical. Forty-two percent of those with a college education felt that way.[41]

All these negative attitudes toward labor leaders and trade unionism are somewhat understandable, given the American people's continuing love affair with competition and the adversary system and their adulation of individualism's credo of self-help. They are probably also generated, at least to some extent, by the rather unsavory reputations of certain labor leaders. It is curious, though, that the American public has rarely, if ever, called most businessmen crooks, even though some have been publicly exposed as having engaged in criminal and highly unethical behavior.

The general lack of enthusiasm for trade unions in America is also clearly evident from the fact that only a small percentage of the national work force has taken out membership in them (only 22 percent of the total work force in 1979), and by the fact that unions have recently lost 48 percent of their representation elections. This latter statistic is especially impressive if we realize that unions will not generally enter into a representation election unless they consider that their chances of winning are favorable. Admittedly, such a large number of failures has also resulted from the increasingly sophisticated countercampaigns that are being conducted by a growing corps of antiunion consulting firms and that are better financed.

Equally illustrative of the lack of union popularity is the low rate of unionization among clerical workers, and its virtual absence among lower- and middle-range administrative personnel (including management). Particularly at this point in time, when the American economy is moving more rapidly from a manufacturing to a service economy, the reluctance and distaste on the part of white-collar workers may be a bad omen for unions of the future.[42]

Granted that the trends and attitudes just cited have multiple and varied causes, they cannot be shrugged off. They do at least suggest that any proposals for workplace reform that can readily be identified as desired by or beneficial to the trade-union movement will have very little chance of being legislated and accepted by the general public or by the American business community.

ORGANIZED LABOR'S PERSPECTIVE ON INDUSTRIAL DEMOCRACY

It has been widely asserted that the introduction of worker-participation practices in the United States will be resisted more by trade unionists than by corporate management. The review of Stateside participative-management experiments presented in a later chapter seems to suggest that to be a valid assertion. What needs to be done here, though, is to review some of the prevailing labor views on industrial democracy, and to determine whether European forms of worker participation in management could become acceptable to American trade unionists.

The key to understanding American labor's view is a thorough awareness of the nation's basic model of industrial relations. That model is based on several premises:[43]

1. Employees have a right to form, to belong to, and to govern labor unions of their choice; employers have a right to belong to their own representative organizations;
2. Employees are expected to leave management free to manage its business, and employers have a responsibility to refrain from dominating the union(s) of their employees;
3. Wages, hours, and other terms and conditions of employment shall be contained in a written, legally enforceable contract arrived at through a process of collective bargaining;
4. Provisions shall also be made for procedures to handle employee grievances, complaints, and claims to fair treatment;
5. Overt conflict in the form of strikes and lockouts are accepted as a regrettable, but often unavoidable, last step in the resolution of differences.

American trade unionists, rather than challenging the essential features of the nation's social, economic, and political system, have selected to obtain only economic justice and to do so primarily, if not almost exclusively, only for the employees of individual firms and to do so by bargaining with individual employers. Labor organizers who speak of class struggle and/or who advocate radical reforms of the system have never received overwhelming support in the United States, whether they were the Wobblies (the Industrial Workers of the World), the Eugene Debses (the Socialists), or the Walter Reuthers (the late United Auto Workers Union president).

As suggested before, many American workers see their personal fortunes at the end of the rainbow. Most of them do not see themselves frozen into a certain social class. Neither do they feel themselves confronting a managerial class that is made up exclusively of the well-born and the well-bred. American workers perceive a considerable proportion of managers as "good old boys" who were just smart or lucky enough to have made it. They may be envious of their ability to spend more conspicuously. However, American workers who, through collective bargaining, have gotten themselves a bigger slice of pie have done their share of conspicuous spending. Thus, they simply do not see managers as their class enemies. What most workers see are the guys you bargain with and play the game of "get-what-you-can" with; they are like the buddies one plays poker with...except they are the guys who have been winning!

A few years ago, William W. Winpisinger, president of the International Machinists Union, said the same thing in another way when he observed that it was not "that American unions have no political goals...our politics, like our bargaining, have been strictly pragmatic and nonideological. We have no interest in replacing free enterprise with a more utopian system." What was striking about his comment was that he appeared to see only two alternative ways of structuring corporate decision making: collective bargaining or public ownership and governmental dominance. He went on to say: "We would much prefer to bargain with private employers than with government bureaucrats." The quote ended with these words: "and we believe workers can receive a better share of the fruits of the enterprise at bargaining tables than in board rooms."[44] The IMU president appeared to assume, as many do, that the ultimate objective of workers is "a better share of the fruits of enterprise" and not necessarily a sense of dignity or shared ownership or responsibility. As Thomas R. Donahue, executive assistant to George Meany put it: "We do not seek to be partner in management—to be, most likely, the junior partner in success and the senior partner in failure."[45] As Winpisinger put it on another occasion: "You must be on one side or the other to maximize your effectiveness. That is the way we will continue to do it in the U.S. for a long time to come."[46]

Everett Kassalow places labor's perspective against the backdrop of American egalitarianism. He quotes Lipset to make his main point:

...an open class system leads workers to resent inequalities in income and status between themselves and others more frequently than does an ascriptively stratified system. America's equalitarian value system, by more broadly and less clearly defining the range of groups with which members may legitimately compare themselves, may make for a more free-flowing discontent among workers than in Europe.[47]

Accordingly, most American workers do not recognize managers as having a God-given, or natural, right to be wealthier. Thus, even though American labor is not class conscious, it views particular managements with much greater expressed animosity than do European laborers.

Not all American trade unionists have rejected the possibility of worker representatives on corporate boards. The issue, for example, was raised by Leonard Woodcock in May 1976, when he projected that the UAW negotiating team would bring up the subject in the July 1976 contract-renewal negotiations with Chrysler Corporation. Douglas Fraser announced that summer that the auto firm itself had prompted the introduction of the issue by offering spots for worker representatives on the Chrysler-U.K. board to British trade unionists. (More will be said about that incident in Chapter 7.) Fraser also readily admitted that codetermination (or worker "presence," as he preferred to call it) was not such a burning issue to auto workers that they would be willing to go on strike for it. In fact, it appeared as if the UAW proposed it at that time partially to prod the company to work toward reform of the corporation's governance by choosing more active outside directors.[48] In 1979, Fraser was offered a position on Chrysler's board as part of the company's attempt to survive financially and to keep labor appeased.

The UAW vice-president in charge of the General Motors negotiations, Irving Bluestone, made several rather interesting observations. In May 1977, he said: "When the U.S. worker eventually realizes how important the decision making at the top level is to him at the job level (the level which is currently at the center of the worker's bargaining interest), he will press for that too."[49] Several years before, *Forbes* Magazine quoted him as having observed that:

We are on the threshold of what will become the second stage of the road to industrial democracy. We've gone a long way in getting a bigger share of economic well-being for our workers through collective bargaining. But we're struggling to get a voice in the big decisions that affect the workingman's welfare. The second stage of the road to industrial democracy will be to challenge certain management prerogatives. Our contracts contain hundreds of provisions protecting the rights of workers, but they still leave to management the sole responsibility about products, location of plants and all the rest. The time is now right for direct worker participation in the decision-making process.[50]

Shortly after Bluestone made this particular analysis, in 1974, "The Changing World of Work Conference" at Berkeley, comprised of some fifty trade unionists, issued a document that called upon unions to broaden their perspectives and to develop further experiments in self-managing work teams and other forms of worker participation. The document confirmed that "our traditional adversary relationship between management and labor discourages such concepts but need not block them."[51]

One of the more recent urgings—that American trade unionists consider bargaining for greater participatory opportunities—was contained in a 1979 *New York Times* guest editorial by Bruce Stokes of World Watch Institute. Stokes suggested that unions consider "accepting peacefully a ceiling on pay raises in return for greater worker participation," whether that would be in the corporate boardroom or in the form of greater day-to-day worker control on the shop floor. He suggested that such a move, and the consequent effective execution of such opportunities, would help unions carve out for themselves new roles that would help them recoup from their dwindling share of the U.S. work force. He assumed that such a bargain would also improve the competitive trade position of American industry.[52] The greater labor-management cooperation that would be involved in such opportunities could not help but favorably affect worker morale and it certainly would not hurt productivity.

What makes all this speculation about the feasability of union influence on the corporate board even more interesting is the fact that employee (including union) pension funds own an increasingly larger share of the stocks of the nation's leading corporations and banks. Peter Drucker pointed out in 1976 that pension funds for employees of private-sector enterprises were already holding 25 percent of American equity capital. Pension funds for government employees, teachers, and self-employed persons held another 10 percent. He also predicted that "within ten years employee funds will own a majority of all but the truly 'small' businesses, and may own as much as two-thirds of the big ones."[53] Even though Drucker's predictions are rather alarmist, particularly when one considers that most of the pension funds are not directly union-administered, there lies within this reality a possible bridgehead for labor to claim the right to be represented on the corporate boards of directors of key multinationals. And labor certainly might not hesitate to lay such a claim if jobs become scarcer, whether as a result of automation or because production jobs are exported to low-cost labor markets and less-unionized countries in the Third and Fourth worlds.

Very specific examples of how union leaders may use their shareholding power to obtain representation on company boards are given by Rifkin and Barber in their very provocative book on *Pension Politics and Power in the 1980s*. They tell of how, in the 1977 annual board meeting of American Telephone and Telegraph, Roger Wenthold, the president of Local No. 81 of the International Federation of Professional and Technical Engineers, introduced a resolution calling for a representative of one of the company's unions to be placed on the board of directors. (A.T. and T. employees reportedly also control one of the largest single-ownership blocs of shares in the company.)

A similar resolution was presented to the Chrysler Corporation board that same year. However, the committee representing more than one hundred thousand shares of company stock held by the UAW, Local No. 412 found their motion omitted from the shareholders-meeting agenda. The Securities and Exchange Commission "allows a company to omit from its proxy, material proposals relating to an election to office."[54] It is clearly possible, nevertheless, that similar resolutions will keep cropping up, and that the SEC may change its rules on this question.

CONCLUSIONS

It seems logical to conclude that even though many traditional values will prevail for some years to come, some most interesting changes are occurring in the way management and labor look at worker involvement in corporate decision making. Americans may remain optimistic, individualistic, conservative, and materialistic. They are, at the same time, increasingly concerned about such nonmaterial grounds for job satisfaction as respect by one's employer and the meaningfulness of one's work. Similarly, corporate managers will remain concerned about maximizing profits and will have suppressive restraints placed on them by the increasingly bureaucratic nature of the large business organization. They are also becoming increasingly interested in the theories of the human-relations school of labor management and in the employee-rights movement. The same can be said of trade-union leadership. They may fear co-optation and the collapse of collective bargaining; yet, their pension-fund holdings are placing them in a situation where they have a direct stake in the welfare of giant banks and corporations. They may well have reached the point at which they will discover that behind-the-scenes or occasional pressure politics at stockholder meetings may not be as productive as constant direct participation in decision making.

The American perspective is changing.

NOTES

1. "Our Society in 1985 — Business May Not Like It," *Harvard Business Review* 53 (Nov.-Dec. 1975): 143-44. Seventy-three percent of the American readers who responded preferred this ideology over an admittedly limited choice of a so-called communitarian ideology (p. 147).

2. M. R. Cooper, B. S. Morgan, P. M. Foley, and L. B. Kaplan, "Changing Employee Values: Deepening Discontent?" *Harvard Business Review* 57 (Jan.-Feb. 1979): 117-25. Similar observations have been made in the Secretary of Health, Education, and Welfare's Special Task Force report entitled *Work in America* (Cambridge: M.I.T. Press, 1973), and by a variety of other writers.

3. Richard M. Pfeffer's guest columns on "The Worker as Commodity," *The New York Times*, April 30 and May 2, 1975. Similar observations are made by Robert Schrank in *Ten Thousand Working Days* (Cambridge: M.I.T. Press, 1978).

4. Reported in David Vogel and Leonard Silk, *Ethics and Profits* (New York: Simon and Schuster, 1976), pp. 21-22.

5. *Gallup Public Opinion Index*, June 1979, pp. 18 and 19.

6. Maynard S. Seider, "American Big Business Ideology: A Content Analysis of Executive Speeches," *American Sociological Review* 39 (Dec. 1974): 807. It is important to recognize that Seider's primary intent was to determine the relative significance of the notion of social responsibility and, particularly, to determine the differences between orientations in various industrial sectors. For example, while the classical-creed themes were used 52 percent of the time by all speakers, utility, car manufacturing, and bank officials used them 73 percent, 67 percent, and 67 percent respectively. Aerospace-industry officials emphasized the nationalistic themes 59 percent as compared to 30 percent for the classical creed (p. 809).

7. Kamal M. Abouzeid and Charles N. Weaver, "Social Responsibility in the Corporate Goal Hierarchy," *Business Horizons*, 21 (June 1978): 30 and 33.

8. David Vogel, "Why Businessmen Distrust Their State: The Political Consciousness of American Corporate Executives," *British Journal of Political Science* 8 (Jan. 1978): 45.

9. Ibid., pp. 59-65.

10. Statements made by top corporate executives at Conference Board conferences in 1974 and 1975 to explore the social and political role of business. David Vogel and Leonard Silk, who reported and analyzed the views and attitudes expressed, are careful to point out that these statements are not to be read as representative of all conference participants. They are nevertheless symptomatic of a considerable degree of elitism and skepticism about the common man that permeates corporate management circles. The quoted statements are reported in *Ethics and Profits*, p. 180.

11. Mason Haire, Edsin E. Ghiselli, and Lyman Porter, *Managerial Thinking: An International Study* (New York: John Wiley and Sons, 1966), pp. 21-33 and p. 172.

12. Vogel, "Why Businessmen Distrust Their State," p. 64.

13. Ibid., pp. 71-72.

14. Frederick W. Taylor, *Scientific Management* (New York: Harper and Brothers, 1947).

15. Max Ways, "The American Kind of Worker Participation," *Fortune* 94 (Oct. 1976): 169.

16. A classic analysis of these varied and changing perspectives is contained in Reinhard Bendix, *Work and Authority in Industry* (Berkeley: University of California Press, 1974), pp. 287-319.

17. An excellent discussion of American behavioral scientific management thinking is contained in David Jenkins, *Job Power* (New York: Penguin Books, 1973), pp. 240-41.

18. See the observations by Robert Zager in his "European and American Developments in Personnel Strategy," in N. H. Cuthbert and K. H. Howlans, *Company Industrial Relations Policies* (London: Longmans, 1973), pp. 240-41.

19. The Detroit area surveys of 1958 and 1971 found this to be the case. See Otis D. Duncan, Howard Schuman, and Beverly Duncan, *Social Change in a Metropolitican Community* (New York: Russell Sage Foundation, 1973), pp. 73-74, as cited in Rosabeth Moss Kanter's "Work in a New America," *Daedalus* 107 (Winter 1978): 56.

20. The study cited in Kanter's article was Raymond A. Katzell and Daniel Yankelovitch, *Productivity and Job Satisfaction* (New York: Psychological Corporation, 1975), pp. 98-101.

21. Quoted in Theo Nichols, *Ownership, Control and Ideology* (London: George Allen and Unwin, 1969), p. 161.

22. *The Economist*, May 29, 1976, p. 87.

23. The typology of ethnocentric- and geocentric-company cultures is derived from Amos Perlmutter. See "The Tortuous Evolution of the Multinational Corporation," *Columbia Journal of World Business* 4 (Jan.-Feb. 1969).

24. A nice capsule discussion of the movement is Alan Westin's guest column, "A Move Toward Employee Rights," *The New York Times*, April 3, 1978. A more elaborate discussion is found in David Ewing's book, *Freedom Inside the Organization* (New York: E. P. Dutton, 1977).

25. David Ewing, "What Business Thinks About Employee Rights,"*Harvard Business Review* 55 (Sept.-Oct. 1977): 81-94.

26. Ibid., p. 84.

27. David Ewing, "Who Wants Corporate Democracy?" *Harvard Business Review* 49 (Nov.-Dec. 1971): 25-27.

28. Ewing, "What Business Thinks," p. 84.

29. Ibid., pp. 83 and 85.

30. One thing to remember is that many respondents are much more willing to give employees certain voting privileges if the participation were limited to employees classed as managerial. Ewing, "Who Wants Corporate Democracy?" pp. 27, 28.

31. Ibid., pp. 28 and 146.

32. Joel Seligman, "Battle for Corporate Democracy," *The New York Times*, June 12, 1977.

33. Thomas Mullaney, "Governance of U.S. Companies: Proposals on Reform Likely Soon," *The New York Times*, May 24, 1978. Also see Sumner Marcus and Kenneth D. Walters, "Assault on Managerial Autonomy," *Harvard Business Review* 56 (Jan.-Feb. 1978): 57-66.

34. It will be shown in Chapter 7 that a number of American managers have discovered the potential of using worker participation to prevent unionization of the firm's employees. An aversion to unions may thus lead these people to champion the democratization of the workplace.

35. Reinhard Bendix, *Work and Authority in Industry: Ideologies of Management in the Course of Industrialization* (Berkeley: University of California Press, 1974), p. 271.

36. The frustrating impact of labor unions on a company's competitive position is of course due to the decentralized collective-bargaining system operative in the United States. Each firm has to face its own union bargaining agents. There are no nationwide or associationwide employer-organization leaders who negotiate for the whole nation or the whole industry's wage rates and fringe-benefits package. See Derek C. Bok and John T. Dunlop's explanation of the context of American management opinion about trade unions in the *Labor and the American Community* (New York: Simon and Schuster, 1970), pp. 34-36.

37. *Gallup Public Opinion Index*, August 1978 and June 1979.

38. Bok and Dunlop, p. 13.

39. *Gallop Public Opinion Index*, August 1978, p. 20.

40. Ibid., June 1979, p. 95.

41. Ibid., January 1978, pp. 8 and 26.

42. *The New York Times*, November 15, 1979.

43. The following five points are partially quoted, partially paraphrased and condensed from two of Milton Derber's recent writings: "Collective Bargaining: The American Approach to Industrial Democracy," in the *Annals of the American Academy of Political and Social Science* 431 (May 1977): 84; and "Collective Bargaining, Mutuality and Workers' Participation in Management: An International Analysis," a paper presented at the Fifth World Congress of the International Industrial Relations Association, Paris, 3-7 September 1979. For a more thorough discussion of the American model, see Derber's classic, *The American Idea of Industrial Democracy* (Urbana: University of Illinois Press, 1970).

44. As quoted in an article by James Ellenberger, "The Realities of Co-Determination," *American Federationist* 10 (Oct. 1977): 15.

45. Harry B. Ellis, "Workers on the Board: Productive Help or Hindrance," *Christian Science Monitor*, May 18, 1977, p. 14.

46. As quoted in "Co-determination: When Workers Help Manage," *Business Week*, July 14, 1975, p. 133.

47. Everett M. Kassalow, *Trade Unions and Industrial Relations* (New York: Random House, 1970), p. 152.

48. "U.S. Unions Aren't Sold on Having Workers on the Board," *Industry Week* 190 (September 6, 1976): 30.

49. Ellis, "Workers on the Board," p. 14.

50. "Fairy Tale or Wave of the Future," *Forbes* 110 (Nov. 1, 1972): 50.

51. Described and quoted in Nancy Foy and Herman Gadon, "Worker Participation: Contrasts in Three Countries," *Harvard Business Review* 54 (May-June 1976): 82.

52. Bruce Stokes, "More Worker Power," *The New York Times*, January 23, 1979.

53. Peter Drucker, "Pension Fund 'Socialism'," *Public Interest* 42 (Winter 1976): 3.

54. Jeremy Rifkin and Randy Barber, *The North Will Rise Again: Pension Politics and Power in the 1980s* (Boston: Beacon Press, 1978), p. 163.

3

THE INDUSTRIAL-RELATIONS REPUTATION OF AMERICAN MULTINATIONALS

The criticisms voiced against American multinational corporations doing business in Europe have been many and varied, ranging from comments that are quite sweeping in nature to those that are very specific. Typical of the broader alarms are cries about the role played by American firms in the so-called Americanization of Europe. Members of the European intelligentsia, for example, blame U.S.-owned enterprises for importing the technology and value system that has produced mass society. Members of the traditional elites are especially harsh in their condemnation of the widespread hedonism that they see to be a direct spin-off of the gospel-of-salvation-through-mass-consumption. Another sweeping criticism originates with certain public officials and opinion leaders who perceive American firms to be closely sponsored and/or controlled by their home government, and, as such, they blame them for the erosion of European economic and political independence.

Some complaints are much more specific, however. They include such things as the precipitous closings of industrial plants and the frequent refusal of U.S.-owned firms to recognize the right of local trade unions to represent company workers. What is so interesting about these specific criticisms is that many have tended to deal with industrial-relations questions; that fact alone would warrant a closer examination of them here. Such a closer look should, however, also help explain why trade unionists have frequently singled out American multinationals for their criticisms of international business enterprises, and why organized labor in Europe has played such a leading role in pressuring national and European Community officials to bring about reforms in local industrial-relations systems and in the structuring of corporate governance.

THE LABOR RELATIONS OF MULTINATIONAL CORPORATIONS

Nat Weinberg was quite correct when he observed that the labor problems generated by the emergence of the multinational enterprise were more significant for their scale and complexity than for their newness and their difference of character.[1] Any time jobs are created, whether at home or abroad, the new employees will soon begin to raise questions about such things as the probable length of their employment, the relative ease with which they might be dismissed, their compensation (particularly in comparison to people who do similar work elsewhere), and the conditions under which they are expected to work. The mere airing of such concerns can easily lead to the emergence of employee unionization when management appears to ignore the workers' pleas or to treat them too lightly. Whenever frustration rises to that level, employees will naturally find much more satisfaction and strength in common, rather than individual, action. Unionization will certainly occur earlier and with deeper passion when job security in the workplace turns out to be unusually low, when management is perceived to depart significantly from locally accepted grievance and negotiation procedures, and when the community's definitions of economic justice are persistently and substantially violated.

The industrial-relations experience of multinational corporations conforms to this type of scenario. There are, nevertheless, certain complaints that are voiced more often against multinationals than against other firms. For example, a very common grievance is the assertion that multinational enterprises, because of their size and greater mobility, tend to rationalize their production. Accordingly, it is alleged, when a multinational company feels that a certain subsidiary or plant is no longer efficient and cannot be turned around, or when it believes that it has become too much of a problem to continue operations in a certain location, it will pull up stakes and relocate in a more profitable or hospitable environment. Witness, for example, the transfer of most of the production of radio, television, and other electronic components from the United States to such low labor-cost locations as Taiwan, South Korea, Ireland, and the Mexican border areas — a relocation of some one hundred thousand jobs.[2] Critics are also quick to point out that many such relocations have been to areas where trade unions are either nonexistent or are severely restricted.

Even though it is not as easy to relocate an operation as many critics imply, and it is virtually impossible in some types of industry and under certain organizational and environmental circumstances, enough incidents have occurred to create the impression that they are commonplace.[3] These widely publicized cases certainly have aggravated the labor problems of multinational corporations. What has angered trade unionists especially is the manner in which many of the relocation decisions were made (without any form of consultation with host-country officials and trade unionists) and the apparently inadequate consideration given by corporate officials to the welfare of the employees and the local economies involved. There is also considerable frustration about the capability of multinationals to transfer production temporarily to a subsidiary or plant not embroiled in the same industrial dispute or bargaining cycle or to use the threat of such a transfer as a bargaining chip.

The second major concern of trade unionists relates to the frequent unwillingness of multinationals to follow established collective-bargaining procedures. Many trade unionists actually accuse firms of having engaged in stonewalling tactics, of seeking to prevent the unionization of their workers. It has also been charged that labor negotiators have been deprived of needed information as well as contact with those company officials who ultimately will make labor-contract decisions. While the refusal to recognize unions appears to be a trait more peculiar to companies of certain nationalities, and particularly of those headquartered in the United States, other kinds of stonewalling are allegedly practiced by all multinationals, regardless of their country of origin. For instance, it is noteworthy that a considerable portion of recent European investments in the United States has occurred in states that have right-to-work laws or that have very low levels of unionization.

In this issue area, as was the case with the relocation issue, the adversary parties perceive the situation somewhat differently. Management representatives, for example, point out that the substantially varying legal and social circumstances in the several host countries make industrial relations the most decentralized of all corporate-decision areas. A Ford official called it "one of the most indigenous and nationally oriented functions" of his company's management.[4] Not only are subsidiary managers said to be the ones who make contract decisions (rather than officials at corporate headquarters), they are also represented as being pragmatic enough to adjust to local expectations and practices. There appear to be considerable differences, however, among firms: those with a singular product line, those whose production is highly integrated, those whose overseas sales are less important than sales at home, and those whose company culture is antiunion are markedly more nonconformist.[5]

What makes the nonconformity issue somewhat confusing is the fact that a number of trade unionists have insisted that the traditional definitions of the scope of collective bargaining and industrial relations have been too narrow. Charles Levinson, for instance, argues that headquarter decisions concerning investment and production rationalization have more serious consequences for the workers than the shorter-range questions of wages, fringe benefits, and working conditions.[6] If and when such a broad definition of collective bargaining becomes increasingly popular, trade unionists will logically insist more and more on dealing with headquarters management and will resent being limited to contracts with subsidiary officials.

Regardless of how broad or narrow the subject matter of industrial relations will be defined, an increasing number of observers assert that corporate decision making on industrial-relations issues has been substantially more centralized than is generally claimed by management. They also suggest that the trend is toward even greater centralization, and their suggestion is based on the recognition that most direct foreign investments are not simply made to return a quick, short-term profit. The majority are intended to establish a firm in a promising market, to take advantage of investment incentives extended by the host government, and/or to meet competitors in their home market. Most of these are long-term company objectives or are designed to meet longer-range goals.

Long-term objectives not only require efficient use of the company's resources (including its human resources) and a considerable amount of integrated planning, they also necessitate that collective-bargaining procedures be handled carefully and in such a way that the firm's long-term objectives will not be endangered. Under such imperatives, the multinational's corporate headquarters can be expected to play a formidable role in reviewing and coordinating the labor-relations activities of the various subsidiaries.

There is another reason why multinational corporations are centralizing their industrial-relations decision-making powers more. As the trade-union movement has sharply increased its transnational activities, concessions made by one subsidiary are not simply items to be considered in total corporate planning at one point in time; they also become precedents with which other subsidiaries will surely be confronted.[7]

The third major complaint against multinational corporations relates to the frequency with which they reportedly violate standards of social and economic justice. Apparently, corporate-headquarters executives and expatriate subsidiary managers can be very parochial. Not only are a number of them unfamiliar with local practice, they are also generally guilty of simply transposing to the foreign operation the kind of labor-relations practices they were familiar with at home. Such indiscriminate transfer of home-country practices has caused more unnecessary conflicts than one could possibly imagine.

A good example of this is the attempt by a number of American firms in Europe to obtain fixed-term labor contracts, which trade unionists have fought fiercely because they are convinced that the introduction of this apparently logical and innocuous practice would surely bring with it several other alien customs. Not the least of these would be the stipulation that strikes would have to be limited to contract-negotiating time, a requirement that would drastically alter existing worker prerogatives and existing power relationships. Such a stipulation would give management a much better opportunity periodically to prepare for negotiation rather than have to defend company practices and be accountable to the workers at all times. Making this sort of change is like introducing the American system of periodic elections—a unique feature of the separation-of-powers system of government—into European politics and abandoning the possibility of a government having to stand for election any time it loses the confidence of the people's legislative representatives.

As implied before, local standards of social and economic justice were especially and most dramatically violated every time a multinational announced the closing of a plant in Western Europe without first having consulted with the parties to be affected. Particularly when there was a clash between cultural values, protesting trade unionists found their national governments especially responsive to their pleas that multinational corporations be regulated. It is not surprising, therefore, to see how cautious most firms have become about such matters. They now earnestly try to avoid the kind of incidents that give their adversaries the opportunity to pose new martyrs.

Not all multinational corporations are equally tenacious in following the industrial-relations standards they are familiar with at home. As suggested in an earlier chapter, certain firms are clearly more ethnocentric than others, and there seem to be variations among them that coincide with their country of origin. American multinationals, for example, are generally perceived to be least adaptive to local culture. Various researchers have found that, as Bomers put it, American firms "take as point of departure their own industrial relations policies and adjust them to local rules, procedures and policies and to do so only to the extent that is obligatory and practical." In contrast, other European-based multinationals are said to adopt industrial policies that are more distinctly similar to those followed by comparable local firms in the countries where they operate.[8]

Ironically, ethnocentrism is not a characteristic exclusive only to business firms. One of the main problems facing the international trade-union movement, for example, is a virtual lack of solidarity among the workers of different countries. Not only are laborers divided among themselves in terms of their preferences for local industrial-relations practices and national loyalties, they also exhibit deep rifts along religious-confessional and political-ideological lines. Thus, while it may be easy for trade unionists to criticize multinational corporations for clinging to their home-country values, they find it difficult to eliminate that problem from their own ranks.

THE LABOR RELATIONS OF THE AMERICAN FIRMS

The fact that American enterprises in the European Community have acquired a special reputation of being antiworker and anti-trade union is indicated, not only in union publications, but it is also evident from the results of opinion surveys of other segments of European societies. For example, in 1970, John Fayerweather, questioning national legislators, senior civil servants, heads of large business firms, and labor-union officials in Great Britain, France, and Canada, found that the British and French respondents rated foreign firms, which were overwhelmingly American, less willing to extend recognition to labor unions than were national firms.[9]

About that same time, Conrad Jamison, having interviewed high civil servants in Britain, found that 46 percent of the respondents disagreed with the statement that "One thing American firms are particularly good at is labour relations." Only 22 percent registered agreement.[10] When a sample of British senior business executives were asked the same question in 1975 for ITT-Europe (within the context of a five-nation study commissioned by that firm), they were somewhat less critical. Nevertheless, 37 percent judged U.S. MNCs to be *not* particularly good at labor relations, compared to 31 percent who thought they did well. The disapproval-approval ratio was even worse in the responses given by German businessmen: 35 percent to 23 percent. French respondents were also quite critical: only 28 percent rated American firms favorably. Interesting, though, were the pronouncements by the Italian and Spanish executives, who were distinctly more positive.[11]

A U.S. Information Agency survey of independent professionals, government officials, and business executives in nine West European countries found that about half the respondents in all nine countries felt that U.S. multinational firms tend to ignore accepted European business practices, which presumably would include European labor-relations practices. A considerable number of respondents in that echelon of European elites also indicated that, in their judgment, U.S. MNC management failed to judge properly the work of non-American employees.[12]

It certainly is possible that opinions such as these may have been artificially inflated by a certain amount of anti-American publicity and/or by competitor envy. They do suggest, though, that there is a problem. And a sufficient number and variety of unfortunate incidents have occurred in West European countries that make such negative conclusions at least partly understandable.

The existence of a distinct problem was also indicated in a compilation of international business blunders committed by American firms. In that study, it was found that 84 percent of the recorded "personnel" blunders occurred in Europe, and that "personnel" errors comprised almost half the serious mistakes made by American firms there. The compilers of this study included in that category poorly handled management decisions, such as those on plant closings.[13]

Most of the unfortunate incidents that have contributed to the somewhat tainted reputation of American multinationals in Western Europe fit into three general categories: (1) refusal or reluctance to recognize trade unions; (2) abrupt plant withdrawals and worker layoffs; and (3) efforts to decentralize the collective-bargaining process.

Several observations should be made before these grievances are examined in more detail. First, most academic observers believe that the majority of foreign-owned multinationals operating in Western Europe conduct their labor relations in conformity with local standards.[14] This generalization does not prove the conformity to be equal among multinationals of different nationality. And, it is also quite possible that such a high rate of conformity may have resulted as much from the strictness of local labor-law enforcement and from the determination and power of local employer associations and trade unions in certain countries as from management's spontaneous preference for following established local practices.

It is also important to point out that the labor-relations reputations and practices of American subsidiaries have varied from country to country, from time to time, and from company to company. Such a variance is partly attributed to the reality that some countries, and particularly Great Britain, have had very few restrictive labor laws, while others were very strict. Equally influential have been the differences in the degree of social-economic cleavage prevailing in the various locations. There seems to be an invisible line running diagonally from the northwest to the southeast of Western Europe, which places Great Britain, southern Belgium, France, and Italy in the zone in which the class struggle is much more pronounced than it is on the other side of that line. Not only is there a greater probability that conflict will occur in these more deeply cleavaged societies, but in actual conflict situations, there is less willingness to compromise, and the mass media are apt to be much more ardently involved in the public dialogue. This, in turn, relates to the presence in these countries of some very active anticapitalist forces. Never having been able to gain power, having been out of power for some time, or when in power finding themselves unable to achieve the radical reforms they desired, these groups have, at times, made American multinationals the targets of their frustrations. Paradoxically, certain American managers have appeared to relish this sort of conflict environment and have found themselves tempted to "teach the radicals a lesson" or to give them the "action" they desired.

Variations in the industrial-relations behavior of American multinationals in different countries are also related to other features of the local industrial-relations systems. For example, while Great Britain has more than six hundred active trade unions, unionism in Germany is dominated by a few very powerful labor organizations.[15] Thus, when management at Ford's Dagenham (Britain) plant has to deal with twenty-one unions, while its sister plants in Germany basically deal only with the German Metalworkers (IG Metall), the situation in Britain is apt to be much more volatile, and Ford management there would be much more inclined to be impatient and insist on doing things its own way.

Another feature of the trade-union system that has had considerable impact is the role and stature of such entities as shop stewards. In Britain, for example, a virtual dual system of industrial relations exists. Employers there have to deal with practically autonomous shop stewards as well as with national union leaders. Not only are American managers unaccustomed to the apparent confusion that can result from such duality, they have a terrible time learning to appreciate it.[16]

The situation in Britain has probably also been somewhat more difficult than in most other northwest European countries because England has attracted a disproportionate share of ethnocentric American companies. Firms that were new to overseas production have tended to settle there first. To them, it seemed that the British culture was more like that at home, a perspective that led them to follow Stateside industrial-relations practices in an environment that had, nevertheless, totally different industrial-relations traditions.

Not only do American practices vary from country to country, but important changes have also taken place over time. For example, the situation in the seventies was substantially different from that in the sixties. Individual countries, like Great Britain, have expanded the scope of their labor legislation, and American firms themselves have become more adaptive. European trade unionists attribute this increased adaptiveness to the firms' having gained experience, and they are especially cognizant of the increased activity and effectiveness of international management consulting firms. Undoubtedly, some of the adjustment must also have been made by the European trade unionists and workers themselves. They have become more willing to compromise as they saw European-based multinationals expand their production overseas and as they observed American multinationals disinvest themselves and begin to concentrate their European operations. Jobs are jobs, and sometimes nationalistic, ideological reasoning has to give way to pragmatic considerations.

Not all American firms have had the same labor-relations experience and reputation. Some differences appear to have resulted from the type of technology employed by the enterprise. Labor-intensive industries, for example, have logically had to be more adaptive to local traditions than have capital-intensive ones because labor stability and productivity is clearly very important to them. One would expect the same from capital-intensive industries that have highly rationalized their production—that is, that have parceled out their production process among specialized plants in different locations. This type of firm is clearly very vulnerable to having its production process dislocated by a local work stoppage in one of the integral plants. What one would logically expect is not what seems to be happening.

The rationalization of production has tended to bring about greater centralization of corporate decision making, has placed greater distance between central management and local operations managers, and has, as suggested before, strengthened ethnocentric tendencies. A number of highly rationalized firms seem enamored with the scientific nature of their organizational scheme and project their corporate industrial technology to be superior to that of the various plant locations. They feel it their mission to update local practices rather than to compromise their proven policies, a state of mind that has created a greater probability of clashes with host-country unionists.

As observed earlier, American firms, like Japanese firms, have been particularly apt to operate their overseas labor relations according to Stateside practices because they are less multinational in orientation than are European-based international business enterprises. Kassalow argues that this is because the home markets in both these countries are so predominant in the sales and production activities of their multinationals that corporate headquarters see their overseas operations as "mere extensions of their domestic markets" and, consequently, of their home country's way of doing business. What makes their ethnocentrism even more striking is the fact that both home countries have unique labor-relations systems.[17]

When it comes to specific trade-unionist complaints against American firms, one of the first to be mentioned is their general antiunionist posture, as evidenced most strikingly in their widespread refusal to recognize the right of unions to represent their workers. Complaints of this nature have been especially widespread in Britain, even though Gennard and Steuer concluded that "non-recognition of manual worker trade unions by foreign-owned firms is no less common than amongst domestic firms." The same authors add, however, that when compared to British firms of similar size, particularly for the post-World War II period, American firms have definitely been more recalcitrant.[18]

The companies against which this accusation has been made most frequently in Britain are: International Business Machines, Kodak, Gillette, Caterpillar, Firestone, Texas Instruments, and Roberts Arundel (a name that is notorious for a variety of reasons, some of which will be discussed later). IBM and Texas Instruments are typical of industries that have a relatively large proportion of white-collar employees, and of companies that have developed industrial-relations programs that seek to minimize the social distance between managers and workers. They have also been apt to satisfy their workers, particularly their white-collar workers, with comparatively higher levels of compensation and amenities. IBM, for example, measures the salaries of twelve comparable firms in Britain, including those in the oil and chemical industries (both of which are renowned for their higher-than-average wages and their low level of unionization) and then pegs its salaries just above them.[19] With a record of no strikes in twenty-five years, the company has been successful in staving off labor-union recognition. One of the most remarkable company victories came on March 31, 1977, when only 566 of the company's 13,000 employees voted in favor of having unions negotiate in their behalf. Trade unionists have argued, albeit unsuccessfully, that IBM's employees would not be able to enjoy their higher pay standards unless the company had been forced to peg its wages to those paid by unionized firms.[20]

IBM and Texas Instruments are also typical of those firms that have Stateside policies of nonrecognition. For years, even the Ford Motor Company, which is now heavily unionized, fitted into this category as well. Ford's labor-relations reputation in Britain and elsewhere closely reflected Henry Ford's 1937 edict that the firm would never recognize the Autoworkers Union or any other similar organization as a partner in negotiation— a policy the company did not abandon until wartime circumstances made such recognition necessary in 1944.[21] What this type of company posture can mean may well be reflected by comparing the industrial-relations experience of Ford and General Motors in Britain. The General Motors plant in Luton had accepted unions and had established a grievance committee, consisting mostly of workers, long before 1944. The company also has experienced very few work stoppages, even though they have generally paid lower wages than does Ford.

The determination of American firms to prevent the unionization of its workers (and in this case, of its supervisory personnel) is illustrated by some of the documents released in the fall of 1977 by the British Association of Scientific, Technical and Managerial Staffs, which sought to represent the supervisory work force of the Du Pont Chemical Company's Northern Ireland facilities. One of these documents, entitled "Departmental Programme for No Union Recognition," suggests, for example: "Identify the union aspirations of each individual foreman, assign the supervisor who will consult with him and determine the best communication programme to convince him of no union recognition." Department managers were also advised to make the foreman feel that he is part of management, to take a "sincere and personal interest" in him and his family, and to shower him with praise rather than chastisement.[22]

The nonrecognition postures of the various American firms in Europe are not just the result of a conscious commitment on their part to keep the workers so happy that they will not become interested in being represented by trade unions. They are as much, if not more so, an extension of the industrial-relations system the companies were used to at home. In the States, for example, employers will generally not be inclined to recognize labor unions in their workplaces unless and until their workers have, by majority secret ballot, elected to do so. That kind of legalistic labor-relations tradition makes the recalcitrance by American subsidiary managers to seemingly loose labor-relations practices very understandable.

What has complicated things even more in such places as Britain is the fact that recent labor legislation, which supposedly was designed to put some order in labor-management relations, did not make employer obligations as clear-cut and as definitive as they are in the United States. For example, IBM management calculated that even though it agreed to the 1977 employee vote, it still might be able to thwart union organizing efforts by appealing the rather gray provisions of the Employment Protection and the Trade Union and Labour Relations acts.[23]

A certain amount of American reticence undoubtedly also results from the fact that, in a number of countries, the company would have to deal with a variety of unions, which means that management would, not only have to deal with the common kinds of labor disputes, but it would also have to cope with jurisdictional disputes as well. Most managers prefer to prevent such a complicated situation at all costs, or they will at least try to postpone them as long as possible. The irony of that posture is, of course, that company recalcitrance merely adds fuel to the already existing distrust and polarization and may even bring about greater anticompany solidarity among the workers organized in the various potentially conflicting unions.

Many American managers are even more critical of trade unionists in Europe than they are of those in the United States because they perceive them to be more antagonistic toward the free-enterprise system. Not only do West European socialist and communist labor leaders villify the American multinationals as the vanguard of the forces of evil that undermine global economic and social justice, but Americans do not feel very comfortable dealing with adversaries who use that kind of rhetoric, and they certainly do not want to contribute to their economic success.

The ideological antagonism felt by these multinational corporation executives is very similar to the negative attitude many American businessmen had toward the late Walter Reuther and his associates in the industrial-union movement. These men were readily identified as socialists, if not un-American, and were sharply contrasted with the more pragmatic, economically motivated craft unionists like George Meany and Frank Fitzsimmons, whose loyalty to the American way of life and free enterprise could hardly be questioned.

American subsidiaries in Britain have not been the only ones reluctant to recognize trade unions; Kassalow reported that several significant incidents have occurred in the Netherlands as well. Some of these took place in the Rotterdam area, an area of very rapid industrialization, which lacked the kind of established working class and industrial-relations culture that existed in the older industrial complex around Amsterdam. In addition, American subsidiaries in Holland have shown particular reluctance to deal with unions in petroleum and in engineering.[24]

U.S. multinationals have been especially opposed to staff or white-collar unions, a tendency that is again directly related to Stateside practices. Until recently, white-collar workers and supervisory personnel have rarely been organized in the States. Employers have generally persisted in considering them to be part of management. Even American trade unions themselves seem to promote the separation between white and blue collars. In their negotiations, they have placed much greater emphasis on differentiations in pay and privileges for workers of various levels of skill and responsibility than is done by European trade unionists. American labor leaders appear to remain true to the American dream that all men can improve themselves, and that workers should be encouraged to become owners rather than remain mere employees. It is not surprising, therefore, that when American companies are confronted with demands for union recognition by supervisory personnel, they have generally been extremely reluctant to comply with such requests.

Even though Nigel McCrae was quite correct in observing that union recognition is frequently just a polemical issue, in the eyes of European trade unionists and social commentators, American management's posture is considered to be evidence of the determination of U.S. multinationals to undermine local customs and traditions.[25]

The second major area of labor-relations complaints against American multinationals concerns the practice of precipitous closing of plants and apparent ease with which large numbers of workers are laid off. These obviously hurtful consequences of corporate investment and production decisions are predominantly interpreted as reflecting the fact that American firms have the maximization of profits as their primary commitment, and that they have little or no consideration for the welfare of the workers and the economies of individual communities, regions, and nations.

Few European trade-union leaders and government officials argue against the necessity for a firm to relocate and/or cut back when a market becomes saturated or when vigorous competition makes the continuation of local production a losing proposition. Nevertheless, it is widely believed in Europe that the loss of a significant number of jobs disrupts local or national planning and welfare, and that such a possibility, at minimum, necessitates thorough consultation between the parties affected. It is felt that a concerted, honest attempt by union leaders and government officials to ascertain that such an action is really necessary will not only prevent unnecessary backlash, it may also prevent the company from having to face legal action and accusations of mismanagement.[26]

One distinct impediment in the effective communication about this issue is the fact that large enterprises (including American multinationals) value highly their mobility of operations. It is ironic that this same mobility made it possible for American firms to invest in the EC countries and respond more readily to the investment incentives offered by host governments than local firms can.

Resentments about shutdown and layoffs have been especially bitter when they involved established local enterprises that had only recently been acquired by American firms. In such cases, trade unionists have not necessarily been the only, or even the major, complainants. While labor leaders have labeled such cases typical examples of Yankee opportunism and callousness, and/or have felt frustrated and angered about their inability to affect company-headquarter decisions, the government officials who issued the takeover permit feel betrayed and, therefore, feel little obligation to save the company from any undue embarrassment and discomfort.

There are a number of legendary cases of closings and layoffs by American firms. One of the most notorious is that of Roberts-Arundel. The Roberts Company of Sanford, N.C., a textile-machinery producer, in 1965 acquired Arundel-Couthard, a British competitor. The new firm, Roberts-Arundel, Ltd., quickly closed four of the older firm's five plants and immediately ran into difficulties in the remaining Southgate-Stockport facility. Even though the actual number of jobs lost was not very great, the firm's difficulties were greatly compounded by several other changes that management wanted to make. The tragic comedy of errors (mostly managerial) resulted in the decision by Mr. Roberts to sell out and abandon the whole project, a decision that, in turn, angered local interests.[27]

Also frequently cited are the cases, in France, of General Electric, Remington Rand, and General Motors. General Electric, immediately upon acquisition of the computer firm Machines Bull, laid off five hundred of that firm's fifteen hundred employees. Remington, seeking to rationalize production in its various European facilities, dismissed eight hundred of the company's twelve hundred workers in Lyon. And General Motors, in 1967, having found that its Frigidaire appliances had been competed out of the French market, decided to close its Gennevilliers plant, resulting in the loss of 685 jobs there.[28] Valéry Giscard d'Estaing, then minister of finance, was only one of many French government officials and journalists who judged these decisions to be callous and reflective of the American firms' ignorance of French labor-relations traditions and practices.[29]

Some years ago, Schlitz Brewing Company declared bankruptcy in Belgium and withdrew after two years of unprofitable operation. That action was also definitely considered to be precipitous and representative of the American "financial mentality" and "lack of consideration for employees, suppliers and customers." Boddewyn suggests that "the Belgian way would have been to smooth over things with government subsidies in one way or the other to tide Schlitz over, or to facilitate the selling of the brewery to another interest."[30]

What appears to be the predominant problem in all these cases, in the eyes of European critics, is the virtual absence in the American culture of a sense of *noblesse oblige*, a sense of responsibility by the wealthy for the less fortunate or by the employer toward his employees. However, it might be just as accurate to place part of the blame on the corporate form of business organization. With a limited-liability structure and increasingly impersonal ledger-balance-oriented managerial elites, profit maximization can easily become the exclusive and predominant company goal. That sort of orientation will generally allow humaneness only when it pays off.

What magnifies the impact of these plant closings and mass layoffs even more are the apparent threats of similar possibilities in deliberate as well as casual remarks by American business executives. For instance, European trade-union circles constantly cite Ford Company officials and their apparent threats to relocate from such locations as Great Britain, and they connect these statements with company decisions to build extensively (including a $350-million Fiesta plant) in Spain, a location known more for its low labor costs than for its tremendous market potential.[31] Henry Ford II, while traveling through Asia during his British company's 1971 strike, was also reported to have said that the production of certain components of the Escort and Cortina models, which were being manufactured in Britain at that time and then shipped to Asia for assembly, would be shifted to Asia, and that such would be achieved deliberately though slowly.[32] During a subsequent visit to London, in conversations with Prime Minister Heath, Mr. Ford tied such a decision to the condition of whether the company's labor problems in Britain would show improvements. He reportedly also threatened to move production from Dagenham to West Germany.[33] Similar observations about dissatisfaction with local conditions and the fact that these might well lead to shifts in investment and/or production were made again by Ford in 1973 and in 1975.[34] Rhetoric of this kind certainly must have done its share to produce the kind of strained industrial relations Ford has experienced in several of its European locations.[35]

Chrysler Company officials had a somewhat similar record in England, although their threats of withdrawal produced a slightly different result. The blunt statements by John Riccardo (then president of the American Chrysler Corporation) in 1975 and the Labour government's fears of the loss of twenty-five thousand jobs produced an interesting relationship between Chrysler and the British government, whereby the company was being backed until 1980 with a maximum of £162.5 million in grants and loans. Although Chrysler's labor relations were not actually smooth after its liaison with the British government, the conditions of that bail-out agreement forced Chrysler to conform more to British labor-relations standards, a changeover that reduced by 95 percent the number of man-hours lost through disputes (from February 1976 to February 1977).[36]

Many American subsidiaries have discovered that layoffs can be very expensive and cumbersome in Europe and, in some cases, almost impossible. In France, for example, employers have for years been required to inform the Department of Labor of any contemplated plant closings and layoffs. Along with this notification should be submitted detailed information on each employee to be released. No one can be laid off until the department has examined the request in light of the local and national employment situations and until it has given its approval to the company action. The same general procedures are followed in the Netherlands. In Germany, if a dismissal is held to be "harsh from a social point of view," it may, in fact, be set aside in court.

Consultation and approval there involves a tripartite body of government, union, and industry representatives. German employers are also required to grant an employee who is about to be dismissed time off with pay to enable him to seek employment elsewhere. In Denmark and France, employers are required to pay severance allowances.[37]

The Council of Ministers of the EEC, on December 17, 1974, tried to deal with the layoff problem on a more comprehensive scale when it approved a directive that sought to bring about greater coordination between national redundancy (layoff) laws, thereby seeking to alleviate firms by allocating jobs to areas from which they could more easily be withdrawn.[38] Two years later, the ministers of labor and social affairs approved a directive concerning the safeguarding of employees' rights and advantages in the event of transfers of undertakings, establishments, and parts of establishments. This particular directive urges member states to assure workers their continued rights from existing contracts of employment and to forbid the dismissal in the event of transfers of undertakings.[39]

The relative difficulty of laying off workers in Europe (as compared to the situation in the States) is well illustrated by the 1976 report of the president of Eaton Corporation, in which he indicated that his firm was only allowed to cut its overseas work force from nineteen thousand to eighteen thousand, while the company reduced its American employment from thirty-one thousand to twenty-five thousand.[40]

The third major grievance against American firms in Western Europe centers on the tendency of a number of them to refuse to participate in established contract-negotiating practices. Here, again, the problem seems to be a matter of transposing Stateside industrial-relations practices. While in most European countries, basic contract bargaining is centralized (that is, negotiations are conducted between national or regional unions or groups of unions and employer associations), the American pattern has predominantly been a single firm negotiating with a single union. A good example of the European pattern is the British metalworking industry, which has operated since 1898 under a bargaining system made up of the forty-six-hundred-member Engineering Employers Federation and the Confederation of Ship-building and Engineering Unions, which is composed of some thirty-four national unions.[41] Agreements resulting from such broadscale negotiations clearly lack the sort of details that will satisfy the specific requirements of the different subsectors and firms. American firms could well object to them for that reason alone. However, supplementary contracts can be and are being negotiated. The main objection seems to be that centralized bargaining requires the surrender of a significant portion of management's prerogative to execute freely its right of private property. Many Americans also consider it too collectivist a practice.

In this area of grievances against American companies (deviations from the established negotiating patterns), it is again in Great Britain where the most serious incidents have been reported. Particularly publicized have been the decentralization initiatives of all three major automobile manufacturers (Ford, Chrysler, and Vauxhall-GM), several oil companies (Esso/Exxon and Mobil Oil), two food processors (Heinz and Kellogg), two metal processors (International Nickel and Alcan), and Massey-Ferguson, Kodak, and Woolworth.[42]

The situation is substantially different with American firms operating on the Continent. For example, Ford bargains collectively at the national level in West Germany and has been doing so since 1963, even though the company still refuses to do so in Great Britain. The same is true of General Motors (Adam Opel).[43] In fact, even normally nonconformist IBM participates in the collective bargaining of its German industrial association.

In Belgium and France, employers in most industries have little choice as to whether they want to belong to employer associations and thus will participate in central bargaining procedures. Roger Blanpain, in fact, suggested that it is in their self-interest to do so. Since, in a number of cases, collective agreements entered into by the appropriate employers' association in Belgium are even binding upon nonmember employers, multinationals who do not join the association and refuse to participate in the centralized bargaining would be totally at the mercy of the negotiations conducted by others.[44] Accordingly, most American firms do belong.

The pressure by American multinationals to decentralize collective bargaining is no longer the issue it used to be, although it has definitely contributed to the unpleasant memories MNC critics have. First, a number of union leaders have become more interested in promoting multinational bargaining—that is, bargaining between the multinational firm's headquarters and the combined unions from the firm's various plant locations. More importantly, European employers and government officials, and even some union officials, have begun to see the benefits of plant-level bargaining. American firms have thus spearheaded what may well have been inevitable and desirable changes in established European practice.[45]

Even though participation or nonparticipation in centralized contract negotiations is virtually synonymous with belonging or not belonging to employer associations, the two aspects can and should be separated. For example, all eighteen U.S.-owned rubber companies operating in Britain were members of the British Rubber Manufacturers Association, even though the major American rubber-company subsidiaries are well-known for their refusal to recognize unions.[46] This paradoxical situation calls attention to the fact that industry or employer associations are advantageous for many reasons other than as vehicles for collective bargaining. In a number of EEC countries, they are important channels of communication with the government's planning and fiscal-policy agencies. They are also viable lobbying organizations for their sector of the national economy. They are particularly viable because the labor unions tend to have very close connections with socialist parties, which, in turn, are either in the legislative majority or participate in governing coalitions. This latter political reality particularly helps explain why most American subsidiaries are members of their employer associations, even in Britain, even though some of these firms were not necessarily association members before they were acquired by American interests.[47]

A number of trade unionists have complained about a fourth labor practice by American multinationals: the use of migrant or guest workers. They point out that in some electric and automotive firms, the proportion of guest workers (Turks, Italians, Portuguese, Algerians) reaches 20, 30, and even 50 percent, a pattern that can obviously help keep labor costs down and keep labor relations benign. Daniel Benedict charges that Chrysler used guest workers in France to keep local trade unions weak and frightened.[48] It has also been suggested that multinational corporations have made widespread use of migrant workers because national governments in Western Europe will protect them less avidly than they do their own workers. Thus, a company will not be criticized as severely when they lay off guest workers or when they relocate a plant that is mostly staffed by migrants. Some communities may even welcome their departure. Guest workers can be and have been sent home; they are also more willing to find work by moving elsewhere. Some trade unionists have charged that the use of guest workers has not just been a way to obtain a labor force not otherwise available; they claim that multinational management may have perpetuated their use even when host economies no longer enjoyed full employment and labor shortages.

CONCLUSIONS

The industrial-relations reputation of American firms has certainly not been totally negative. Many Europeans, both from management and labor, appreciate the fact that American management technology has helped increase worker productivity; introduce a fixed, hourly-wage pay system; shorten the work week; raise the level of compensation; make available a large array of useful goods and services; and generally raise the standard of living and the social mobility of workers.

At the same time, though, American firms have generally been identified as antiworker and antitrade union. The level of appreciation for their policies toward union recognition, collective bargaining, and adherence to local standards of justice is not very high. This kind of reputation has been a key element in the dynamics of the European movement toward greater direct worker participation in business-enterprise decisions.

NOTES

1. Nat Weinberg, "The Multinational Corporation and Labor," in Abdul A. Said and Luiz R. Simmons, eds., *The New Sovereigns: Multinational Corporations as World Powers* (Englewood Cliffs, N.J.: Prentice-Hall, 1975), p. 92.

2. This issue was discussed at considerable length by Jacob Clayman, secretary-treasurer of the Industrial Union Department of the AFL-CIO, before the Senate Foreign Relations Committee's Subcommittee on Multinational Corporations (94th Congress, hearings on July 21, December 9, and December 10, 1975). The irony of this example and numerous parallel cases is that these products are then imported into the home country (the country from which the jobs were removed).

3. For more detailed discussion of the problems inherent in relocation, see: *Multinational Enterprises and Social Policy* (Geneva: International Labour Office, 1973); Christopher Tugendhat, *The Multinationals* (London: Eyre and Spottiswoode, 1971); *Multinational Enterprises: The Reality of Their Social Policies and Practices* (Geneva: International Organization of Employers, 1974); and *Host Countries and Multinational Corporations* (Washington, D.C.: U.S. Chamber of Commerce, 1975).

4. Robert Copp, "The Multinational Corporation and Industrial Relations," *Monthly Labor Review* 96 (Aug. 1973): 453. This is the text of Mr. Copp's remarks at the 1973 annual spring meeting of the Industrial Relations Research Association.

5. B. C. Roberts, "Factors Influencing the Organization and Style of Management and Their Effect on the Pattern of Industrial Relations in Multi-national Corporations," in Hans Günter, ed., *Transnational Industrial Relations* (London: Macmillan-St. Martin's Press, 1972), pp. 118-19. Everett Kassalow, in his paper "Multinational Corporations and Their Impact on Industrial Relations" (presented at the International Conference on Trends in Industrial and Labour Relations, held in Montreal in May 1976), suggests also that companies with fairly standardized technologies, such as petroleum refining and automobile manufacturing, will be more likely "to lean more heavily" on subsidiaries than is the case in such industries as food processing or light electronics, both of which are labor-intensive.

6. As quoted in John Allen James et al., "Multinational Trade Unions Muscle Their Strength," *European Business* 39 (Autumn 1973): 40. This same judgment is also made by Paul Malles in *Trends in Industrial Relations Systems of Continental Europe* (Ottawa: Task Force on Labour Relations, 1969), p. 157.

7. Duane Kujawa, *International Labor Relations in the Automobile Industry* (New York: Praeger Publishers, 1971), pp. 18-27.

8. G. B. J. Bomers, *Multinational Corporations and Industrial Relations: A Comparative Study of West Germany and the Netherlands* (Assen, Netherlands: Van Gorcum, 1976), p. 128.

9. John Fayerweather, "Elite Attitudes Toward Multinational Firms: A Study of Britain, France, and Canada," *International Studies Quarterly* 16 (Dec. 1972): 472-90. British trade-union leaders rated American firms as very distinctly less willing to extend recognition.

10. Twenty-two percent neither agreed nor disagreed, and 8 percent said they did not know. Compare with Michael Hodges, *Multinational Corporations and National Government: A Case Study of the United Kingdom's Experience, 1964-1970* (Lexington, Mass.: Lexington Books, D. C. Heath, 1974).

11. ITT, *European Attitudes to Multinationals*, prepared by Landell Mills Associates, London, April 1976.

12. "Europeans Offer 'Split Image' of U.S. Multinationals," *Industry Week* 74 (July 17, 1972): 26.

13. David E. Ricks, Marilyn Y. C. Fu, and Jeffrey S. Arpan, *International Business Blunders* (Columbus, Ohio: Grid, Inc., 1974), p. 74.

14. For example, Hans Günter, "Labor and Multinational Corporations in Western Europe: Some Problems and Prospects," in Duane Kujawa, ed., *International Labor and the Multinational Enterprise* (New York: Praeger Publishers, 1975), p. 148; International Labour Organisation, *Multinationals in Western Europe: The Industrial Relations Experience* (Geneva: ILO, 1975), p. 3.

15. Samuel Silkin, "American Investment and European Cultures: Conflict and Cooperation," in Alfred Kamin, ed., *Western European Labor and the American Corporation* (Washington, D.C.: Bureau of National Affairs, 1970), p. 447; Günter, "Labor and Multinational Corporations in Western Europe, p. 176.

16. Milton Derber, "Labor-Management Relations in the Metalworking Industries of Three Countries," *Journal of Industrial Relations* 13 (March 1971): 3-4. Also see the *Donovan Report* (The Report of the Royal Commission on Trade Unions and Employer Associations, 1965-1968), (London: Her Majesty's Stationery Office, Cmnd. 3623, 1968).

17. Everett Kassalow, "Multinational Corporations and Their Impact on Industrial Relations," p. 21.

18. John Gennard and A. M. Steuer, "The Industrial Relations of Foreign-Owned Subsidiaries in the United Kingdom," *British Journal of Industrial Relations* 9 (July 1971): 155.

19. *The Times*, February 20, 1977. Also see Nancy Foy and Herman Gadon, *The IBM World* (London: Eyre, Methuen, 1974), for a detailed description of the company and its philosophy of personnel management.

20. *The Times*, June 13, 1977.

21. F. Lundberg, as cited in Ernst Piehl, *Multinazionale Konzerne und Internationale Gewerkschaftsbewegung* (Frankfurt: Europäische Verlagsanwalt, 1973), pp. 150 ff.

22. *The Times*, November 4, 1977.

23. *The Times*, February 20, 1977.

24. ILO, *Multinationals in Western Europe*, pp. 4-5.

25. Nigel McCrae, "Report on Research Findings Relating to Great Britain," prepared for the Research Meeting on Multinational Corporations and Labour, International Institute for Labor Studies, Geneva, 5-7 December 1973 (Geneva: IILS-International Educational Materials Exchange, #4 131), p. 11. He logically suggests that automatic union recognition would be poor management strategy, considering the adversary relationships and tactics of class-conscious societies.

26. Paul Heise, "The Multinational Corporation and Industrial Relations: The American Approach Compared with the European," *Industrial Relations-Relations Industrielles* 28, no. 31 (1973): 42.

27. Silkin, "American Investment and European Cultures," p. 443; and ILO, *Multinationals in Western Europe*, pp. 12-14.

28. John H. Dunning, *The Role of American Investment in the British Economy* (London: PEP-Broadsheet 507, 1969), p. 154; Ricks, Fu, and Arpan, *International*

Business Blunders, p. 60; and Daniel Benedict, "Labour and the Multinationals" (Paper presented at the International Conference on Trends in Industrial and Labour Relations, Montreal, May 1976), p. 6.

29. *Christian Science Monitor*, October 6, 1962.

30. J. Boddewyn, "Issues Between the Multinational Corporation and Host Governments: The European Case," in A. Capoor and Phillip D. Grubb, *The International Enterprise in Transition* (Princeton, N.J.: Darwin Press, 1972), p. 435.

31. The Spanish government granted Ford the investment permit under the condition that at least two-thirds of its production be exported. See Ben A. Sharman, "Multinational Corporations and the International Metal Workers Federation," *Labor Law Journal* 24 (Aug. 1973): 470.

32. ILO, *Multinationals in Western Europe*, p. 21; and Benedict, "Labour and the Multinationals."

33. Sharman, p. 470.

34. ILO, *Multinationals in Western Europe*, p. 22.

35. See Piehl, pp. 150-61, for a general history of Ford's labor-relations experiences in Europe.

36. See John M. Starrels, "The Dilemmas of Planning: Chrysler and the Wilson Government: Or, How Labour Came to Love the Automobile" (Paper presented at the annual meeting of the American Political Science Association, Chicago, September 1976).

37. Shearer, p. 115, and Teague, "I.L.O.'s World Watch on Labor Standards," pp. 28-29.

38. *The Protection of Workers in Multinational Companies* (EEC: European Documentation, Trade Union Series, 1976/1), pp. 6 ff.

39. European Commission, *Report on the Development of the Social Situation in the Communities in 1976* (April 1977): 9-10.

40. *The Economist*, April 17, 1976.

41. Milton Derber, "Labor-Management Relations in the Metalworking Industries of Three Countries," *Journal of Industrial Relations* 13 (March 1971): 2-7.

42. Gennard and Steuer, p. 153.

43. Robert Copp, "Ford Motor Company as a Multinational Employer," *Monthly Labor Review* 96 (Aug. 1973): 59-60; Gennard and Steuer, p. 155.

44. Roger Blanpain, "Multinational Corporations as Agents of Change and Innovation in Industrial Relations," as quoted in ILO, *Multinationals in Western Europe*, p. 10.

45. Union people and other representatives of workers at the plant level have always felt a need for special grievance and other provisions to make the national contract "operative" at their particular plant.

46. Gennard and Steuer, p. 153.

47. Ibid.

48. Benedict, "Labour and the Multinationals," p. 9. Joseph Mire suggests that employers have turned to foreign workers because they had great difficulty attracting nationals to do undesirable jobs, such as assembly-line operation. ("Improving Working Life: The Role of European Unions," *Monthly Labor Review* 97 [Sept. 1974]: 3-4.)

4

LIMITED WORKER-PARTICIPATION
EXPERIMENTS IN THE UNITED STATES

Most trade unionists, European as well as American, believe that American workers participate only very occasionally and indirectly in corporate decision making (through the process of collective bargaining) and, then, only on a very limited number of issues. This may be the case for the bulk of American workers; it is not for all of them. A number of American firms — among them, several multinational corporations — have indeed introduced workplace reforms that give employees a variety of opportunities to participate in decision making in a more direct fashion.

This chapter seeks to describe broadly the evolution of the workplace-reform movement in the United States, to illustrate the kind of practices adopted by a number of multinationals in their Stateside operations, and to examine ways in which such third parties as local and national governments have sought to stimulate reform. A brief look will also be taken at the labor-management style of subsidiaries of foreign multinationals (especially the Japanese) operative in the United States and the impact these may have on American firms.

We should not proceed, however, until we mention some of the arguments presented by the defenders of the American way of labor management. First, such advocates are apt to label European worker-participation practices as unnatural and artificial. Max Ways, for example, decries the fact that the U.S. media have frequently made it appear as if the United States lags behind in worker participation.[1] He feels that such allegations are only valid if "worker participation [were] narrowly defined as the kind that arises out of confrontation and class struggle and is decided by political strictures imposed on companies [as a result of] labor union pressure." The expectation of the latter kind of participation is said to ignore a "much broader, deeper and sounder" type of participation that occurs "through the evolution of the economic system."

Ways suggests, for example, that very significant improvements have been made since 1900 in the quality of jobs in America. Workers, who were previously paid only for their brawn or their automated performance of clearly defined tasks, are said to be paid more frequently now for using their increased knowledge, their power of reason, their communicative skill, and their sensitivity in interpersonal relations. Thus, since today's holders of better jobs are more responsible for the way the work is done, they are said to participate in shaping the course their firm and the whole national economy will take more than their predecessors ever did.

Ways also argues that organizational growth, technological change, and increased organizational complexity have made it imperative that corporate decision making be decentralized and delegated. With automation having eliminated scores of tedious and repetitive jobs, and with work having become increasingly specialized, the argument runs, a manager would rarely want to, or be able to, tell a subordinate exactly how to do his job. Thus, he suggests, the worker of today has a considerable amount of influence in his firm.

The key question, however, is whether today's workers feel they really have much say in matters that count. The arguments presented are apt to satisfy them as much as the average consumer is convinced that he is the one who decides in the market place what will be produced and how such products will be priced. In both cases, the conviction will undoubtedly prevail that their input in the business's decision-making process is miniscule compared to that of corporate management.

THE EVOLUTION OF THE WORKPLACE-REFORM MOVEMENT

American experiments in worker participation are not just a product of the last several decades. Even while Frederick W. Taylor's theories of scientific management (with their built-in preference for hierarchical organization) were fast rising in popularity, several firms were already establishing labor-management consultation structures. In 1923, for example, the Baltimore and Ohio Railroad and the Machinists Union organized joint management-worker committees for that firm's repair shops. Although the committees were nothing more than screening mechanisms for employee suggestions, they turned out to be quite active. In the first fifteen years of their existence, they processed some thirty-one thousand suggestions, dealing with such a range of questions as the improvement of efficiency, the reduction of waste, the expansion of the business, and ways to achieve better working conditions in the shops. This Baltimore and Ohio experiment was paralleled by a number of firms in the garment industry.[2] Two other early and interesting experiments are still operating today. One of these is at Baltimore's McCormick and Co., processors of spices and other food products.[3] Charles Willoughby, nephew of the company's founder, assumed control of the firm in 1932 with the strong conviction that his uncle's distrust-ridden, dictatorial management practices had to be replaced if the company were to survive. The new company president raised the wages, reduced the working hours, and instituted a system of employee boards. Even though these multiple management boards at McCormick have been composed exclusively of middle management and have elected their members by a system of co-optation rather than by direct election, they have certainly decentralized company decision making. They have established a precedent that, according to some of the firm's contemporary executives, ought to be extended to include the lower ranks of company employees.[4]

Another case of practices that were initiated during the depression is that of the Lincoln Electric Company, a maker of arc-welding equipment in Cleveland, Ohio. James F. Lincoln set the plan in operation in 1933, when the company was operating at a sizable loss. It is based on the premise that a company is a team and that the head of the company is merely the leader of the team. Every individual member of the team is expected to realize that he or she carries responsibility. One of the prime responsibilities of management, according to Lincoln, is to stimulate in the employees "a strong desire to develop their latent abilities."

Worker participation at Lincoln Electric does not occur through consultative structures. Its workers share in a significant way in the company's earnings and are left to manage their own task performance. Their financial benefits come through a system of productivity bonuses that are based on measurements of quantitative and qualitative productivity. The fact that workers are basically self-motivated and make their own decisions as to how their work tasks should be performed has apparently produced a side benefit: it has reduced the amount of overhead the company would have to expend for supervision and inspection.

Also established during the thirties were the labor-management committees of the Tennessee Valley Authority and various applications of the so-called Scanlon Plan. The TVA committees were intended to build worker morale, to reduce waste, to promote employee health and safety, and to increase efficiency. One distinct benefit of the joint committee consultations, according to William Black, Jr., administrator of the TVA labor-management relations program, is that, as a result of the employee representatives' knowing what management is doing and why, workers have been "more excited about their work, much more involved in it, and much more productive."[5]

The most widely practiced employee-participation plan, designed in the thirties but increasingly popular in the sixties, is the arrangement developed by Joseph Scanlon, cost accountant, steel worker, trade-union leader, and M.I.T. lecturer. In 1937, when Scanlon, then a local union president, was confronted with his employer's virtual business failure, he got together with Clinton Golden of the Pittsburgh Steelworkers Union headquarters. The two of them devised a three-pronged arrangement: (1) open and frank consultations on goals, problems, and ideas; (2) the optimization of human potential; and (3) a bonus system based on enterprise as well as on individual productivity.[6]

Most of the more than one hundred U.S. firms that have adopted the Scanlon Plan facilitate the projected consultations through a two-tiered system of committees: the departmental production committees, and the company-wide screening or coordinating committee. The production committees are generally made up of two or more employees, elected by their peers or appointed by the union local, and a management representative, usually the foreman, office manager, or chief engineer. The management representative chairs the committee, which is given full authority to solve the unit's production problems, to devise procedures that will increase unit efficiency, and to put into immediate operation worker suggestions, as long as they will not affect other departments and will not require large expenditures of money. If the plant is unionized, extreme care is usually taken that the committee will stay away from union business, grievances, wages, and other basic collective-bargaining issues.

The screening or coordinating committee is normally composed of an equal number of representatives from the production committees and from company management. The company's top executive generally serves as chairman of this committee. In a unionized shop, the president of the local will be a member as well. While the other worker-members are usually designated by their respective production committees, they can be elected directly by the workers or by the union leadership.

The tasks of the screening or coordinating committee are relatively clear-cut: determine the bases and size of the bonus; communicate the company's current competitive standing, its prospects, and its problems; and screen suggestions that deal with issues that extend beyond one department. It also sits as a court of appeal for considering suggestions that were not adopted by production committees but that the sponsors would like to see given a second consideration.

Several key points about Scanlon committees need to be kept in mind. First, they are clearly only consultative; management retains its decision-making prerogatives. Second, a majority of the companies employing the Scanlon Plan are not unionized. In fact, trade unionists tend to be of the opinion— and several businessmen have admitted— that some firms have adopted the plan to avoid having unions in the shop.[7] A third feature is important as well: the plan is based on the premise that the individual's prime motivation for working is to earn money. A number of people have raised the question of whether the plan is therefore as vulnerable to failure as are ordinary incentive-payment techniques and profit-sharing plans.[8] The defenders of the plan have a valid argument when they point out that the bonus system is not individually calculated, as incentive systems are, and thus does not tend to atomize the workplace. And incentive systems and profit-sharing plans do not involve a system of consultation committees, while the Scanlon Plan does. Thus, even though workers may originally find their materialist motivations activated by Scanlon's bonus plan, it is likely that, as the plan continues operation, they will see themselves more and more as members of the team and will consider their firm to be *their* business as well as that of management. That latter point is supported somewhat by the findings of Goodman, Wakeley, and Roh, who asked workers whether they would like to be representatives on a production committee: nearly 40 percent of the employees interviewed answered in the positive. That is not a bad percentage when we realize that committee membership would only mean more work, more time spent, and more responsibility, and that usually no extra monetary compensation is given for accepting such a membership assignment.[9]

The most elaborate and inclusive system of labor-management consultation was devised during World War II by the War Production Board.[10] Launched on February 27, 1942, as part of President Roosevelt's War Production Drive, the concept of the so-called Labor Management Production Drive Committees was enthusiastically endorsed by the CIO and AFL. The National Association of Manufacturers leadership was more reluctant, though. It did, in fact, raise the question of whether the proposal was not an acceptance of labor's desire to enter the field of management's prerogatives; a number of companies withheld their cooperation on those grounds. The president of a leading car-manufacturing firm went on record, saying that he could only accept the committees if they served as clearing houses for suggestions to improve production. He also insisted that they be purely advisory.[11]

At the high point of their existence (1944), there were some five thousand plant committees representing over seven million workers. Most observers of the committees are rather reserved about the degree of their effectiveness. Apparently, only several hundred of them made any sort of significant contribution to productivity.[12] Most of the committees seemed to limit their activities to organizing car pools, blood banks, and bond drives, and the bulk of them evaporated as soon as the war ended. As soon as victory had been won, the "victory committees" seemed to have lost their reason to exist.

The plant-level victory committees did not just stand by themselves; they were designed to be integral parts of a nationwide structure of consultation. Some observers suggest that the wartime experience with district-level committees contributed to the emergence of the currently existing area and/or city labor-management committees. For example, the first postwar area committee came about in February 1946 in Toledo, Ohio, a city that, during the thirties, had experienced some particularly bitter and violent confrontations between management and labor.[13] Not long after, Louisville, Kentucky, established its committee. In both cases, the committees that have remained in operation are tripartite, with equal representation for management, labor, and the general community. Their primary tasks are to prevent unnecessary cleavage in the community and to promote the economic development of the area. Even though the Toledo and Louisville committees have been relatively successful, local committees did not really begin to function until recently in a number of towns. Area committees became popular again in the early seventies partly because of the establishment and activities of the National Commission for Productivity and its successor institutions (which will be discussed later). Many of these later experiments were inspired by what was achieved in Jamestown, N.Y.

Jamestown had undergone a very serious economic decline, and its mayor, Stanley N. Lundine, in his inaugural address in January 1972, called upon labor and management to commit themselves to reverse that trend. Having set their first priority as the raising of productivity, the Jamestown Area Labor-Management Committee effectively strove to allocate community resources more efficiently and, above all, to lay a basis for open dialogue and trust among the previously antagonistic industrial camps of the area. Under the guidance of Professor Richard Walton of Harvard University, eight basic requirements for quality work were adopted as guidelines for areawide as well as in-plant activity. They are:

1. Adequate and fair compensation,
2. Safe and healthy working conditions,
3. Immediate opportunity to develop and use human capacities,
4. Future opportunity for growth and security,
5. *Social integration in the work organization,**
6. *Constitutionalism in the work organization,**
7. Work relative to the total life span,
8. Relevance to the larger society.[14]

All the quality-of-work projects that have been sponsored by the Jamestown Area Committee were specifically developed in plant-level labor-management committees. In this part of the program, the area committee was merely the facilitator and coordinator; its main task was to encourage an atmosphere of understanding and a common recognition of the need to improve work quality.

The Jamestown plant-level labor-management committees faced two problems. First, they had to make sure that they did not interfere with the collective-bargaining process and with established grievance procedures. Unions were logically concerned about their jurisdiction and about the

*Author's italics.

possibility that the committees could be used to undermine them. The second problem related to the occasional drift and lack of communication between labor-union leadership and rank-and-file workers. Just as union leaders can become suspicious about what is intended, so, too, can workers, who need to understand that productivity-directed schemes do not necessarily turn out to be instruments of exploitation.

Labor-management consultation structures have also been established at the level of industrial sectors or sets of enterprises engaged in the same kind of business. The most publicized example of an industry wide program is that of the steel industry. In the wake of apparently fruitful work by the industry's Human Relations Committee from 1959 to 1964, and the increased competition from imported steel, the ten leading steel companies and the United Steelworkers Union decided, in 1971, to establish an industry-wide joint productivity committee. In 1974, at the plant level, it established the so-called Employment Security and Productivity Committees. By 1978, some 230 plant committees were reported to be in operation.[15]

These steel-industry committees have been strictly consultative. They are composed of union officials (the local president, the chairman, and the secretary of the grievance committee, and the grievance-committee members most concerned with the topics scheduled for consideration) and company officials (the plant manager, the executive in charge of industrial relations, the plant's industrial engineer, and the area or district superintendent). Their agenda embraces a variety of subjects, all of which relate to productivity improvement and job security: excessive absenteeism; reduction of rejects, waste, rework, and scrap; saving of materials and energy; equipment maintenance; and downtime. They also discuss the competitive environment of the company and the industry, including foreign competition—one of the prime reasons for their having been established.

A number of workers have been quite critical of the committees. They feel that too much committee time has been spent analyzing the behavior of the workers, and that the emphasis appears to be on speeding up the workers and eventually phasing many out of their jobs.

PARTICIPATIVE MANAGEMENT IN PARTICULAR AMERICAN MULTINATIONALS

A number of workplace reforms have been introduced in the Stateside plants and offices of American firms that are active internationally. Distinctly limited in number, these reforms have been operative in only a small number of a company's Stateside plants, and have led to the establishment of labor-management committees with distinctly differing kinds of jurisdiction. A variety of industries are included: automobiles, automobile parts, rubber tires, chemical products, food products, and electronic instruments, to name but a few.

The American multinational corporation that has been most extensively involved in Stateside workplace reform is General Motors. Most of GM's reforms have come about since 1971, the year in which Stephen Fuller was appointed to the newly created position of vice-president for personnel administration and development. Fuller, who had been an associate dean of the Harvard Business School for five years, was given the assignment to develop a program that would increase work efficiency and job satisfaction. An organization development (O.D.) staff was created to facilitate plant-level reforms rather than to impose them from above.

One of the company's earliest work-reform projects occurred at Tarrytown, New York.[16] The plant, which had been plagued for years by excessive absenteeism and labor turnover and which had turned into a virtual labor-management combat zone, was in serious trouble by April 1971. Things were so bad that the plant manager decided the place just had to be turned around; there was no other way to go but up.

His first initiative was to solicit the support of some of the key UAW officials. Then he allowed the workers in the Hard Trim and Soft Trim Departments to participate in planning their departments' move and reorganization. This worked out so well that he followed the same procedure the next year with the Chassis Department. Similar worker-participation schemes were also introduced at the General Motors assembly plant in Lakewood, Georgia.

Although the success of the Tarrytown and Lakewood experiments undoubtedly played their part in encouraging corporate officials to continue their commitment to workplace reform, many observers have suggested that the greater stimulus came as a result of the Lordstown strike. In the spring of 1972, the predominantly young work force at that Ohio GM plant went out on strike to protest what they called the boredom and dehumanization of the plant's assembly work.[17] What made that strike such a landmark was the fact that the Lordstown plant was the company's newest and supposedly best-engineered workplace. It was clearly unavoidable that during the next year's contract negotiations, GM and the UAW would have to agree on a systematic plan to improve the quality of work life for the company's employees. This they did by establishing a national QWL (quality-of-work-life) Committee.

Even though General Motors' management insists that its labor-management experiments are more than just changes in the organization of work, and are directly motivated to obtain increased productivity, many experiments appear to be severely limited in the way in which they involve the workers in actual decision making.

There are a number of other General Motors plants, though, where workers have been given direct problem-solving responsibilities. Max Ways reports, for example, how a 46-percent glass-breakage rate in one plant drove supervisors to utter despair; they just did not seem able to deal with the issue. Consequently, the workers were given the responsibility of solving the dilemma, and they did. They began to identify the causes of the breakage, such as poorly and improperly aligned car bodies, and they solved the problem by calling it to the attention of the workers at that part of the assembly line.[18] A somewhat similar problem-solving situation developed at the Oldsmobile Division in Detroit. The problem was not necessarily turned over to the workers, but the solving of it—after a series of interviews had helped identify some seventy contributory causes—was assigned to a task force composed of foremen and workers. At the Indiana plant of the Delco Division, employees participate in setting goals regarding such issues as absenteeism, quality of work, and wastage. Through discussion groups, workers there are mobilized to solve work problems and to meet plant goals.[19]

An example of a work-group system at General Motors is the scheme at the Fisher Body Plant, No. 2, at Grand Rapids, Michigan. The twenty-five hundred employees (plant and office) are divided into six so-called business teams, with each unit being composed of the total array of functional specialists and workers that is typical of a smaller individual firm. As a consequence, communication between supervisors and workers is much better and, more importantly, distinctly different from what it used to be. Worker grievances have decreased, and the level of trust has risen sharply.[20]

Something more should be said about the Tarrytown plant. What began in 1971 as an experiment in two departments, had become a plantwide program involving some thirty-eight hundred workers and supervisors by 1977. After more than thirty-three hundred workers were trained in 1978 to develop effective problem-solving skills, they were given the opportunity to become involved in the plant's preparation for the changeover to the production of the all-new 1980 X model. Since then, GM's Tarrytown plant has increasingly been cited as one of the company's best-run sites, and as a prototype of what can happen to a production facility once workers and managers communicate with one another and discover the mutual benefits of a work culture of trust and dignity.

The company's general experience with quality-of-work-life projects are well capsuled in observations by two of its executives: one, by Fuller; the other, by Dominic Conklin, the plant manager of the Fisher Body Plant, No. 2. Fuller is quoted as having observed that "the employee doesn't necessarily want to make your [management's] decisions, but he wants to make decisions that affect his work. Fifteen or twenty years ago he didn't see this as part of his role." In assessing that this change is good for the country, he continued: "You can't have a nation divided; a non-thinking work force and a thinking electorate."[21]

Conklin observed that the company has benefited from smoother contract negotiations, from increased worker interest in being trained for supervisory positions, and from greater teamwork and better worker morale. What benefits management most is that it is now free to manage the organization more, in such areas as long-range planning, legislative relations, and community activities. The managers do not have to be singularly preoccupied with running the plant anymore.[22]

The Eaton Corporation in Cleveland, Ohio, is another American multinational that has attempted to improve the quality of work life in some of its Stateside operations. This highly diversified firm, which manufactures such varied products as automobile engine valves and fork-lift trucks, has received publicity for two of its programs. One is a vertical communication system, which was built around "kaffee-klatsches" between supervisors and workers and impromptu shop floor interviews of workers by management people. In the plant where this program was put into operation, absenteeism decreased sharply, the turnover rate dropped, and off-the-street applications increased to such an extent that recruiting ads were no longer necessary.[23]

The other Eaton experiment was conducted in Kearney, Nebraska, when a new plant was established there in 1970. Sensing Kearney to be a rather intimate town with a rapid-fire system of informal communication, management realized that its labor-management practices would quickly become known in the community. It, therefore, went out of its way to make sure that some of the conventional discriminatory practices were eliminated and that the workers were given tasks to perform that were not normally assigned to them. Thus, white- and blue-collar employees were treated alike. Office workers would no longer be subjected to work on probation, have disciplinary rules posted in the plant, punch time clocks, and be subjected to disciplinary reprimands. Blue-collar workers were involved in showing visitors through the plant, and were placed on safety, work process, and other committees. Dan Scobel, Eaton manager of industrial relations, reported that the "Kearney thing" has been introduced in another half dozen plants. Hesitation by the managements of these plants has only allowed modified versions, though. As he observed, he is "a little worried about these hybrids; it's like we're saying: 'We trust you—but only so far.'" The interesting thing is that Eaton has only experimented with these forms of worker participation in their nonunion plants. Scobel expressed fears about the job-description disputes and inflexibility of practices that are apt to arise in unionized shops.[24]

An internationally active chemical company that has engaged in labor-management experiments is Monsanto. Jenkins reports their success with two methods: shared goal-setting and joint training. The goals are set through a sequence of discussions among employees and their superiors. The first discussion is to set production goals and the methods by which the units plan to achieve these. Consequent meetings are evaluative and may lead to adjustments in goals and work methods. As J. I. Johnston is reported to have observed: "The worker develops an understanding of what the business is about, and the foreman understands how he can help the operators. But it only works if you mean it — and make sure the operator has enough information. What we're driving at is self-determination and self-control."[25] Monsanto also conducts joint training programs that involve both supervisory and rank-and-file personnel. Their common experience in training and problem solving cannot help but improve mutual appreciation and respect.

Although trade unionists may charge that Monsanto has used its labor-management experiments to undercut prospective organization of the workers (that certainly was part of the motivation that led to the innovations at the Long Beach, California, plant), the charge is not necessarily true in all circumstances. For example, the plant manager in Bridgeport, New Jersey, became fascinated with participative-management theories. He, undoubtedly, was not adverse to possible morale and productivity boosts. Whatever his motivation, he organized the plant into autonomous product teams that set their own goals and evaluate their own results. By 1973, 30 to 40 percent of the Monsanto work force was in some way involved in some kind of work-reform project. A number of the company's plants in which the projects are operative are unionized.

A most interesting program has been introduced in some of Procter & Gamble's plants.[26] That firm's experiments began in Lima, Ohio, in the late sixties. The P & G operation there was rather small: it employed about 125 people and produced two products — one by continuous process, the other in batches. The most outstanding features of the high-technology, high-automation Lima operation are that there are no job classifications, each individual in the community determines his own skill development, and everyone continues to share responsibility for day-to-day operation. The plant operates without time clocks, and everyone receives a simple salary according to pay scales worked out among the workers themselves. The Lima plant is a so-called open-system environment, under which workers are free to interact with anyone outside the plant whom they feel will help them improve the plant operation — whether that is with people at corporate headquarters, with consultants, or with suppliers. Features of the Lima system have also been designed into several newer P & G plants, and they have been successfully introduced in some of the company's older facilities.

Heinz-USA is another MNC that has several labor-management programs in operation. It started in 1972 at Freemont, Ohio, with a three-tiered consultation structure: in a free-for-all discussion format, stewards and management representatives meet weekly; union leaders and key management personnel meet monthly; and all 550 employees meet together annually.[27] Five of the remaining seven plants in the Heinz-USA Division joined the program in 1974 by setting up joint union-management committees to discuss mutual concerns on a regular basis. These committees of twelve members (six each from management and from the Amalgamated Meat Cutters and Butcher Workmen Union) have, at times, established task forces to work on problems in particular departments.[28] The company's Holland, Michigan, plant has a six-man committee (meeting monthly) through which management funnels information to the four hundred employees, and in which representatives of the Retail, Wholesale, and Department Store Employees Union's Local No. 705 discuss any worker concerns they care to bring up.[29]

The AMCBW also participates in labor-management committees at Oscar Mayer and Company, Inc. Four of that company's nine plants consider their joint meetings "institutions," and say that they "would not know what to do without them." Their quarterly committee meetings apparently have been held since 1966.[30]

In 1975, the seven hundred workers at the National Biscuit Company's Houston plant voted to participate in a quality-of-work-life project, which today operates through a site committee, a steering committee, and five permanent subcommittees. The site committee is composed of nine labor and nine management members and meets weekly. A steering committee of four management representatives from the company's international headquarters and three union representatives meets every month. In addition, there is a subcommittee for every plant department. Management and labor have equal representation and have their alternating cochairmen. The subcommittees have undertaken numerous projects, including reorganizing machine diagrams to simplify machine repair and maintenance, improved quality control in the manufacturing process, expanded social activities, and better security in the parking lots.[31]

Armco Steel Corporation has two plants in Ohio—the Washington Courthouse plant with four hundred employees, and the Zanesville plant with five hundred employees—each with a productivity committee. Set up in 1971, the Washington Courthouse and Zanesville committees have three representatives each from management and from the company union (the Armco Employees Independent Federation, Inc.). They meet monthly for the singular purpose of productivity improvement. The Butler, Pennsylvania, arrangement is a little more interesting, both in terms of the committee makeup (three to represent the hourly employees, three for the salaried employees, and three for management) and the manner in which the two respective unions nominate and elect their representatives (nominated by the union executive councils, elected by the union memberships). Armco's Middletown,

Ohio, plant, with eight thousand employees, has a joint labor-management committee with both a labor-representative majority (four versus three for management) and broader jurisdiction (plant and personnel problems). Management has rated the Middletown committee only "moderately successful," however.[32]

At Falconer, New York, the Carborundum plant has a labor-management committee that meets once every two months. Composed of six labor and six management people, it discusses such issues as redesign and expansion of the plant, quality control, and worker safety. Committee minutes are posted on the employee bulletin boards.[33]

A vehicle of employee involvement in management decision making that became particularly popular in 1979 and 1980 is the quality-control circle. Ironically, the idea for these regularly convening small groups, trained to spot and solve production problems, was conceived by U.S. business consultants, but they began to be practiced by American firms after they had proven to be successful with their Japanese competitors.[34]

By February 1980, some sixty-five companies were reported to have active quality circles, four times as many as a year before. The companies using the procedure then included some of the biggest names in American business. General Motors, for example, had some one hundred circles operating in various plants of its Buick, Chevrolet, Cadillac, Oldsmobile, and Fisher Body divisions. International Harvester's solar-turbines division in San Diego projected to increase its circles from twenty-two to fifty. Reportedly, circles were also operative at Northrop, Lockheed, Rockwell International, Phillips Petroleum, Ford, and Aetna Life and Casualty Company.

The general format of the quality-circles program is that a plant first establishes a steering committee made up of labor and management representatives. This steering committee then decides which area of the plant could benefit from a circle. Eight to ten workers are recruited to meet weekly with their immediate supervisor and with a personnel or industrial-relations specialist who is to train the workers in elementary data gathering and in statistics. The process culminates with the group investigating existing problem situations and presenting its ideas on how these could be solved. Jeff Beardsley, the president of a business-consulting firm in San Diego, reports that there have been few instances where management has not accepted the recommendations made by a circle.

An American-based multinational that projects itself to be particularly employee oriented, but about which trade unionists generally do not have many kind things to say, is IBM. What one French trade unionist is reported to have called the company's "socialistic paternalism" is a system of employee relations designed to reflect the premise that "people" are the company's greatest asset.[35] The program involves paying relatively high wages and salaries, extending such elaborate fringe benefits as a pension plan paid for by the company, pleasure-oriented educational opportunities, special banquets and award ceremonies, and, not least of all, company country clubs, sports stadiums, and tennis courts. The company does not provide structured worker input in company decision making, however. Its traditional concept of worker participation has been its open-door policy, a practice used by many enterprises, which, however, tends to sound much better than it works. While an open-door policy may be successful in a small company and possibly even among white-collar workers in a larger firm, it does not tend to involve shop workers and lower-level white-collar workers in the larger-sized firms.

Another multinational that is generally the target of trade-unionist criticism is Texas Instruments. Although many people tend to categorize its personnel policies with those of IBM, this firm does actively seek and obtain a high degree of worker participation in production planning and control. Basic to TI's participation procedure is a continuous cycle of meetings between groups of workers and their supervisors. These meetings are intended to do three things: (1) identify problems in the work methods of the group; (2) assign the responsibility for solving them to different members of the group (supervisor or worker); and (3) hear progress reports on the solution of the problems identified in earlier meetings.[36]

Many anecdotes are being told about the effectiveness of this procedure. One deals with a case in which the company that had mistakenly bid less than the actual manufacturing costs of some radar equipment, was awarded the contract, and immediately began to lose large sums of money. Reportedly, the foreman selected ten of his assemblers, explained the situation to them, and asked them for their suggestions. They sat down together, broke the job down into its operations, studied each of them, and made some forty suggestions that they thought could bring production time down from one hundred thirty-eight man-hours to eighty-six, which was fourteen less than needed to make the operation profitable. The foreman, having stuck his neck out, most reluctantly let them try it that way. It actually turned out that the assembly time was reduced to seventy-five hours. The assemblers then asked for another meeting, during which they cut the time to fifty-seven hours. The job eventually ended up taking thirty-two hours![37]

Texas Instruments, like several of the others we discussed, has made it common practice to use the same pay and fringe-benefit policy for its white- and blue-collar employees. Accordingly, the company culture is generally described as nonelitist. The firm apparently does not sport any sort of ostentatious indicators of pecking order, such as a scale of plushness of offices, separate management dining rooms, and parking places expressly designated for executives. That sort of egalitarian culture undoubtedly contributes to making Texas Instruments' participation schemes work.

What is most striking about TI's procedures is the high percentage of company employees participating in the program and the continuous nature of the team-meeting cycle. Seventy-three percent of the firm's manufacturing employees and 49 percent of other employees are apparently grouped into production teams. Those are considerably higher percentages than virtually every other firm engaged in labor-management programs. The other major difference with programs in other firms — except for those using the Scanlon Plan — is the almost-permanent nature of TI's production consultations. This latter feature almost makes it seem as if the Texas Instruments structure is not much different from the West European works councils. There clearly remain some very distinct differences, though. First, TI management determines who shall be in the groups, and it decides how long each of them stays operative. The workers do not elect representatives, and the designated workers do not generally get to talk about shopwide issues. The groups, therefore, are only productivity and efficiency teams. They do produce better worker morale, but it is questionable whether anyone would want to argue that the program is intended to encourage basic changes in the distribution of power within the firm.

The participative-management program at Texas Instruments and most of the other programs discussed in this section have been highly suspect to many outside observers. There are two main reasons: first, they have been mostly initiated by management; and, second, the majority of them are located in nonunionized plants.[38] Milton Derber summarized these apprehensions when he labeled them "a late twentieth-century revision of Taylorism, a new model of scientific management based on recent psychological theories about job satisfaction and communications instead of engineering concepts."[39] It may be too early to warrant such comprehensive conclusions about them, however. They could become the stepping-stone toward a broader worker participation in the future.

OTHER TECHNIQUES OF WORKER INVOLVEMENT IN THE ENTERPRISE

One technique employed by some firms to give their employees an opportunity to obtain justice in cases where they feel themselves treated unfairly is the office of ombudsman. This Swedish innovation of the early nineteenth century has been introduced into several large American corporations. Ewing reports that the procedure was first tried in the sixties in several high-technology companies, as well as in some science-based service organizations and in interdisciplinary think tanks.[40] The best-known cases are the Xerox Corporation, General Electric's Aircraft Engine Group, and the Grumman Aerospace Corporation.

At Xerox, employees with grievances, after first having attempted to find satisfaction through their supervisors or the personnel department, must submit a written complaint to the ombudsman, who reports directly to the appropriate division president, if necessary. Grumman, which apparently calls its ombudsmen "plant coordinators," has them in more than thirty of their plants, dealing with a broad variety of employee concerns.

Frederica Dunn's experience as General Electric's first ombudsman is rather interesting; it certainly shows what was envisioned and what the results can be. When she joined the Aircraft Engine Group in 1973, she was charged with reviewing the grievance procedures and developing programs to correct any deficiencies in them. She was to improve labor-management communication, avoid unnecessary complaints, work to reverse clearly unfair decisions, and assure an impartial outlet for employee grievances.[41]

After having reviewed some 150 cases dealing with promotional opportunities and job search, Dunn had collected sufficient data to warrant forming an employee panel to study the company's method of filling professional jobs. As a result, the company now has a staffing system that includes the posting of all positions not controlled by the unions. Another direct result of her work is the fact that managers now make sure they can justify their actions. The possibility that they could end up in an argument or that their mistakes would become known to the executive vice-president in charge seems to be a good deterrent against their sloppy management of human resources.

A number of American firms have kept track of worker attitudes through employee surveys. Such surveys are conducted periodically, only once, or sporadically—at the time of substantive change in company policy or practice.[42] Almost all large firms are reported to have conducted at least one such survey at some point in time. In some companies, including some of the largest multinational corporations, periodic surveys are said to be a key element in the company's information-gathering system.[43]

The main problem with employee surveys appears to be the reluctance of some managers to let their decisions really be influenced by the data obtained. Where such reluctance prevails, management risks being accused of hypocrisy, the sort of alienation that certainly does not promote workplace stability.[44] Surveys have not only proven themselves helpful in identifying problem areas, they have, at times, led to effective worker participation in company decision making. One large American-based multinational, for example, publishes the general survey results and then gives each group an oral report on its own responses so that the unit can compare itself with the others in the plant. Company employees are also given an opportunity to suggest solutions for the problems identified through the survey. This use of the survey clearly suggests that the employee survey can also be, and is sometimes used as, a device to help labor-management committee (or works-council) members be informed about the opinions and attitudes of the people they are to represent.

Surveys are not the only method by which management keeps up with the moods and grievances of workers. In the middle seventies, for example, company house organs (periodic publications by firms for their employees) became freer in printing letters from employees that are critical of the company and its management employees. Stessin, for example, tells of how the American Airlines house organ runs an "op-ed" page on which employees have challenged the comparatively top-heavy management structure of the company. Union officials have been given the opportunity to label the company's contracting for strike insurance "an anti-union strategy designed to make a sham of collective bargaining."[45] Even though the number of firms that allow their house organs to be used for such public criticism is still very limited, a 1976 Syracuse University study reported that company publications no longer tend to be devoted only to personal news, idle chitchat, and the perennial "president's column" extolling the virtues of free enterprise.

General Electric's Re-Entry and Environmental Systems Division in Philadelphia employs a hotline, a technique that is apparently also used by several other companies. Any division employee who desires to do so can pick up the telephone, dial a certain company extension, and ask any question he desires. Not only does management provide an instant answer to the question, but the subjects of the queries are fed into the company's computer, enabling supervisors in the various company plants to obtain printouts indicating worker concerns. The fact that, in 1976 alone, more than one hundred ten thousand calls were handled suggests how needed and useful this communication system may have been.

IBM uses a letter-writing system. Employees who sign their letters of inquiry or comment are answered by a management person who does not learn their name. The response is sent to the employee's home address through the public mail; the whole process is handled through the Speak-Up Office, which keeps the letters under lock and key and guarantees total anonymity.

During 1976, some thirteen thousand letters were received by the office. The bulk of these were answered within twenty-four hours. In those cases where more time was required, the employee received a clear indication as to when an answer would be given. Unsigned letters dealing with topics of broader interest have been printed in IBM's house organ.

Mobil Oil operates a so-called direct response information exchange with a budget of some $60 million. One of its programs is the Executive Forum, through which videotaped interview sessions are produced several times a year. These sessions involve randomly selected workers asking questions of members of the firm's board of directors.

Even though many corporate managers have serious reservations, if not outright objections, about involving rank-and-file workers in business decisions that go beyond the production process they are immediately involved in and in rather insubstantial fringe-benefits issues, many of them enthusiastically endorse employee stock ownership. Managers do not perceive of employee stock-ownership plans (ESOPs) only in purely pragmatic terms—that is, as a method by which large, capital-intensive companies are enabled to raise capital cheaply. They expect the plan to give workers a greater sense of proprietorship and responsibility, both of which are important elements in heightening worker morale and productivity. ESOPs were particularly stimulated by the Employment Retirement Security Act of 1974 and the Tax Reduction Act of 1975. Some two hundred firms quickly established them. The legislation allowed them to set up an employee stock-ownership trust, to borrow the money from the bank (to buy the stock and thus increase the firm's capital), to increase the fund by 15 percent each year, and to have these payments exempted from taxation.[46]

ESOPs generally give participants voting rights on the company stock purchased; however, such entitlement does not begin until retirement, death, or separation from the company. Thus, the worker's participation is strictly indirect (through a general trust fund), significantly delayed, and only involves ownership and not influence or control over corporate decisions. Worker stock-ownership programs that have stood out by their effectiveness have been those in which employees bought up all their companies' stock. Such occasions, in turn, have predominantly tended to be cases in which parent firms wanted to unload or close a plant, or cases in which a firm seemed doomed to go bankrupt.

GOVERNMENTAL INITIATIVES AND PROGRAMS

Even though virtually all the experiments to improve labor-management interaction described in this chapter were initiated privately (mostly by corporations and some by organized labor), a considerable number of them have benefited from technical assistance and/or financial support by public governments. Such was clearly the case with certain local and regional labor-management committees as the one in Jamestown, New York. However, support has not been extended only by local governments; the federal government has been involved as well. President Nixon first initiated federal action through the establishment, in 1971, of the National Commission on Productivity, which was soon charged to include in its activities the encouragement of more general tripartite (labor-management-public) committees.[47]

Four years later, the commission, which had been renamed the National Commission for Productivity and Work Quality in 1974, was reconstructed to become the National Center for Productivity and Quality of Work Life, and it was provided an annual budget of about $5 million, a level of funding that was guaranteed for three years. The life of the center, though, turned out to be of short duration. It was not funded again in 1978, and, upon its demise, its responsibilities were reassigned to the Federal Mediation and Conciliation Service, which already had provided extensive technical assistance services before the National Center even came into operation.

During its short-lived existence, the National Center tended to focus on the dissemination of information, both to the general public and to relevant parties. One example of its public-information activities was a three-part series of articles under the title "Workplace 2000," which appeared in a number of local newspapers in 1978. This Associated Press feature story was clearly a spin-off from the center's releases, one example of which was the February 1976 pamphlet *Recent Initiatives in Labor-Management Co-operation*. A certain amount of information also reached the public as a result of the center's 1978 publication of the *Directory of Labor-Management Committees*, cited earlier.

Another typical center activity was the periodic convening of union-management conferences, such as the 1977 Chicago Conference on Quality of Working Life and Productivity: The Double Pay-Off, which focused on the labor-management experiments of the General Motors Fisher Body Plant, of Harman International and the United Auto Workers in Bolivar, Tennessee, and of Citibank of New York. Most of the center's conferences were co-sponsored by trade unions and by such private organizations as the Work in America Institute, headquartered in Scarsdale, New York.[48]

The center also extended technical assistance and, in a very few instances, limited funding to business firms and local governments that were interested in instituting joint committees or autonomous work groups. The Jamestown Area Labor-Management Committee, for example, received such funding. Most of the center's work was parallel to that done by the Federal Mediation and Conciliation Service, which may be one reason the work was reassigned to the FMCS. The service, for instance, has been cosponsoring its own series of conferences. Typical of that series was the Third Annual Conference of Area Labor-Management Committees, cosponsored with the New York State School of Industrial and Labor Relations of Cornell University, which was held in Buffalo, New York, November 13 through 15, 1978. This particular conference resulted in the establishment of a national association of area labor-management committees.[49]

By year-end 1977, the FMCS's mediators reportedly organized and contributed to the formation and operation of 269 labor-management committees.[50] The increased popularity of such committees at the plant level motivated the service to publish an instructional pamphlet for management and unionists. This pamphlet not only describes how one determines the need for a labor-management committee, the benefits for both sides, and guidelines for bringing it about, but it also reports that each year more than one hundred labor-management committees are formed with the assistance of the service.[51]

A key person in shaping the federal government's commitment to a program of labor-management cooperation has been Senator Jacob Javits, Republican from New York. In 1975, not only did he cosponsor (with Senators Charles Percy and Sam Nunn) the legislation that established and funded the National Center for Productivity and Quality of Working Life, but he was finally instrumental in the attachment of the Labor-Management Cooperation Act of 1978 to that year's CETA (Comprehensive Employment and Training Act) reauthorization act.

The 1978 act was based on the proposed, but never enacted, Human Resources Act of 1977, a bill authored by Representative Stanley Lundine (Democrat, New York), the former mayor of Jamestown who had been a key figure in organizing that area's labor-management committee (see above). Its sevenfold purpose is:

1. To improve communication between representatives of labor and management;
2. To provide workers and employers with opportunities to study and explore new and innovative approaches to achieve organizational effectiveness;
3. To assist workers and employers in solving problems of mutual concern not susceptible to resolution within the collective-bargaining process;
4. To study and explore ways of eliminating potential problems which reduce the competitiveness and inhibit the economic development of the plant, area, or industry;
5. To enhance the involvement of workers in making decisions that affect their working lives;
6. To expand and improve working relationships between workers and managers; and
7. To encourage free collective-bargaining by establishing continuing mechanisms for communication between employers and their employees through Federal assistance to the formation and operation of labor-management committees.[52]

Through amendments in the Taft-Hartley Act, the Federal Mediation and Conciliation Service was authorized and directed to provide assistance in establishing and operating plant-, area-, and industrywide labor-management committees and to enter into contracts or make grants to fulfill this mission. For the fiscal year 1979, funding was provided in the amount of $10 million.

Although the 1978 act was much less ambitious than what had been projected in its progenitor, H.R. 2596, and is of smaller scale than provided for the center, it may well turn out to be the beginning of a broader federal government commitment in the future.

EXPERIMENTAL BUSINESS EDUCATION IN
PARTICIPATIVE MANAGEMENT

Mention should also be made of the New School for Democratic Management in San Francisco. This alternative business school was organized in 1977 under the directorship of David Olsen, formerly a professor of philosophy at Tufts University. With a faculty of five full-time and one hundred part-time staff members, the New School has mostly been financed by grants (70 percent of its budget). Although most of the 675 students who enrolled in the school's courses in 1978 took only two courses, varying in length from one week to three months, Olsen eventually hopes to offer an accredited master's degree in business administration.

Of particular significance are the school's technical assistance and consulting services. In 1977, for example, the city of Springfield, Ohio, (population eighty thousand) had the school help implement a program of increased worker autonomy among the city's nine-hundred-person work force. Springfield's personnel director reportedly contracted for the school's services because he saw "increased workplace democracy as the wave of the future, particularly in the public sector."[53]

THE MANAGEMENT STYLE OF JAPANESE SUBSIDIARIES
IN THE UNITED STATES

American workplace-reform projects, as suggested during the description of the quality-control circles, are not products solely of American values and initiatives. An increasing number of Stateside managers have worked overseas and have thus, at minimum, become acquainted with alternative ways of organizing the plant and the firm. That subject is obviously the focus of this study and will be described in more detail later.

Reform has also been stimulated by the Stateside presence of subsidiaries owned by foreign multinationals, particularly by those that are operated by home-country standards and practices. Especially interesting and widely publicized in this respect has been the management style practiced by American affiliates of Japanese multinationals. It is somewhat ironically assumed, although not systematically investigated, that West European firms have generally managed their operations in the United States in accordance with the American code of business conduct. This should not be surprising, considering our earlier observations about the greater adaptiveness of European multinationals and the comparatively more pronounced ethnocentrism of Japanese and of American firms.

Although it has been correctly argued that Japanese and American management styles are not as different as has generally been projected, particularly in the amount of worker participation in consultative decision making, there are some distinct differences in how firms of these two nationalities manage their workers.[54] For example, most Japanese-managed subsidiaries in the United States tend to spend more on staffing (twice as much as American firms), on cross-training, on company social and recreational programs, and on janitorial services. Employees of Japanese subsidiaries have also exhibited a comparatively higher degree of job satisfaction and more positive work attitudes, as reflected in less counterproductive behavior by workers in these subsidiaries.[55]

The labor-relations practices that remain generally identified as the most unique features of the Japanese labor-relations systems are lifetime employment, seniority wages, and company unions.[56] All these features are derived from the Japanese point of view that the business firm is as much a community of people as it is a vehicle for making profits for investors and owners. Thus, when a person becomes an employee of a Japanese firm, the company is apt to assume that it provides (as far as humanly possible) employment rather than hiring and firing workers as business opportunities warrant. Japanese management is also more apt to provide cross-training in order that job reassignment will be easier and boredom may become less of a problem. In addition, managers are perceived more as facilitators than as commanding officers: they spend more time with the workers (including group calisthenics); wear the same company uniform; encourage lateral communication, particularly among middle managers; and prefer group decisions that create commitments for those who help make them. Permanent workers are treated by Japanese managers as if they were citizens of the firm rather than as aliens admitted on a temporary work permit.

A story told by the president of Fujitsu America, Inc., illustrates what the Japanese management style can mean in a specific American location.[57] He described how the subsidiary had been making a certain subassembly for the Amdahl Corporation. The same product was made at one of the company's plants in Japan. In 1977, the MNC's corporate management noticed that the subassemblies made by the American subsidiary had ten times as many defects as those made in Japan. Mr. Nakayama, therefore, immediately initiated a cycle of weekly meetings in which the American managers were encouraged to discuss their problems openly and seek to solve them together. As a result of these meetings, the subsidiary's management identified their problems as carelessness, poor handling of delicate parts, inaccurate testing equipment, and improper placement of parts to be tested. They also resolved to deal with these issues. In the end, the Fujitsu America product became even better than the one made in the company's Japanese home factories.

It will be interesting to see whether the recent and presumably increasing shift by Japanese firms in the United States from trading, retail business, and banking to manufacturing will accelerate this cultural transfer process. As Johnson and Ouchi have suggested, Americans may learn from the Japanese that even though ten thousand individualistic and competitive John Waynes could be accommodated in the frontier society of the early West, "millions of John Waynes employed under ten thousand corporate roofs may not, in the long run, prove workable."[58]

Several Japanese firms have gone beyond the described paternalistic practices of Japanese management and have begun to formalize worker-participation practices. For example, when, in the mid-sixties, the recession made it necessary to find something to do for lifetime employees, the Japanese steel industry introduced *jishu kanri* (workers' voluntary control). Under this system, more than eight thousand small groups, such as the Zero Defects Group of Nippon Steel's Iota Works, have been developing better procedures for quality control, cost saving, and energy conservation. Apparently, some seven million workers take part in *jishu kanri*, and their work has resulted in corporate savings of more than $100 million in U.S. currency.

In the summer of 1978, Matsushita set up a system under which management is obligated to consult with worker representatives on all corporate policy decisions. This three-tiered system, called *keiei sanka* (participation in management), does not give workers a voice on company boards; it appears to come quite close, however, to the German and Dutch systems of worker participation. What would really be ironic would be the introduction of European-style worker-participation practices in the United States by the subsidiaries of Japanese rather than European multinational corporations.

CONCLUSIONS

Although virtually all American business firms still operate by the code of nonparticipative, nondemocratic politics, a number of interesting modifications have begun to occur. Whether the described workplace reforms are called examples of human-relations management practices, participative management, productivity and quality circles, or quality-of-worklife projects, many of them actually have brought shop-floor workers into different roles and relationships with their superiors and co-workers.

Also significant has been the way in which the initiative for such projects has not remained exclusively with corporate management. Some trade unionists, although hesitant at first, have increasingly endorsed quality-of-worklife projects—as long as they would not undermine the collective bargaining process and trade unionism, and would not turn out to be simply another way to increase worker output to maximize company profits at the cost of the worker's welfare. And, finally, the federal and some local governments have been particularly prone to recognize that increased labor-management cooperation may well be the only way ailing firms and economies can avoid going under in an increasingly competitive global business environment.[59] Especially striking is the impact multinational competition has had: Japanese business success, for example, has helped drive U.S. managers to copy some of their practices.

NOTES

1. Max Ways, "The American Kind of Worker Participation," *Fortune* 94 (Oct. 1976): 168-82.
2. Harry M. Douty, *Labor-Management-Productivity Committees in American Industry* (Washington, D.C.: National Commission on Productivity and Work Quality, 1975).
3. Both experiments discussed here are described in David Jenkins's classic *Job Power: Blue- and White-Collar Democracy* (New York: Penguin Books, 1973), pp. 116-222.
4. The McCormick Company also employs a profit-sharing plan.
5. William L. Batt, Jr., and Edgar Weinberg, "Labor-Management Cooperation Today," *Harvard Business Review* 56 (Jan.-Feb. 1978): 104, and Martin Patchen, "Labor-Management Consultation at TVA: Its Impact on Employees," in Ervin Williams, ed., *Participative Management: Concepts, Theory, and Implementation* (Atlanta: School of Business Administration, Georgia State University, 1976), pp. 151-74.
6. The literature on the Scanlon Plan is quite prolific. Most complete is Fred G. Lisieur, ed., *The Scanlon Plan: A Frontier in Labor-Management* (Cambridge: M.I.T. Press, 1958). Also see D. McGregor, *The Human Side of the Enterprise* (New York: McGraw-Hill, 1960), pp. 110-31; Fred G. Lisieur and Elbridge S. Pucket, "The Scanlon Plan Has Proved Itself," *Harvard Business Review* 47 (Sept.-Oct. 1969): 109-18; R. Hill, "Working on the Scanlon Plan," *International Management* 29 (Oct. 1974): 39-43; and Henry Tracy, "Scanlon Plans: Leading Edge in Labor-Management Cooperation," *World of Work Report* 2 (March 1977): 25, 32-34.
7. For example, see Richard Ruch's observation reported in the *Christian Science Monitor* article, "Workers on the Board: Productivity Help or Hindrance?" May 18, 1977, p. 15.
8. For example, see Jenkins, p. 224.
9. Robert K. Goodman, J. H. Wakeley, and R. H. Ruh, "What Employees Think of the Scanlon Plan," *Personnel* 49 (Sept.-Oct. 1972): 28.
10. An International Labour Office study authored by Carol Riegelman, *Labour-Management Co-operation in United States War Production* (Montreal: International Labour Office, 1948), pp. 185 ff.
11. Ibid., p. 187.
12. Milton Derber, "Collective Bargaining: The American Approach to Industrial Democracy," *Annals of the American Academy of Political and Social Science* 431 (May 1977): 85.
13. Peter Nye, "A History of Labor-Management Committees," *Nation's Cities* 16 (April 1978): 21.
14. *Three Productive Years*, the three-year report of the Labor-Management Committee of the Jamestown Area, p. 8. The italicization of criteria 4 and 5 is mine. They most directly relate to the issue of worker participation at the plant level.
15. *Directory of Labor-Management Committees*, 2d ed. (Washington, D.C.: National Center for Productivity and Quality of Working Life, 1978), p. 162, and Derber, p. 89.
16. D. Clutterback, "General Motors Strives to Motivate Its Workers," *Interna-*

tional Management 30 (Jan. 1975): 14. Also see G. Lodge and Karen Henderson's description in Benjamin C. Roberts, ed., *Toward Industrial Democracy: Europe, Japan and the United States* (Montclair, N.J.: Allenheld, Osmun, 1979), pp. 250-83.

17. The Lordstown strike is consistently cited as America's prime example of a worker rebellion against a lack of personal control over one's work and fate. See, for example, Rosabeth Moss Kanter's "Work in a New America," *Daedalus* 107 (Winter 1978): 62.

18. Ways, p. 176.

19. The latter two experiments are described briefly in Clutterback, p. 17.

20. David Robison, "General Motors Business Teams Advance QWL (Quality of Work Life) at Fisher Body Plants," *World of Work Report* 2 (July 1977): 73, 80-81.

21. Ways, pp. 176 and 180.

22. Robison, p. 81.

23. Lawrence Stessin, "Management Tunes in on Employee Gripes," *The New York Times*, October 16, 1977, Sect. 3, p. 2.

24. Jenkins, pp. 211-14.

25. Ibid., p. 204.

26. The description of the Procter and Gamble experiment is exclusively derived from Jenkins, pp. 231-35.

27. *Directory of Labor-Management Committees*, p. 133.

28. Ibid., p. 45.

29. Ibid., p. 69.

30. Ibid., p. 30.

31. Ibid., p. 173.

32. Ibid., pp. 137, 143, 145, and 150.

33. Ibid., pp. 103-104.

34. *Wall Street Journal*, February 21, 1980, p. 40.

35. See William Rodgers, *Think: A Biography of the Watsons and I.B.M.* (New York: Stein and Day, 1969), and Thomas Watson, Jr., *A Business and Its Beliefs: The Ideas That Helped Build I.B.M.* (New York: McGraw-Hill, 1963).

36. The TI system is explained in some detail in William J. Roche and Neil L. MacKinnon, "Motivating People with Meaningful Work," *Harvard Business Review* 48 (May-June 1970): 97-110, and is summarized in Lodge and Henderson, pp. 258-59.

37. Told by M. Scott Myers, TI's personnel director, in his "Increasing Employee Motivation," in Harold M. F. Rush, ed., *Managing Change* (New York: National Industrial Conference Board, 1970).

38. Jack Barbash, "The Work Humanization Movement: U.S. and European Experience Compared," in Benjamin Martin and Everett M. Kassalow, eds., *Labor Relations in Advanced Industrial Societies: Issues and Problems* (Washington, D.C.: Carnegie Endowment for International Peace, 1980), p. 187.

39. Derber, p. 91.

40. David Ewing, *Freedom Inside the Organization* (New York: E. P. Dutton, 1977), p. 168.

41. Frederica H. Dunn, "The View From the Ombudsman's Chair," *The New York Times*, May 1, 1976.

42. A 1973 Conference Board study found that as many as 71 percent of their

sample of so-called OD-practicing American and Canadian firms used the survey method. Even 38 percent of the 102 non-OD companies reported using them. Harold M. F. Rush, "A Non-Partisan View of Participative Management," *Conference Board Record* 10 (April 1973): 35.

43. Geert H. Hofstede, "Employee Surveys: A Tool for Participation," *European Business* 39 (Autumn 1973): 65.

44. Rush reports how a company psychologist complained, in fact, that the company collected information it really did not want to hear, and how management, therefore, ignored the findings. He ended up saying: "Then they wonder why we continue to have discontent, grievances, and strikes. It would be better not to ask the employees what they believe and feel than to ask them and do nothing. For this reason, I wish we didn't go through the motions of collecting attitudinal data. At least we wouldn't be insulting the employees." Rush, p. 35.

45. Stessin, p. 2. Most of the information in this section is derived from the Stessin article.

46. Lodge and Henderson, pp. 255-56. Also interesting is James O'Toole's analysis in "The Uneven Record of Employee Ownership," *Harvard Business Review* 57 Nov.-Dec. 1979): 185-97. O'Toole reports that as many as three thousand American companies promoted employee stock ownership by mid-1979. Some of the larger firms with ESOPs are Mobil, American Telephone and Telegraph, and Atlantic Richfield.

47. *Congressional Quarterly, 27th Annual Almanac*, 92nd Cong., 1st sess., 1971, p. 460.

48. The institute's board of directors is headed by Clark Kerr and has Jerome M. Rosow as its president. Other members are leading union leaders (such as Irving Bluestone and William Winpisinger), business executives, and academicians.

49. The National Association of Area Labor-Management Committees, Box 118, Fairfax, Va., 22030.

50. Federal Mediation and Conciliation Service, *Thirtieth Annual Report: Fiscal Year, 1977* (Washington, D.C.: Government Printing Office, 1978).

51. *Labor Management Committee: Planning for Progress* (Washington, D.C.: Government Printing Office, 1978), p. 3.

52. Public Law 95-524, October 27, 1978, *Ninety-Two Statutes-at-Large*, pp. 2020-21.

53. *The New York Times*, January 4, 1979, p. D 12.

54. Richard Tanner Pascale, "Communication and Decision Making Across Cultures: Japanese and American Comparisons," *Administrative Science Quarterly* 23 (March 1978): 91-108.

55. Richard Tanner Pascale, "Personnel Practices and Employee Attitudes: A Study of Japanese- and American-Managed Firms in the United States," *Human Relations* 31, no. 7 (1978): 597-615.

56. Organization for Economic Cooperation and Development, *The Development of Industrial Relations Systems: Some Implications of the Japanese Experience* (Paris: OECD, 1977), p. 10.

57. Richard Tanner Johnson and William G. Ouchi, "Made in America (Under Japanese Management)," *Harvard Business Review* 52 (Sept.-Oct. 1974): 61-69.

58. *The Economist*, December 9, 1978, p. 91.

59. *The New York Times*, March 17, 1978.

5

WEST EUROPEAN TRADE UNIONISM AND ITS RESPONSES TO THE PRESENCE AND PRACTICES OF U.S. MULTINATIONALS

The activities of American multinational corporations doing business in Western Europe obviously have not gone unchallenged. They have not only been confronted with increasingly aggressive and effective competition by local and other multinational firms, they are also challenged by the decisions and actions of European trade unions, governments, and European Community authorities. Of these three, the trade unions may well have been the most significant; most of the attempts by European public authorities at regulating multinational business have been the consequence of trade-union initiatives. This chapter, therefore, reviews the general features of European trade unionism, especially as compared to the organized labor movement in the United States. It will also describe the ways in which the particular trade-union systems of the several regions and countries of the European Community differ from one another, and the structures and strategies through which transnational trade unionism has sought to balance the power of multinational enterprises.

Even though the trade-union systems of the various regions and countries in Europe are distinctly different from one another, they do have certain features in common. West European trade unions, for example, have been much more than purely economic organizations. They are, first, manifestations of the underlying social-class system. As such, they are very responsive to class-conscious ideologies such as Marxism, whose symbol systems do more than call for superficial economic and political reforms; they seek to bring about a complete overhaul of society's institutions. When this type of rejection of the established order combined with the awareness that the working class was experiencing extensive social and political deprivations, European trade unions readily became the creators of virtual "substitute societies."[1] European trade unions helped workers develop and maintain their own separate countercultures, and simultaneously sought to provide the workers and their families the educational, recreational, and social opportunities from which they were being excluded in their elitist societies. As a consequence, European workers, for years, would rarely, if ever, deny their trade unions since such a denial would amount to a virtual betrayal of one's own kind of people. That level of class solidarity has only sporadically manifested itself among American workers.

What is interesting is that this sort of appreciation for the trade unions' role in advocating and attaining social, economic, and political justice has not been confined to the members of the European working class. Both the general public and many members of the managerial class in Western Europe have shown very little of the widespread apprehension about organized labor that prevails in the United States. Neither do they become involved in so many union-recognition battles; most European managers accept the union membership of their workers as one of the givens of industrial society.

European trade unions—in addition to being manifestations of the class system—have also been important as vehicles of working-class politics. Unions, and especially national trade-union federations, have either been creatures of working-class parties (as in Germany), or working-class parties have been brought about by the concerted effort of independently organized unions (as in England). This type of umbilical relationship between unions and parties reflects the interest many unionists have in reconstructing their national societies, and their realization that such a radical imperative requires the predominant power of the state. It is also an indication that European trade unionists have consistently felt that economic benefits could be obtained much more successfully through legislative action than through the singular process of collective bargaining. European trade unionists have increasingly realized that strength comes from unity and that unity grows out of the successes that strength make possible. Therefore, it has been through the dual channels of the unions and the political parties that European workers have obtained such fundamental political rights as the right to vote, the right to a free public education, the right to organize freely, the right of free press, and equality under the law.

Even though the West European trade unions and working-class parties have generally been linked together, the trade unions, from their earliest years, have tended to be more moderate and pragmatic than their companion parties. This difference must be related to the earlier secularization of the trade-union movement. Worker political parties emphasized the more long-range and comprehensive goals from the onset, a position they did not really begin to abandon until after World War II, when the earlier politics based mainly on social class began to be supplanted by broad popular politics. The unions, on the other hand, have always had to be more concerned with short-term payoffs and, therefore, readily appeared to compromise their commitment to ideology and working-class solidarity. Consequently, as the national economies grew, as the pie to be shared became larger and larger, and as the welfare state began to mature, trade unionists began to find it increasingly difficult to keep their rank-and-file memberships responsive to their leadership.

When the bulk of the American firms entered the Common Market in the late fifties and the sixties, they encountered a trade-union system that was a curious mixture of the heritage of class politics and of the widespread commitment by West European governments to egalitarianism and the welfare state. In addition, they had to deal with a work force that became increasingly prosperous and white collar. In such a climate, trade unions could not help but encounter even greater problems in recruiting members, and they would soon find themselves pressed to redefine their purposes and postures. Ivor Roberts found, for instance, that the percentage of the work force holding membership in European trade unions decreased from 1950 to 1968, although not drastically, in Germany, Norway, Sweden, Switzerland, and the United Kingdom (five of the seven countries he studied; Austria and Denmark were the other two).[2] That trend occurred even though labor-federation memberships increased at the same time and the degree of unionization exceeded that of the U.S. work force. The sharpest drops in organizational density were in Germany, Sweden, and Switzerland, all three countries where prosperity came earlier than in the other countries studied.

The full employment in the fifties and sixties created another major problem for European trade unions. With the centralization of collective bargaining, which became the hallmark of postwar industrial relations, the unions began to concentrate more on affairs away from the workplace. This allowed both the shop stewards and the works councils, rather than local union officials, to become the prime channels for worker grievances and for the negotiation of shop-floor issues.[3] The gap that began to develop between the workers and the union bureaucracies became even wider when centralized bargaining placed union leaders in the difficult position of being pressured to compromise on worker demands for the sake of harmonizing their particular economic demands with the needs of the total national economy. Time and time again, rank-and-file union members began to feel that their case was betrayed by union bureaucrats who seemed to be too comfortable making common cause with the nation's business elite for such apparently esoteric purposes as balancing the international-payments accounts.[4] It seemed to the members that even worker-party politicians placed the attainment of personal power above servicing those who put them in office. Such estrangement quickly radicalized a considerable segment of the European working class. This certainly was the case as soon as the rate of economic growth began to slow down, the recession set in, oil prices rose, and inflation became a gnawing problem. Even the previously peaceful labor systems such as those of Holland

and Germany experienced drastic increases in the number of shop-floor revolts and strikes. It appeared that European trade-union leaders might be losing control over their members.[5]

The stress that came over West European trade unionism in the late sixties and the seventies was not just due to the increased bureaucratization of the union apparatus and the ever-wider schism between leaders and rank-and-file members. It has even been suggested that it was also partly caused by the fact that a large number of the workers had not experienced the Great Depression nor the reconstruction days of the forties and the fifties. The workers no longer seemed to perceive of unemployment and inflation as policy questions that could be resolved by consensus politics achieved through a process of tripartite consultation. Many of them began to see such issues as symptomatic of severe deficiencies of their nations' institutions. The situation became even more complicated with the subsiding of the cold war, when the workers became increasingly aware about political and social inequalities, about the threats of nuclear and environmental destruction, and about the ironies of such events as the Vietnam War, the 1973 oil embargo, and Watergate. By that time, a significant number of workers seemed to have become convinced that their union leaderships' relative silence on these issues proved that they had become an integral part of the status-quo establishment.[6]

It would be logical to assume that any significant degree of worker alienation would benefit the more radical elements of the labor movement and the parties of the extreme Left. Such was not the case, however. Even though leftist parties did increase their voter appeal somewhat during the seventies, they did not gain an unchallenged upper hand in West European politics. They either obtained a slim majority (Great Britain), had to ally themselves with a minor party to stay in power (Great Britain and Germany), found their support divided (France and Italy), or found themselves kept out of the government even though they attracted a significant portion of the popular vote (Italy). Thus, the Socialists and Communists were never able to bring about the sweeping reforms the more activist elements of the labor movement seemed to expect. Neither did they prove themselves capable of solving the associated problems of recession and inflation.

European trade unions have recently tried to make two significant adaptations to deal with the rank-and-file alienation discussed above. One of these was the development of new bridge-building techniques. Opinion polls, invitations for direct responses to specific questions, frequent educational conferences, better training of union leadership, closer control over works councils, and granting a certain degree of self-determination to locals are all now part and parcel of the arsenal of trade-union strategies and/or rhetoric. In the area of collective bargaining, negotiations are being decentralized so that local plant and enterprise agreements are not left to works councils or nonunion structures, and so that trade unions can again prove their viability on bread-and-butter issues.[7]

Even though many workers in Common Market countries became radicalized in the seventies, and some unions came under the control of ultra-left leadership, that trend was not universal. In Britain, for example, left-wing union leaders and aspirants for union office did not fare very well in 1976. Most spectacular was the triumphant reelection of Frank J. Chapple, England's most outspoken anticommunist leader of the 450,000-member Electrical, Electronics, Telecommunications, and Plumbing Union. Equally significant, in May 1978, was Terry Duffy's election as president of the Engineering Union. He also is a staunch anticommunist.[8]

A somewhat similar trend seemed to be occurring in Italy, where an increasing number of workers turned their back on the more political unions. This behavior, which had mostly been peculiar to the more middle-class workers, was then also being adopted by those workers who were not as well paid. They seemed to join in disavowing the altruistic reform objectives of the bigger, established unions. As such, they did not so much deny radical reform politics as they appropriated to themselves the kind of economic action that the established union leaders called "economic terrorism." The independent economic unions were quickly accused of "fostering corporate interests," in the sense that they were abandoning worker solidarity for the sake of a pot of porridge (getting a better contract for themselves).[9]

While some observers have suggested that there has been a trend away from union membership generally, this is not necessarily the case. It is true that in the summer of 1977 in Britain, the staffs of the three Trust House Forte hotels rejected representation by the General and Transport Workers Union by a vote of more than 88 percent, and that the March 1977 IBM-U.K. vote was equally antiunion, with fewer than 4.5 percent voting in favor of union representation.[10] These events were probably more a reflection of those particular strata of workers, the nature of these industries, and the British disillusionment with unions than the fact that the bulk of European workers are rejecting worker organization.

It may be much more warranted to suggest that the days of cooperation, deference, and patience by the West European worker may be over. The rising impatience and recalcitrance of the workers may be strikingly exemplified by the 1977 refusal of Herr Heinz Oskar Vetter, the formidable chairman of the German Workers Federation (DGB) to continue participating in Germany's so-called Concerted Action Committee. For ten years, this consultative body had brought together representatives of government, trade unions, and employers to maintain and support a national consensus on economic policy. Herr Vetter's threat—that if the employers wanted a fight, "they could have one"—admittedly was a response to the management groups' court challenge of the 1976 Codetermination Act (which will be discussed in a later chapter). It also reflected, however, the kind of frustration that had been building up in the union rank-and-file about the German Socialist party's need to compromise with their conservative coalition partner, the Free Democrats, and the frequent public insinuations by employers that high labor costs had become a prime cause for the stagnation of German economic growth.[11]

The European workers of the late seventies began more and more to look for directly visible payoffs, and they expected these to be social and political as well as financial. What *The Economist* said about Dutch trade unionists did not appear to be true only for them; it observed that they were "not just after...a bigger slice of the growing cake, but were also after a hand in choosing the recipe, mixing and baking as well."[12] The head of one of Britain's biggest companies reportedly described the worker mood in a somewhat different way: "We are sitting on a volcano and we cannot pretend that what happens in the factories is divorced from how the workers and their families feel about the whole industry-based society."[13]

European trade unionism is characterized by several additional features; one of these is multiunion bargaining. In other words, a trade union in Western Europe is not required to obtain the endorsement of a majority of a firm's employees in order to represent the workers, as is the case in the United States. Therefore, it is not uncommon for an employer to have to deal with a number of different unions. Adams has suggested that this fact partly explains the differential in the levels of unionization in Europe and in the United States. Europe's liberal laws of representation helped inflate the rate of union membership among its workers. If European employers were protected from having to deal with minority unions and were also allowed to campaign against unions in recognition elections, fewer European workers would probably be affiliated.[14] Similarly, if the social, political, and legal climate in the United States were more supportive of trade unionism, then more American workers, particularly white-collar and middle-management workers, would probably be members of a union.

The difference between the labor culture of Western Europe and that of the United States also expresses itself through their respective ideological configurations. Unionists in America are generally sold on the free-enterprise system; in fact, they are among the more ardent supporters of the economic and political status quo in American society. Consequently, George Meany and his cohorts had almost more to do with the U.S. withdrawal from the International Labour Organisation than did the American business community. Time and time again, American workers have supported political leaders who championed policies that capitalized on their love of country and "the American way of life." As such, they definitely contributed to the frequent denials of and misunderstandings about the aspirations of working people the world over.

In the 1950s, American workers united themselves into the AFL-CIO, which listed as one of its ten primary goals "protection against Communist subversion" and which shortly thereafter expelled eleven unions from the federation for having engaged in "Communist activities." At the same time, large numbers of workers, especially in those European countries, such as France and Italy, in which workers and employers had not identified themselves to be partners in national reconstruction, cast their ballots for Communist politicians and became members of Communist-dominated trade unions. An additional sizable group of European workers affiliated themselves with Socialist parties and candidates, something that very few American union leaders and members have ever done. Clark Kerr characterized this ideological distinction between West European and American trade unionists well when he observed that while American unions are selling memberships, German unions are selling a new society.[15]

One feature of European trade unionism that should not be overlooked is the fact that European unions are generally organized, sometimes even broadly defined, along industrial rather than craft lines. Thus, all workers in an industry tend to belong to the same union. For example, all Germans who work for firms that manufacture products in which metal is a prime substance, belong to the Metalworkers Union. A side effect of industrial unionism is the tendency for a somewhat greater cohesion between workers in that industry and workers in the same industry in other countries than between workers of various industries in the same country.[16] This latter trend, along with the greater ideological affinity among European trade unionists, partly explains why the transnational labor movement originated and has been most active in Europe.

All these descriptions about West European trade unionism undoubtedly make one suppose that labor relations there must have been highly unstable and costly. Paradoxically, with the striking exceptions of Ireland and Italy, the countries of the European Community have experienced significantly fewer days lost through industrial disputes than have the United States and Canada. In the latter two countries, an annual average of 1,232 and 1,307 days, respectively, were lost between 1963 and 1972. Comparable losses in European Community countries were: Belgium, 291 days; Denmark, 85 days; France, 320 days; Germany, 54 days; Ireland, 1,086; Italy, 1,481, the Netherlands, 36; and the United Kingdom, 546 days.[17] The picture is not much different for the decade 1967 through 1976. These figures are admittedly raw figures, and they are possibly not very accurate; nevertheless, they make the general point. In fact, they understate rather than overstate the situation, particularly if one considers the differences in the rates of unionization in the United States and in these countries. As Kassalow suggests, the time lost due to strikes in the United States would be even higher if Stateside workers were as organized as those in Western Europe.[18]

DIFFERENCES AMONG NATIONAL TRADE-UNION SYSTEMS

Although there are distinct differences among national trade-union systems, not all are purely random; some seem to fall into regional patterns. For example, there seems to be a distinct pattern in the variations between the trade-union systems of the more northern EEC countries and those to the south and west. Germany, the Netherlands, Denmark, and Belgium conduct their industrial relations in definite contrast to the way it is done in Ireland, the United Kingdom, France, and Italy. Many people suggest that one can almost visualize a dividing line running through the North Sea, through central Belgium (almost along its line of linguistic division), along the Rhine River, and then along the western and southern boundaries of Switzerland. In the northern-hemisphere countries of the community, worker and manager attitudes are more conciliatory. Only very few incidents of revolutionary tactics, such as worker occupations of plants, have occurred in these "integrating" industrial-relations systems.[19] As we shall see in the next chapter, these countries have also been much more receptive to such cooperative schemes as worker participation. And finally, as the statistics of workdays lost due to work stoppages suggest, distinctly fewer workdays have been lost in the northern countries than in those to the west and south.

The same regional consistency does not hold, however, when one looks at the first level of comparison—the level of unionization of the nations' work forces. The national rates vary; however, these differences do not follow the distinct geographic patterns. For example, while the average for the total European Economic Community in 1976 was 43 percent, the workers in Denmark and Belgium were organized to some 70 percent. Ireland, Italy, Luxembourg, and the United Kingdom were listed in the range of 50 percent; Germany and the Netherlands around 40 percent; and France slightly more than 20 percent.[20] A number of explanations have been given for these differences. Von Beyme enumerates seven of them: the degree of class-consciousness in the country's past; the occupational structure of the nation's economy; whether the nation's economy is on the up- or downswing; the continuity, degree of centralization, and ideological unity of the nation's unions; the government's wage policy; the legal framework of the national industrial-relations system; and the closeness of the organizational links between the unions and the workers' party.[21]

Adams, building on Blanpain's findings, suggests that the rate of union membership is highest in those countries where the trade unions have a greater influence in intervening on behalf of worker grievances, an observation that gives credence to the premise that workers are more oriented toward their self-interest than to ideology, at least with regard to their decision whether or not to join a trade union.[22] The same premise seems to be supported by the fact that in Denmark and the other Scandinavian countries, the trade-union systems are integral components of the social-security system. Under such circumstances, it makes good practical sense to belong to a union if you want to be eligible to receive unemployment benefits.[23]

The second most common basis for comparing national trade-union systems is the relative rates of concentration in union membership. When this variable is expressed in terms of the number of unions active in the society, the United Kingdom is least concentrated, in that it counted some 488 active unions in 1975. West Germany is rated at the other end of the continuum with about seventeen. What these data ignore, however, is the phenomenon of trade-union federations. For example, in the United Kingdom, only 111 of the total of 488 trade unions were affiliated with the Trade Union Congress, the country's only national trade-union confederation. However, these 111 affiliated unions have a combined membership that amounts to some 87 percent of British trade unionists. In none of the EEC countries is the level of confederation less than 70 percent; in Belgium and Denmark (the same countries that had the highest rate of unionization), virtually all blue-collar workers are organized into the confederation.

The rate of concentration of union membership in a country's national confederation(s) is one of the more important variables. One reason is the fact that a rather consistent amalgamation of trade unions has been occurring in most West European countries. To use the United Kingdom as an example again, in 1900, it counted 1,323 unions; in 1958, there were about 673, a number that decreased to 534 by 1970 and to 488 by 1975.[24] The unions that have been absorbed have mostly been the smaller, unaffiliated ones. The degree of membership concentrated in the national confederations is equally important because in the more integrating industrial-relations systems (Denmark, Holland, Germany especially), the confederations are extremely powerful structures. They are so largely because collective bargaining is so highly centralized in these countries.

The next crucial issue is whether the country has only one trade-union confederation or more. There are two confederations that have a monopoly: the British Trade Union Congress and the Irish Congress of Trade Unions. In two other cases, there are several national confederations, even though one clearly dominates: such is the case with the German Confederation of Trade Unions and the Federation of Danish Trade Unions. A more multiple division exists in France and Italy. In both countries, one confederation, the General Confederation of Labor, encompasses about half of the country's union members. In Italy, the CGIL has a substantial challenger—the Christian Democrat CISL. In addition to these two larger ones, there are several smaller confederations. The situation in France is even more diffused: the CGT has several competing confederations as well as a number of unaffiliated unions; none of these, though, provides much of a counterweight to the CGT.

There are, at the same time, a sufficient number of trade-union organs in France to make that national system highly decentralized. The configurations in Belgium, the Netherlands, and Luxembourg are unique in their own way. In these three countries, the cleavage among labor confederations reflects the kind of tripartite confessional and ideological orientations that impact on most of their societal institutions. In each of them, there is a Social Democrat and a Catholic confederation, complemented with a Liberal confederation in Belgium and a Protestant federation in the Netherlands.

These cleavages in the various national trade-union systems not only foretell problems in coordinating legislative and economic actions, they also clearly suggest a potential for a much more difficult problem: the existence of very definite and deep ideological disagreements and a frequent incapacity even to have dialogue on any issues vital to the working class of these countries. Although confessional cleavages also affect employers and the structuring of their cooperative organizations, management's cohesion has not been undermined in any comparable way by ideological differences. While trade unions and labor federations may be deeply divided about the degree of reform that should be made in the nation's existing political and economic institutions and policies, employers quarrel among themselves mostly about the degree to which they should accommodate to demands for more socioeconomic legislation. They have been quite unanimous, though, in their desire to roll back the infringements that Social Democrat policies have perpetrated on their property rights and privileges. The employers' solidarity tends to be unquestionable; it is the workers who are divided, which contributes to the continuation and the deepening of worker radicalism.

Mention should also be made of the relative power position of particular unions. In Germany, for example, the IG Metall (the Metal Workers Union) constitutes almost one-third of the DGB-affiliated membership and one-fourth of all unionized labor. Their annual settlement usually sets the pattern for the other unions and clarifies the points of general contention.[25] The settlements of the Danish General Workers Union also sets the pattern in Denmark.

Another very significant distinction should be made about trade unionism in the several Common Market countries, which relates to the social distances between labor and management. For instance, The Times quoted a German banker who observed: "When I see British employers and workers together on TV here, I can always tell them apart. In Germany, no such distinction would be obvious." The newspaper's correspondent suggests that this lesser social distance may have resulted partly from the fact that German trade unionists are themselves involved in big-business management, both in the form of works councils and codetermination as well as through such union-owned enterprises as the Bank für Gemeinwerkschaft. The latter does not only rank sixth among nonstate-owned banks, but it has provided financing for such business firms as leading mail-order houses.[26]

The feeling of social separation that Italian, French, and British workers experience could well relate to the low level of worker compensation there. While workers in West German manufacturing industries in 1977 received approximately $5.40 per hour; Italian workers received about $2.75 per hour; French workers, $3.10; and British workers, $3.00. The British workers, in fact, received considerably less than the others in total compensation, including holidays, social insurance, and other benefits. Their total package was about $3.80, compared to $8.70 for the Germans and $5.10 for the Italians and the French.[27] We should remember, though, that the level of worker compensation does not always correlate with the degree of labor stability. As we suggested earlier in this chapter, Belgian workers lost almost six times as many workdays (average per year from 1963 to 1972) as did German workers even though their compensation packages were almost identical. Thus, while the sense of social alienation through lower wages and the propensity to strike may tend to correlate, it is not possible to establish a universal causal relationship.

The national trade-union systems differ in one additional way: in the variation in the trade union's role on the shop floor, particularly in the degree of independence enjoyed by shop stewards. At one extreme, British shop stewards feel more obligated to their work mates than to their union leadership. At the other extreme, works councils in Germany and Holland have either been much more influential than shop-level union officials or the latter have chosen to operate primarily through the works councils. While the British shop steward is not as much of a troublemaker as is frequently alleged, he is definitely a more independent agent than shop stewards elsewhere.[28] British management is not able to play the union representative off against worker delegates on the works council, and it is also much more susceptible to the personality traits and ideological leanings of the steward or council of stewards.

Regardless of the particular circumstances that have made the trade-union systems in the several European Community countries so different from one another, they do vary considerably, and that is the important point. That fact should keep one from making too many hasty generalizations; it should also prevent multinational corporate management from committing the grand error of prescribing for its affiliates a uniform EEC-wide response to trade unionism.

TRANSNATIONAL TRADE UNIONISM AND ITS RESPONSES

One of the primary goals of trade unionists is to balance the power of their adversaries through negotiations. Such a goal, which is never easy to attain, presents some real problems when the adversary's power is over-whelmingly dominant. Just imagine, for example, the plight of British union leaders who seek to negotiate a labor contract for the workers of Vauxhall, the British subsidiary of General Motors. One of the first things they face is the fact that they represent only 5 percent of the automaker's worldwide work force and that the company's global headquarters is not going to stay aloof from their negotiations.[29]

It is not at all surprising, therefore, that the strategies European trade unions adopted to deal with such a dilemma are not much different from those employed by local European firms faced with overwhelming competi-tion from multinational corporations. Business firms responded by com-bining across national boundaries and by supporting the development of a common market (the Economic Community) that allowed free trade and a market of scale. Trade unions formed new transnational combinations, strengthened existing ones, and developed fresh strategies for common action. At the same time, they intensified the pressure on the decision-making structures of the European Community and the Organization for Economic Cooperation and Development. Through these latter, political channels, they tried to ensure that foreign-owned enterprises would not become exempt from local labor laws; to aid in the development of a set of regulations designed to deal with the problems accompanying the spread of multinational enterprises; and to guarantee for workers and their representatives increased participation in corporate decision making.

The oldest, and probably most effective, structures of transnational trade unionism are the so-called international trade secretariats, which seek to mobilize all the workers in the world who are employed in an industry. This is done through the joining together of their national industrial unions. The largest secretariat is the International Metalworkers Federation, the IMF. This Geneva-based organization represents some eleven million workers in the automobile, electrical appliances, shipbuilding, engineering, and steel industries. Component industrial unions of the IMF include the United Auto Workers in the United States and Canada and the IG Metall in Germany. The stature and effectiveness of the IMF is not just the result of its larger budget and staff; it is, not least of all, a reflection of the sophisticated and shrewd leadership of its assistant general secretary, Daniel Benedict, a former UAW official. The European Metalworkers Federation has an IMF daughter organization located in Brussels, through which Günter Köpke has represented the interests of some four million European workers.

An international secretariat that speaks for considerably fewer workers but that has received an equal amount of publicity is the International Federation of Chemical and General Workers, the ICEF.[30] Canadian-born Charles Levinson, an ideologue with rather imaginative ideas about worker goals and strategies, is its spark plug. It was Levinson who was one of the first pamphleteers writing against multinational corporations. To him, the multinationals were the creators of permanent inflation, invulnerable to any governmental controls, to be tamed only by the eventual accession of workers to multinational company boards.[31] Although considered by many of his fellow union leaders as an "enfant terrible," the ICEF general secretary has scored some distinct victories for his workers. Still somewhat legendary, partly due to Levinson's buildup of the incident, is the St. Gobain story.

In 1969, when American workers for the French-owned glass and manufacturing enterprise were renegotiating their contract, they were told that their demands could not be met because the U.S. subsidiary had failed to earn the company any profits from 1966 to 1968. Levinson, who had already brought ICF union delegates together in March to agree upon a common beginning strategy, immediately notified American union leaders that the workers in Germany and Italy had obtained very favorable contracts and that the company's global profits had gone up some 25 percent. The U.S. workers held out and obtained a 9.5-percent wage increase as well as improvements in fringe benefits. The St. Gobain case certainly proved what coordinated bargaining can bring about, particularly in a sector of industry that is highly capital-intensive, a characteristic that makes it especially vulnerable to strike action.

Levinson's achievements have not always been what he purports them to be. In 1976, for example, at the ICEF Congress, he reported that ICEF "appeals had met with active and enthusiastic response from ICEF affiliates through the duration of the lengthy URW [United Rubber Workers] strike." Northrup and Rowan found that no international boycotts, no monitoring of shipments by European and Japanese union members, and no sympathy actions (including by the International Transport Workers Federation and longshore and maritime workers' unions) occurred, however.[32] It is no wonder, therefore, that the ICEF general secretary is not particularly considered a part of the in-group by his peers (international union officials) and is being taken with a considerable grain of salt by multinational management.

Also quite active in multinational labor action are the International Union of Food and Allied Workers Associations (the IUF) and the International Textile, Garment, and Leather Workers Federation (the ITGLWF). The latter, under Charles Ford, has had a virtual uphill battle in a sector that is riddled with runaway enterprises. Nevertheless, Ford can proudly claim that he organized a boycott of Farrah slacks and clothing, which forced the firm to accept unionization of its plants in the southwestern United States.

However significant a number of the strike-support and coordinating actions of the international secretariats may have been, their most significant achievements may well be the establishment of world councils, or working parties. Most of these are creatures of the IMF.³³ These councils came into existence in 1966, when General Motors, Ford, and Chrysler brought together worker representatives from all the plants and operations of each company, those located in the headquarters country as well as those overseas. Company councils presently exist in several other industrial sectors. Many of the world's larger multinational corporations are, in fact, paralleled by world councils.

Although many union leaders hoped that the councils would quickly bring about the negotiation of companywide contracts, that did not happen. The councils have primarily served as disseminators of secretariat-collected information, a task in which they have been quite effective. For example, the IMF has developed a computerized data bank from which local union leaders facing negotiations obtain up-to-date information on contract concessions achieved at other company units, an update on the company's overall economic and financial condition, and any other information deemed advisable.³⁴

Worldwide collective bargaining has not yet been achieved. There have been meetings, however, between world-council representatives and certain management representatives. For example, in Dearborn, Michigan, on February 9, 1973, Ford Company management representatives met with IMF and UAW officials, a meeting that resulted from a request by European union leaders to meet with management of Ford subsidiaries in Europe. The meeting at Ford's world headquarters certainly was not a multinational bargaining session; neither did it turn out to be the first of a successful series of conversations. At a subsequent informal meeting, the Ford labor-relations expert is reported to have stated crisply: "We will not meet with the IMF and its council because we do not have to. We will only do so when you are strong enough in the plants to force us to do so. When that happens we will not be the first company to do so, but we will not be the last either."³⁵ Such conversations as those with Ford, and those held with General Electric, General Motors, and other MNCs have been strictly informal.

The world councils have had more success dealing with Philips Electric (Holland), Brown Bovari (Switzerland), and VFW-Fokker (Holland-Germany). The nationalities represented in this group illustrate again that American firms are not very inclined to follow European "social harmonization" procedures. American management seems unable to abandon the notion that you only sit down with labor when it is contract-negotiating time, and that you, then, only talk about pay and fringe benefits, not about such things as company investment and work organization. It is as if they believe it is more economical to go to a doctor when faced with a medical crisis than to practice preventive medicine.³⁶

Consultations are not singularly disliked by American managers. American trade unionists—with the exception of a number of UAW officials—generally have not been in the vanguard of the transnational trade-union movement, either. In fact, all but one of the sixteen international trade secretariats are located in Europe. This statistic again illustrates the greater determination of European trade-union leaders to promote transnational worker solidarity and their inclination not to limit themselves to purely economic action.

Breaches in worker solidarity are not brought about solely by differences in ideologies and/or tactics; they are somewhat inevitably linked to the economic circumstances prevailing in the unionist's home country. Thus, for example, when UAW officials saw an increasing number of foreign-made cars being imported into the United States in the late sixties, they logically saw considerable benefit in appealing to their brother trade unionists overseas to help counterbalance the exportation of American jobs. German, Japanese, and car workers of other nationalities undoubtedly must have had some difficulty meeting the expectations of their American peers. The situation became almost completely reversed by the late seventies. By that time, European and Japanese manufacturers had begun to set up factories in the States, and it became the turn of European and Japanese workers to express concerns. It is terribly difficult under such changing circumstances for unions to remain consistent in their postures.

An activity in which the international trade secretariats have been very effective has been their training and publications program. The International Metalworkers Federation, for instance, has published detailed studies on virtually all major multinationals in its sector. These studies are then used as basic documentation for seminars on these companies. Such seminars are either held unilaterally (by a national union dealing with one of several of that company's affiliates) or multilaterally (by national unions from several subsidiary countries joining together). Training sessions are also organized on such a range of issues as membership recruitment and the development of a global strategy for bargaining with a certain company.

The personal know-how and the staff resources of the secretariats have been put to a whole new use with the election of several ITS executives to the supervisory boards of American subsidiaries in Germany. Charles Levinson became a member of the Du Pont board upon the nomination of IG Chemie, the German Chemical Workers Union. Ford Werke acquired Herman Rebhan, the American general secretary of the IMF. One of IMF's assistant general secretaries, Werner Thonnessen, was designated to serve on the board of ITT's affiliate Standard Electrik Lorenz. Günter Köpke, the general secretary of the European Metalworkers Federation, was assigned to the board of the German affiliate of the Dutch multinational Philips Electric.

As suggested earlier, Levinson and other transnational trade unionists are not necessarily satisfied with only rendering their personal services at this level of corporate decision making. A number of them feel, as Levinson expressed it, that "the only possible way multinationals can grow while protecting workers at the same time" is for worker representatives to sit on corporate-headquarter boards.[37] That goal will not be attained in the near future, though. The nearest possibility would be for those firms that would primarily be organized as European companies—that is, that would choose to incorporate under the European Community's projected Company Statute. (More will be said about this later.)

An interesting part of transnational trade unionism in Europe is the EEC-level equivalent of the ITS, the so-called European Industrial Committees, which operate in the transport, chemical, metal, food, construction, and textile industries. The most effective of the five committees is the European Metalworkers Federation, which originated in 1963 as the Metal Committee of the European Confederation of Free Trade Unions. Under the leadership of Günter Köpke, EMF has concentrated it activities on three main tasks:

1. Representation of workers' interests in the policy of the European Community,
2. Cooperation and coordination of the unions, especially during collective bargaining negotiations and strike actions, and
3. Discussions and negotiations with employers' organizations on European levels and with boards of management of multinational companies based in the EEC.[38]

Its work has paid off in all three areas. In the fall of 1968, for example, sixty-five hundred Ford employees in Belgium went on strike. EMF contacted the German Metalworkers Union, the works council at the Ford plant at Cologne, the bargaining committee of Ford workers in Britain, and the United Auto Workers in the States. Consequently, pressure was put on the company's world headquarters, on Ford management in Cologne to prevent sending German workers to the Belgian plant, and on the managements of the various subsidiaries to which the company might shift production. The EMF initiative worked. And so it did in 1971, when Belgian, Dutch, and German Ford workers were mobilized to support their fifty thousand British colleagues whose strike resulted in the shifting of production to plants on the Continent.[39]

EMF has also been very persistent in its drive toward multinational bargaining. Previously mentioned discussions with Philips and with Fokker-VFW were initiated by Köpke. The deliberations with Philips ran aground due to rather precipitous attempts to convert them into formal bargaining sessions and to extend them beyond matters of European dimension.

Rowan and Northrup have strongly suggested that EMF may be in a much better position to achieve its goals than is the worldwide IMF. While the EMF already has many problems keeping its ranks united, the diversity within the global IMF is almost insurmountable. More important to the successes of the EMF have been the facts that its organization naturally parallels that of the European Community, that the European Commission officials have been quite responsive, and that most European governments have generally had significant worker-party participation and/or input.[40]

Mentioned so far have been the international trade secretariats, the European industry committees, and the several ITS-sponsored company world councils. The fourth type of transnational trade-union organization—the international confederation—is more comprehensive in nature. As the international secretariats are industrially based, this particular form is as all-inclusive as nationwide labor federations. In fact, the fourth type is nothing but alliances of national confederations. Rather than being primarily engaged in economic activity as the first three are, the international confederations primarily concern themselves with political goals. Thus, they are the ones who seek to mobilize transnational worker solidarity and who seek to have the interests of all working people everywhere considered by and incorporated into the actions of various global international organizations.

The oldest of the three major confederations is the World Confederation of Labor (the WCL, known before 1968 as the Federation of Christian Trade Unions). With headquarters in Brussels and established in 1921, the WCL represents some sixteen million Protestant and Roman Catholic workers. Its European membership of some four million is mainly located in Belgium, the Netherlands, and Luxembourg. In spite of what the confessional label of most of its member unions may suggest to American observers, this confederation has generally taken distinctly anticapitalist, anti-American positions and is generally described as conciliatory toward the revolutionary Marxist unions. Their objectives have been described as being focused on the replacement of "both the capitalistic and Marxist state socialistic societies by more decentralized, self-governing economic and social units coordinated through democratic planning, shared in by all governed groups themselves, and based on the social ownership of the economy."[41] The WCL considers it an integral responsibility of trade unions to prepare workers for their eventual participation in the management of their workplace.

While the WCL is generally considered to be cooperative toward the other world trade-union confederations, a much more independent, if not recalcitrant, line tends to be taken by the World Federation of Trade Unions (the WFTU). This confederation, headquartered in Prague and organized by Soviet initiatives in 1945, claims a membership of more than one hundred sixty million. About half of these are members of Soviet trade unions, and another 42 percent are located in satellite countries; thus, only some 7 or 8 percent of its membership is located in noncommunist countries. Remember, however, that the WFTU's affiliates in France and Italy, the General Confederations of Labor, represent about half the organized workers there. That apparently alarming statistic is only moderated somewhat by the fact that the level of unionization is rather low in France; in Italy, however, it is generally reported to be about 50 percent. WFTU strength in these two countries again reinforces the assertion made several times now: worker attitudes and politics in these two countries is distinctly more radical than in the northern areas of Western Europe.

The WFTU and the WCL have their own counterparts to the international trade secretariats—their trade-union internationals. These TUIs have, at times, undercut the collective-bargaining attempts of the more moderate ITS by such techniques as organizing so-called shop-stewards committees (in Britain) and by withholding strike and boycott support (as in the 1976 U.S. Rubber strike).[42] They are also much more controlled by their sponsoring organization and can thus more easily be mobilized to serve the sponsor's generally more political objectives.[43]

The international labor confederation that is designed to represent the interests of most West European (and other free-world) workers is the ICFTU, the International Confederation of Free Trade Unions. Also headquartered in Brussels, this confederation of reformist, social-democratic national unions came into existence in 1949. In that year, noncommunist unions, which had previously joined the WFTU, left that organization in protest against Moscow's attempts to use them to undermine the Marshall Plan and Western defense efforts, and combined with the AF of L into a more independent organization. The approximately sixty million workers affiliated with ICFTU unions are particularly concentrated in Great Britain, Germany, the Scandinavian countries, and Holland. These are the countries where labor has generally been much more evolutionary than revolutionary in their orientation.

Until 1969, when George Meany pulled the AFL-CIO out of the ICFTU, the organization was frequently handicapped by the American labor leader's anticommunist strategies and by the way in which he played his politics. For example, at a press conference in 1965, Meany not only charged that the organization was bureaucratic and ineffective, he also implied that it was a haven for homosexuals.[44] That, unfortunately, has been the style of politics by which some American union leaders have created virtual havoc in the ranks of free-world labor. Lane Kirkland, Mr. Meany's successor, made some rather undiplomatic remarks himself. In January 1978, he described the difference between West European and American trade unionism by observing: "We are all doing God's work. They in their way, we in His."[45]

What makes the 1969 American withdrawal from the ICFTU even more ironic is the fact that Meany decided to do so, not only because he felt that the confederation was too soft on communism, but also out of rancor that it did not chastise the United Auto Workers for dropping out of the AFL-CIO. Of course, expecting the ICFTU to do that was rather illogical, especially since Walter Reuther had been one of the most active leaders of international trade unionism.

The isolation of American labor could not last forever; its termination could certainly not be postponed until Meany's demise. Thus, in August 1977, after Meany had successfully helped to engineer U.S. withdrawal from the International Labour Organisation, some of his lieutenants apparently were successful in pushing for rapprochement with the ICFTU. The international committee of the AFL-CIO was charged to study whether it should rejoin the confederation. As of this writing, the reconciliation has not yet occurred. There are, nevertheless, indications that it may come about soon.

While the ICFTU had proven it could survive financially without previous sizable U.S. funding, it never thrived to the point that it could choose to teach the American cold warriors a lesson (if such chastisement would ever have been its intention). The confederation has had its own problems, particularly since its success mainly depends on its ability to promote worldwide worker solidarity. It was logical, therefore, that American seats on the ICFTU executive board were never filled, and continued American participation in the activities of its inter-American affiliate was gladly accepted. The doors were always kept open.

Typical of the activities of the international confederations of labor is the ICFTU's adoption of the Multinational Charter—a set of trade-union demands for the legislative control of multinational companies adopted at the Eleventh World Congress, which met in Mexico City, October 17-25, 1975. Among other things, the charter calls for: "legislation obliging multinational concerns to provide detailed financial accounts and other data," the imposition of some fourteen "social obligations" on multinational firms, treaties to control foreign direct investment and takeovers, treaties to deal with restrictive business practices and oligopolistic pricing, and treaties to establish principles and rules for the taxation of multinationals.[46]

The international labor confederation that is possibly the most viable as well as the most important to American investors in the European Community is the European Trade Union Confederation (ETUC), created in 1973 as a successor to the European Confederation of Free Trade Unions. Even though ETUC's predecessor may, by name at least, appear to be merely a regional version of the ICFTU, the European Confederation is not formally or legally related to any global confederation or set of trade secretariats. It has been consolidated to a much greater extent than has any other international confederation. It counts within its ranks, not only the social-democratic unions of Western Europe, but also some of the WFTU (revolutionary Marxist) national labor organizations, particularly the Italian and French General Confederations of Labor.

On February 6, 1975, the Executive Committee of ETUC passed the organization's first substantive resolution on multinational companies. It demanded that national legislatures and the European Assembly ensure the establishment of an "institution or body of information and consultation of employees" if and when such is requested by a trade-union organ.[47] More will be said in the next chapter about this proposal and its effects.

One year later, after the ICFTU's Mexico City Multinational Charter, the Executive Committee adopted an extensive resolution that built upon the authority of the European Community, under the Treaty of Rome, to adopt supranational law.[48] The resolution also suggested that since it was "unlikely that legal norms with worldwide legal force will come into effect in the fore-seeable future...an attempt must be made [to start] somewhere...and that it is best to start where the conditions for the realization of these measures are most favourable." The regulations that were being proposed and demanded should contain three basic elements: (1) a legal definition of the concept multinational firm (*Konzern*), (2) representation of employees at the corporate level of the multinational firm, and (3) an obligation of multinational companies to draw up and publish consolidated annual statements of accounts for the firm.[49] At the confederation's Second Statutory Congress in London, April 22-24, 1976, this larger, representative, organizational body reiterated these demands.[50]

As Roberts suggested, the European Trade Union Confederation can be credited with persuading the European Commission to include provisions guaranteeing the right of worker representation on company boards and the establishment of plant-level and EEC-wide works councils in the draft of the European Company Statute.[51] The nature of this statute and its relevant provisions will be discussed in the next chapter.

CONCLUSIONS

The European trade-union movement is the core element in a concerted campaign, not only to balance the bargaining power of multinational business there, but also to bring about the "democratization" of the national and European economies. It may be disputable as to whether this action program is the result of the sociopolitical heritage of that part of the world or whether it was engendered by the presence in the European Economic Community of American multinational corporations. Few would deny, however, that the trade-unionist commitment to the regulation of international business is real, and that the national and European political power of trade unionists is formidable. There is not much question about the nature and level of commitment that a number of trade unionists have to expand worker participation in enterprise decisions. While the advent of the economic recession may have temporarily delayed the widespread attainment of either of these goals, they certainly have not been removed from labor's agenda for the future.

NOTES

1. Everett M. Kassalow, *Trade Unions and Industrial Relations: An International Comparison* (New York: Random House, 1969), pp. 18-19. Many of the following general observations parallel those made in this classic work.

2. Ivor Roberts, "Trade Union Membership Trends in Seven Western European Countries, 1950-1968," *Industrial Relations Journal* 4 (Winter 1973): 50.

3. Adolf Sturmthal, *Comparative Labor Movements* (Belmont, Calif.: Wadsworth, 1972), pp. 162-63. The impact of works councils on unions in the plant will be discussed in further detail later.

4. Interesting observations about these mood changes are made by Sturmthal, and by Everett M. Kassalow, "Conflict and Cooperation in Europe's Industrial Relations," *Industrial Relations* 13 (May 1974): 156-63. Kassalow points out that the unrest commenced before 1973 and was greatly influenced by the 1968 student strikes.

5. *The Economist*, February 18, 1978.

6. For instance, see Jan Pen, "Trade Union Attitudes Toward Central Wage Policy: Remarks on the Dutch Experience," in Adolf Sturmthal and James G. Scoville, eds., *The International Labor Movement in Transition* (Urbana: University of Illinois Press, 1973), pp. 278-81.

7. See Solomon Barkin, "Summary and Conclusion," in Barkin, ed., *Worker Militancy and Its Consequences, 1965-1975: New Directions in Western Industrial Relations* (New York: Praeger Publishers, Special Studies, 1975), pp. 381 ff.

8. A. H. Raskin, "The Labor Scene: Transformed Attitudes at British Unions," *The New York Times*, July 9, 1976, and *The Economist*, May 6, 1978, pp. 19-20.

9. *The New York Times*, January 30, 1978.

10. *The Times*, June 17, 1977.

11. *The Times*, July 1 and 12, 1977.

12. *The Economist*, February 19, 1977. Holland's unions recently spearheaded another significant change in the worker movement — greater centralization. The two largest labor federations, the NVV and the NKV, merged into the FNV, the Confederation of Dutch Trade Unions.

13. *The New York Times*, July 22, 1976.

14. Roy J. Adams, "Solidarity, Self-Interest and the Unionization Differential Between Europe and North America," *Industrial Relations-Relations Industrielles* 29, no. 3 (1974): 507. It should, in all fairness, be pointed out that more American workers, particularly white-collar and middle-level management people, would be organized if the legal climate in the States were more encouraging.

15. Clark Kerr, "The Trade Union Movement and the Redistribution of Power in Postwar Germany," *The Quarterly Journal of Economics* 68 (Nov. 1954): 537.

16. Anthony Carew, *Democracy and Government in European Trade Unions* (London: George Allen and Unwin, 1976), p. 53.

17. See Barkin, *Worker Militancy*, p. 370. It should be pointed out that the figures for the United States and Canada did include days lost in certain public-utility industries, like gas and electricity, which are not included for the others. The figures cited are per one thousand people employed.

18. Everett M. Kassalow, "Industrial Conflict and Consensus in the U.S. and

Western Europe," in Benjamin Martin and Everett M. Kassalow, eds., *Labor Relations in Advanced Industrial Societies: Issues and Problems* (Washington, D.C.: Carnegie Endowment for International Peace, 1980), pp. 46, 47.

19. W. Albeda, "Trade Union Attitudes and Management Responses," in OECD, *Workers' Participation* (Documents prepared for the International Management Seminar convened by the OECD, Versailles, March 5-8, 1975, pp. 16-21).

20. European Commission, *Report on the Development of the Social Situation in the Communities in 1976* (Brussels: European Commission, 1977), pp. 202-203.

21. Klaus Von Beyme, *Challenge to Power: Trade Unions and Industrial Relations in Capitalist Countries* (London: Sage Publications, 1980), pp. 74-83.

22. Roy J. Adams, "Solidarity, Self-Interest and the Unionization Differential Between Europe and North America," *Industrial Relations — Relations Industrielles*, 29, 3 (1974): 507.

23. Ivor Roberts, p. 53.

24. A. W. J. Thomson and L. C. Hunter, "Great Britain," in John T. Dunlop and Walter Galenson, *Labor in the Twentieth Century* (New York: Academic Press, 1978), pp. 104-105.

25. Kerr, p. 540.

26. *The Times*, October 21, 1977.

27. *The Economist*, February 4, 1978, p. 91.

28. See John F. B. Goodman, "Great Britain: Toward the Social Contract," in Barkin's *Worker Militancy*, pp. 56-57.

29. Daniel Benedict, "Multinational Companies: Their Relations with the Workers," (Report presented at the Conference on Industrial Relations in the European Community, Royal Institute of International Affairs, London, October 4, 1973).

30. Before October 1976, the ICEF was known as the ICF. From 1907, its founding, to 1965, it was named the Factory Workers International. See Herbert R. Northrup and Richard K. Rowan, "Multinational Union Activity in the 1976 U.S. Rubber Tire Strike," *Sloan Management Review* 18 (Spring 1977): 19.

31. Particularly interesting is Levinson's *International Trade Unionism* (London: George Allen and Unwin, 1972).

32. The ICF Conference statement was quoted in the Northrup and Rowan analysis, p. 22.

33. The organizing story and an inventory of the achievements of IMF world councils are told in Richard K. Rowan and Herbert R. Northrup, "Multinational Bargaining in Metals and Electrical Industries: Approaches and Prospects," *Journal of Industrial Relations* 17 (March 1975): 1-29, and by Burton B. Bendiner, the IMF's former coordinator of the World Auto Councils, "A Labor Response to Multinationals: Coordination of Bargaining Goals," *Monthly Labor Review* 101, (July 1978): 9-13. It should be kept in mind that the company councils are supported from two levels of international labor organization — by the secretariats and the so-called industry committees. The latter, few in number, generally represent the workers in a certain industry, such as automobiles, and in a certain geographic area, such as Europe. The latter, for instance, sought to coordinate the drive to eliminate wage differentials within several national regions as well as throughout the entire European car industry. See Christopher Tugendhat, *The Multinationals* (London: Eyre and Spottiswoode, 1971), pp. 185-86.

34. Daniel Benedict gave an interesting inside account of the world-council vehicle in his report, "Labour and Multinationals," to the International Conference on Trends in International and Labor Relations at McGill University, Montreal, 24-28 May, 1976.

35. See Rowan and Northrup's 1975 article and the Bendiner article for accounts of the sequence of attempts at periodic meetings.

36. General Electric, nevertheless, held four meetings with world-council and IMF people between 1966 and 1973 alone. It should also be mentioned that the European companies listed dealt only with Europe-wide trade unionists and issues, not with global company councils.

37. John Alan James et al., "Multinational Trade Unions Muscle Their Strength," *European Business* 39 (Autumn 1973): 40.

38. Günter Köpke, "Union Responses in Continental Europe," in Robert J. Flanagan and Arnold R. Weber, *Bargaining Without Boundaries: The Multinational Corporation and International Labor Relations* (Chicago: University of Chicago Press, 1974), p. 209.

39. Ibid.

40. Herbert C. Northrup and Richard L. Rowan, "Multinational Union Management Consultations: The European Experience," *International Labour Review* 116 (Sept.-Oct. 1977): 153-70.

41. Barkin, *Worker Militancy*, p. 376.

42. Northrup and Rowan, "Multinational Union Activity in the 1976 U.S. Rubber Strike," pp. 19 and 23.

43. See John P. Windmuller, *Labor Internationals* (Ithaca, N.Y.: New York State School of Industrial and Labor Relations, Cornell University, 1969), and Roy Godson, *The Kremlin and Labor* (New York: Crane, Russak, 1977). The latter book is alarmist, yet it contains some generally agreed-upon conclusions.

44. Reported in Robert W. Cox's analysis of the U.S. withdrawal from the International Labour Organisation, another case of Mr. Meany's foreign-policy successes. "Labor and Hegemony," *International Organization* 31 (Summer 1977): 400. Cox also reviews some of the AFL-CIO cooperative activities in Western Europe and Meany's persistent denials of such ties.

45. *The Economist*, February 4, 1978, reported this remark to have been made that week in Davos, Switzerland, at a management symposium for European businessmen.

46. The total charter, with its relevant appendices, consists of some sixty-seven pages. Those dealing specifically with demands concerning worker participation will be cited and discussed later in this study.

47. European Trade Union Confederation, *Supplement to Report on Activities, 1973-1975* (Brussels: ETUC, 1976).

48. Under Article 235 of the Rome Treaty, the European Community can issue regulations. Such regulations are totally binding on the governments of the member states. If it chooses to issue directives, it merely binds the governments to attain a certain directed goal by whatever means they deem appropriate.

49. ETUC, *Supplement*.

50. European Commission, *Report on the Development of the Social Situation in the Communities in 1976* (Brussels: European Commission, 1977), p. 71.

51. B. C. Roberts, "Multinational Collective Bargaining: A European Prospect," *British Journal of Industrial Relations* 11 (March 1973): 14-15.

6

WORKER-PARTICIPATION PRACTICES IN THE EUROPEAN ECONOMIC COMMUNITY

It is somewhat ironic that the first proposal for a democratically organized workshop was reportedly made in the United States, particularly when one considers the marked differences between the ways worker participation in management has evolved in the United States and in Western Europe.[1] The fact that the suggestion, in 1797, was made by a recent immigrant from Europe may have been a foreboding of the fact that it was on the European Continent rather than in the New World that worker-participation practices would develop more fully and distinctly. After all, it was in France that the first self-governing workshop originated and where much of the earlier, more extensive philosophizing about industrial democracy appeared in the writings of such reformers as St. Simon, Proudhon, and Fourier.[2] Paradoxically, French trade unionists chose the Sorelian revolutionary strategy, which advocated the destruction of all existing economic and political institutions and which thus considered worker-participation schemes as sellouts and as subversive tactics by which management sought to undercut the anarchistic spirit of the working class.

The situation developed somewhat differently in Germany. There, the first workers councils were set up on the initiative of employers. These entrepreneurs, having become concerned about the rapidly rising anger of the working class, suggested in 1840 that factories should develop for themselves a sort of basic law, a constitutional order, under which workers would at least be consulted, if not given a direct chance to participate, in managerial decision making. Their philosophy was also incorporated into the Industrial Code submitted to the 1848 Frankfurt National Constitutional Assembly. If it had become the law of the land, paragraphs 42 and 43 of this code would have provided for the election by employees of factory committees, or works councils, composed of employers and employees. These councils were proposed to decide work rules, participate in running the factories' social-welfare programs, and supervise child-labor practices.[3] Even though no statutory basis for works councils was established until the days of World War I, such councils were voluntarily introduced by a number of entrepreneurs and, under a 1905 state statute, were required for mine operations in Prussia that employed more than one hundred persons.

In 1916, the trade unions obtained in the law on patriotic auxiliary service the inclusion of a requirement for separate committees for manual workers and for salaried employees in all enterprises employing more than fifty workers. This statute prescribed industrial and other work for those not serving in the military. Through the handling of workers' grievances, the committees were expected to promote good relations among employees as well as between employees and the firms' management. Two years later, the committees were made compulsory by executive decree for all enterprises employing twenty or more persons. Joint consultation procedures and worker committees were also used during World War I as guarantees of labor peace in Great Britain, France, and Russia.

Germany's broadest legislative base was laid in 1920. That statute, implementing the Weimar Constitution's commitment to worker representation, provided for "coinfluencing" by workers on a limited array of social, economic, and personnel questions. Two years later, the statute was amended to enable the works councils to appoint one or two representatives to serve on the firms' supervisory boards. Thus, worker participation was extended from the shop floor to the level of enterprise organization, where decisions and policies were made affecting entire firms and where the executive directors (the managers) were held responsible for their actions. The precedent for codetermination, or *Mitbestimmung*, had been established. Although the 1920 act as amended was repealed by the Hitler regime in 1933 — at the same time that it dissolved the trade unions — the basis had been laid for the kinds of worker participation that became more permanently established at the end of World War II.[4]

A number of other West European countries passed Weimar-type works-council laws in or about 1920: Austria, Denmark, Norway, Czechoslovakia, and Italy.[5] In some other locations, employee-representing organs for consultation were voluntarily established by several of the larger employers, whether they did so either to preempt trade unions or simply to improve the communication between management and shop-floor workers is not known.

The motivations or philosophical principles behind worker-participation practices are obviously interesting ones. It is undeniable that many supporters of works councils, and of codetermination in particular, have been Social Democrats. Some of them consider the councils an integral part of a societywide network of joint enterprise and consultation. To these people, the shop-floor or plant-level councils are links to regional and national bipartite or tripartite councils (the latter, including representatives of government as well as labor and management). This is what the Weimar Constitution envisioned. Other socialists envision the works councils and worker representation on company boards as either stepping-stones to the nationalization of the nations' basic industries or as the nearest available step to total worker control of productive property.

A certain amount of support has also come from nonsocialist trade-union circles, particularly in those countries and circumstances where the unions could control the nominations and elections of the council members. Under such circumstances, works councils could serve as the de facto plant-level union locals and could thus complement the more centralized, national trade-union structures.

Some have understandably argued that the greatest impetus for worker participation came from the ranks of Christian progressives: from inside and outside the trade unions and from Protestants as well as Roman Catholics. Ever since 1891, when Pope Leo XIII, in his famous encyclical *Rerum Novarum*, condemned laissez-faire economics as un-Christian and declared labor not to be a commodity to be bought or sold on the market, Catholics and socially progressive Protestants have sought to develop ways of cooperative industrial governance.

The period when the works-council phenomenon spread most widely was during and immediately after World War II. Allied countries used labor-management committees to stimulate war production. In areas occupied by Germany—except for France—patriotic elements, among whom were trade unionists and entrepreneurs, worked side by side in the resistance. They had thus learned to set aside those issues that used to divide them. In their new-found spirit of optimism and idealism, the postwar reconstruction seemed to be a chance to create new consensus-inducing processes and structures. Such a consensus was expected both to insure greater national productivity and to prevent the return of earlier bitterness and animosities. We should also mention that the International Labour Organisation, the ILO, placed the issue of worker representation on management boards on its agenda for 1941. In the Philadelphia Declaration of 1944, the organization declared worker-management collaboration as one of the integral principles of the organization.[6] Also at this level of politics, postwar reconstruction was seen as an opportunity to redefine traditional structures of authority.

As soon as the Hitler regime was dismantled in Germany, the workers in a number of that country's industrial centers elected themselves works councils. The trade unionists who led them in this endeavor had at least three objectives: first, they wanted to lay the basis for the recovery of the rights of workers as defined in the Weimar Constitution and statutes; second, they tried to help prevent the recurrence of nazism and the concomitant misuses of economic power; third, they intended to obligate the occupation authorities to accept trade-union-based works councils, particularly since trade unions beyond the plant level had been outlawed for at least five years.

Particularly interesting were the different reactions to the issue by American and British military authorities. When the states of Hesse and Baden-Württemberg passed statutes providing for worker participation in corporate decision making, American authorities there suspended such provisions with the suggestion that such issues should be postponed until a national government was organized. The British, meanwhile, offered trade unionists the opportunity to participate in the management of the coal and steel industries of the Ruhr Valley. They even provided for labor's selection of personnel directors. American reluctance, if not opposition, to the reintroduction of Weimar-type worker participation was not sufficient to keep the Allied Control Council for Germany from regulating the organization and operation of works councils in those enterprises where employers and employees agreed on the desirability of such structures.[7]

Corporate shareholders and entrepreneurs did not fight the apparent resurrection of industrial democracy in Germany. They not only saw the benefit of gaining employee support to enable them to achieve desired optimum productivity, but they also recognized them as the lesser of two evils. Work councils, and even codetermination, were much less a threat to their ownership and management rights than the possibilities of Allied divestiture and nationalization by a socialist reconstruction government. In fact, it could even be argued that German management leaders once again—as they did in the 1890s—foresaw the possibility that alleviating worker grievances might prevent worker radicalization and, in particular, the laboring class's determination to have a socialist government.

One additional impetus to the widespread introduction of worker participation in Western Europe was the fact that most governments in the region were entirely controlled or dominated by either Social Democrat or Catholic progressive parties. Parties of the very conservative Right did not fare well in the wake of that area's experience with authoritarianism from the right. Of all the national legislatures, France took the lead in February 1945 in prescribing works councils. Norway followed suit in November; Sweden, in the next year; Belgium, in 1948; the Netherlands, in 1950; and the Federal Republic of Germany, in 1952. Germany distinctly outdid the others by also providing for the parity representation of workers on the boards of coal and steel industries and for minority (one-third) codetermination on the supervisory boards of companies whose stocks were traded on the stock market.

Worker representation in the management structures of all or some state-owned enterprises began to appear as well in Austria, Belgium, France, Ireland, Italy, Norway, Switzerland, and the United Kingdom. Their method of selection, their number, their name, their degree of influence, and the number of years that such representational practices have been operative have varied, however, from industry to industry and from country to country. Works councils, enterprise committees, and codetermination have come about in a variety of ways: they were established by law in Austria, Belgium, Finland,

France, Germany, Italy, and the Netherlands; while they came about through central collective-bargaining agreements in Denmark, Norway, and Sweden; and through a limited number of single-company bargaining agreements in Italy, Switzerland, and the United Kingdom. Other differences in national and industry practices resulted in variations in the composition of councils, the degree of dominance by trade unions, the actual functions assigned to worker representatives, the range of enterprises in which they became required, the variations in actual compliance with the local legal requirements, and the spread of such practices in environments where they were strictly optional.

Generally, practices changed only slightly during the fifties. Where changes did occur during the sixties, they generally amounted to an increase in works-council responsibilities and authority. That decade produced distinctly stronger pressure politics for the expansion of worker participation in general and for worker participation on company boards in particular. It is difficult to judge what led to the buildup of such pressures. It might have been the attainment of full employment; persistent monitoring by the International Labour Organisation; research work done under sponsorship of the Swedish Federation of Employers at the School of Economics at Stockholm, the 1966-initiated research project of the International Institute of Labour Studies (under the leadership of Robert W. Cox and Kenneth F. Walker); or the tumultuous events of 1968.[8] Whatever the causes, the pressures for change were at work, and they could not help stimulate further expansion during the seventies, with the probability that further evolution will occur in the future.

VARIOUS NATIONAL REQUIREMENTS AND PRACTICES[9]

Germany

The German system of worker participation is the most extensive: it ranges from works councils on the shop floors of 98 percent of the country's manufacturing enterprises (and 75 percent of its wholesale and retail enterprises) to equal employee representation on the supervisory boards of the approximately six hundred fifty companies that employ more than two thousand people to the definitive majority of worker representatives on the supervisory boards and a personnel director approved by worker representatives in coal, iron, and steel firms.

A works council (*Betriebsrat*) is required for each firm or plant with five or more employees, and the size of the council varies with the number of employees. Members of the councils do not have to be union members, and they are to be elected every three years by all employees, regardless of whether they are members of the union or not. Hourly-wage-earning employees (blue-collar workers) and salaried employees (white-collar workers up to the level of senior executives) must be represented proportionally. These constituencies can elect their representatives separately or jointly.[10] Partners, shareholders, and senior executives are not eligible to be elected or to participate in the election. The German works councils are therefore really *workers'* councils. Although the initiative for establishing workers' councils is expected to be exercised by management, any three employees or any union representing company workers can demand that employees be balloted to determine whether a majority favors organizing a council.

The councils have four types of powers: administrative, codeterminative, consultative, and informative. They administer such company social services as kindergartens, vacation homes, and the emergency loan fund. They participate directly in the development of personnel policy, including the terms of employment (working hours, method of payment, job-performance-evaluation procedures, and piece rates); in decisions concerning hiring, firing, reassignment, or training, and how such training programs shall be executed; and in the development of a social-compensation plan for workers unnecessarily disadvantaged as a result of projected job relocations or organizational changes. Management has the obligation to consult the workers councils on all business decisions that add new jobs, change existing ones, and damage the interests of current workers.

The right of the councils to be informed at an appropriate time on a great variety of economic and financial dimensions of the firms is the most tenuous of all. It is vitally important to the employees' leadership to know the general financial condition of the firms, their comparative production and sales positions, their planned investments, their rationalization plans, anticipated mergers, contractions, organizational changes, and new manufacturing processes. The record of employer compliance with this obligation to inform their councils has not been unblemished. For example, when Axelrod Springer, the publisher of *Der Spiegel* and numerous newspapers and other periodicals, bought the newspaper the *Münchener Mercur*, the latter's works councillors first heard about the planned merger when they read about it in their paper.[11]

Plants with more than one hundred employees are expected to establish a special works-council committee, the economic committee, for the purpose of receiving such information. At the same time, management must be protected against divulgence of company trade or business secrets by works councillors. In companies that operate multiple plants, a central company council must be established. These councils are composed of two representatives (one hourly-wage and one salaried employee) from the works councils of the various plants. The voting strength of these representatives is proportionate to the number of electors they represent at the plant level. The central company council is charged with the annual convening of a company conference, made up of senior councillors, which will primarily hear management reports on the state of the company.[12] Overarching company councils can be established upon company-council and/or works-council initiatives, when the business firm is a large conglomerate and when it could be contended that the investment and production decisions made at that high a command level are at least as important as those made at the plant or the company level.

The workers councils are closely monitored by the German trade unions. In fact, the average percentage of elected council members that belong to DGB-affiliated unions has been about 80 percent, with significant variations from industry to industry. More than 90 percent of the councillors in the railways and mining sectors have been union members, while in the banking and finance sector, the average has been only slightly more than 60 percent (from 1965-1972).[13] Council chairmen have apparently almost all been unionists. Workers who are union members are also more apt to participate in council elections than are nonunion workers (91 percent versus 71 percent of the chemical workers).[14]

Unions are obviously concerned that the workers councils might supersede union bargaining rights and undercut worker interest in union membership. Equally worrisome to unions is the possibility that the councils might create an independent worker aristocracy that is more loyal to the firm than to the members of their social class. They also fear that the "institutionalization" of the council may inflame the radicalization of the younger workers. For example, the larger the enterprise, the more professional the chairman and the senior council members seem to become, and the less frequently corporate management representatives participate in council meetings. When the chairmen and councillors no longer work on the shop floor—that is, they spend all their time on council work—and when management seems to employ them more as middlemen and buffers between themselves and the workers than as worker spokesmen, shop workers begin to view their representatives as more attuned to management than to the rank-and-file workers. With the high rate of union participation in the councils, the younger workers apparently also tend to equate the union bureaucracy with the councils, and they begin to see both as being far removed from their everyday lives and concerns. One example of the sort of rebellion that can result from such perceptions occurred in October 1978, at a Daimler-Benz factory, when a union-backed slate was able to win only 24 out of 47 council seats. That happened while 95 percent of the plant's ninety-five thousand workers were members of the union. The leader of the worker insurgency, a 49-year-old welder, said: "The established works council has too often given into the company's logic. Work councils in big companies often seem to separate themselves from the workers and become managers."[15]

The trade unions have tried to compensate for this alienation by providing for the election of shop stewards (*Vertrauensmann*), who are charged with collecting union dues, recruiting new members, passing out union literature, recruiting union candidates for works-council election, organizing union meetings, and serving as grievance middlemen between individual workers and the works council. Since 1972, the unions have also been able to initiate a variety of actions that allow them to enter into council and company business in areas from which they were previously excluded. If one-fourth of the members of the council agree, union officials can even take part in council sessions in the role of advisors.

Worker representation on German company boards takes one of three forms. The oldest form has been the variety of codetermination that exists in the coal, iron, and steel industries, the sector judged to be basic to the national economy (*Montan-industrie*). The supervisory boards (*Aufsichtsrat*) of enterprises that have more than one thousand workers must be composed of equal numbers of employee and stockholder representatives. These then select a "neutral" additional member who is empowered to vote only in case of a tie.

Both the labor and the stockholder factions of the boards must reserve one of their seats for a person who is not connected to the union or the company and who does not hold any stock in the company. The "outsider" worker representative and two others are nominated by the union(s) upon consultation with the workers council. The latter shall have one representative selected by its wage-paid members and one by its salaried members. It has been customary for the union nominations to be divided between the majority union in the firm and the national labor federation (the DGB), with the federation selecting the "outsider" labor representative. The board chairman is elected by the board itself; most of these have turned out to be stockholder representatives.

This whole system of selection and representation is complex; however, not just for the sake of complexity. It clearly seeks to provide optimum representation to the various constituencies in the firm and the public. And, more importantly, it is designed to prevent excessive bifurcation of the supervisory board.[16]

A company's supervisory board is one of a two-tiered structure of corporate organization, a format that has prevailed in Germany since the late nineteenth century and that is practiced in several other West European countries. Its primary task is to select a board of managers (*Vorstand*) for whom it sets policy and whose execution of such policies it oversees. The supervisory board, originally elected by the stockholders, may not include anyone who is also on the board of managers.

The board of managers in the coal, iron, and steel industry enterprises is generally composed of three members. One of these, the personnel director

(*Arbeitsdirektor*), can only be appointed or removed with approval by a majority of the employee representatives on the supervisory board. (This position will be discussed later.)

The codetermination system operative in the other sectors of the economy is generally comparable. There are, however, some subtle, yet significant, differences beyond the size of the enterprises involved. Companies that employ between five hundred and two thousand employees, which are not corporations in which family members exclusively hold the stock, are required to have employee representatives make up only one-third of the supervisory board. The worker representatives must be employees of the firm rather than full-time union employees who do not have direct ties to the firm. In the codetermination of the coal, iron, and steel industries and of the larger firms, some of the employee representatives are "outsiders." One employee representative (there are usually two on the boards, most of which have six members) must be a wage-paid (blue-collar) worker and the second a salaried (white-collar) worker. Both of them must be directly elected by their peers. While the supervisory boards of the two thousand to three thousand firms in this category also select a personnel director to serve on the board of managers, employee representatives do not have any special privileges in this selection process.

The third form of codetermination that exists in business enterprises employing more than two thousand persons appears to provide parity representation for employees and stockholders, but it is not the case. The formula for employee representation calls for a proportional representation of "supervisory" salaried employees (executives) as well as hourly-wage and salaried employees. Each group, including the executives, is guaranteed to have at least one representative. In order to protect further the interests of the shareholders, the board chairman and the vice-chairman must be elected by a two-thirds vote. When such a margin is impossible, the shareholder representatives will select the chairman and the employee faction selects the vice-chairman. The third preventative of true parity lies in the power of the board chairman to cast a second, and thus deciding, vote in case of two successive tie votes on an issue. A fourth "qualifier" is the fact that the personnel director is selected, as are the other members of the management board, by a majority of the supervisory board. No special influence is given to the employee faction of the board.

The law provides for the possibility that the trade union that represents the largest number of company workers can appoint two or three of the employee representatives; the actual number would depend on the size of the board. These union appointees do not have to be employees of the firm, but the rest of the employee representatives are expected to be employees and are to be directly elected by the firm's employees. This particular feature of the codetermination system has created some interesting possibilities for German and international trade unions. First, the larger German unions, such as IG Metall and IG Chemie, could be able to control more company directorships than could Germany's largest banks. IG Metall, for example, has its national president, two other union officials, and five other union members serving as eight of the nine worker representatives on the supervisory board of Volkswagen, the first board organized under the 1976 law.[17] By methodical assignment and by limiting to two the number of directorships each union leader can hold, the unions can spread their officialdom over the key industries and thus have access to the "commanding heights" of their sector of the national economy. By bringing in top international trade unionists like Herman Rebhan, and Daniel Benedict of the International Metalworkers Federation, they can also speak up more directly on global and regional company policies and thus come one step closer to dealing with some of the frustrations organized labor has had vis-à-vis the multinational enterprise.

Experience with this third system of codetermination, which came into effect in 1978, is still too limited to allow definitive conclusions about its efficacy. Some possible hints could come from the so-called Biedenkopf Report of 1970,[18] which concluded that *Mitbestimmung*, or codetermination, had not resulted in any sort of boardroom or company-policy revolutions, nor any serious breaches of confidence or anticompany initiatives. It showed, as have a number of other writings on the subject, that most boardroom decisions are verifications of informal negotiations and consultations that occur outside that context. Stockholder representatives and management do their share of caucusing and so do the council members, who double as board members and union officials. Apparently, the two sides, either with or without the services of the neutral member of the board in the coal, iron, and steel industries, do a considerable amount of checking with each other before things become a confrontation in order to avoid complete breakdowns.

Apparently, there are ways in which management can circumvent possible confrontations in the boardroom. In the fall of 1979, for example, AEG-Telefunken was faced with the need to cut thirteen thousand jobs. Even though company management would have been able to outvote IG Metall and the employee representatives on the board, it chose not to bring the issue before the board. Union officials charged that management kept the information within the presidium of the board. This executive committee, from which trade-union representatives were excluded, presumably could better guarantee secrecy of company policy.[19]

The main effect of codetermination appears to be a tendency for company policies to reflect social and labor considerations as well as those of a purely financial and technical nature.[20] A number of specific instances can be cited to show that worker participation on the supervisory board can be beneficial. Ball tells, for example, how the projections of VW car sales by trade-union officials proved to have been more accurate than those made by the company's professional management. Thus, after the unions had grudgingly gone along with a management initiative to lay off workers, which required the payment of liberal severance payments, the company found itself having to rehire the same workers. This provided a handsome bonus for those who had been laid off, but it did not help the company's production costs.[21] The union could also make a good argument that its pressure to remove Rudolf Leiding from VW's top management position proved to be a service to the company. His successor, Toni Schmucker, who was much more amiable to labor and to fellow managers, was able to lead the company to the almost imperative decision to build an assembly plant in the United States, a decision that helped the company get back into the black. In spite of codetermination, a number of other German firms have been equally capable of proceeding with vigorous overseas investments and thus guaranteeing themselves continued growth. Early in 1977, Bayer Chemicals announced a five-year investment plan for the United States. Walter Glasner, the North Rhine leader of the Chemical Workers and a member of the Bayer Company board, quickly endorsed the decision, with the observation that he had no fear for the jobs of German chemical workers. He projected that the American Bayer plants would undoubtedly need German-made raw materials and semimanufactured goods, and added that the American market offered tremendous new opportunities for the firm.[22] His foresight has proven to be correct.

The third method of worker participation is the personnel director, which was first mentioned under the discussion of codetermination in the coal, iron, and steel industries. This management officer, who has tended to be a former union official, particularly in that sector, has primary responsibility for developing and monitoring the company's wage and salary policies. He also handles the kind of administrative functions that normally accrue to personnel managers and industrial-relations staffers. Thus, even though the personnel director is one among a limited number of persons charged with running the company's operations, he must be particularly sensitive to balancing the interests of the employees with those of the firm. The success of the firm is dependent to a great degree on his ability to retain the confidence of his fellow managers, the works council, the worker representatives on the supervisory board, and the unions.

At this point, it is somewhat difficult to predict what changes might be made in the German legislation concerning codetermination. There apparently will not be any significant rollback. The German Constitutional Court in March 1979 dismissed what seemed to be a most substantive challenge of the 1976 statute, which provided for codetermination, as described above, for enterprises employing more than two thousand workers. That challenge will be discussed in more detail in the next chapter. The court, however, suggested that *Mitbestimmung* might well present constitutionality problems if it actually did provide for parity representation. It thus appears to be somewhat unlikely that substantial changes will be made in the near future.

The Netherlands

The Dutch system of worker participation is considerably simpler than that of Germany. Nevertheless, it is generally perceived to be the second most effective arrangement in the European Community.

Works councils (*ondernemingsraad*) must be established in all entities that employ at least one hundred persons. However, firms in the construction, ocean shipping, mining, and railway industries are exempted. Any employer organization or trade union that can be considered representative of management, or the workers of a firm that employs between twenty-five and one-hundred persons, may request that the law also be applied in their firm. All firms of this size and larger were prescribed to have councils, but on a somewhat optional basis, from 1948 until 1971 when they were made compulsory.

The council is composed of three to twenty-five employee representatives, who are to be directly elected by the workers to represent the various organizational departments.[23] Consultative meetings with the general manager shall be held at least six times per year and can be convened at the request of either the council or management.

Nominations for council membership can be made by unions in consultation with their membership. They can also be made by a petition signed by thirty workers or by one-third of the employees, if that is a smaller number. Regardless, about three-fourths of the works councils have union members making up at least two-thirds of their membership.[24]

The Dutch works councils have three kinds of power: They participate directly by consenting to decisions regarding working hours, holidays, safety and health regulations, and pensions, profit-sharing, and savings plans. This power of codetermination has only existed since 1971. Management is required to consult with the council on such key economic questions as layoffs, plant shutdowns, expansions, cutbacks, relocations, reorganizations and/or mergers. The council must also be consulted on such social questions as training, job evaluation, compensation, plant discipline, and social-welfare services. The law is explicit in requiring that the advice of the works council be obtained *prior* to making decisions on these subjects. This obligation may only be waived on some of the issues, and only if compelling reasons such as a need for secrecy, company interest, or the interests of other parties require. The possibility that this escape provision can be abused for such purposes as obfuscation is somewhat ameliorated by the legal provision that works councils may go to court if they feel management would not have decided the way it did if it had reasonably considered the interests involved in the matter.

If companies operate more than one plant, the works councils of the several plants can, by majority vote, demand the creation of a companywide works council (*centrale ondernemingsraad*). The same thing holds true if the company is part of a conglomerate or group.

Several things can be said about the way the Dutch councils work. First, the trade unions until recently have not been able to dominate the works-council system. They felt that a number of councils were in fact dominated by management. They have, therefore, established their own plant structures, through which they have sought to emphasize the "natural contradictions" between the interests of the firm and those of the workers. They have also sought to direct themselves exclusively to the bread-and-butter issues that concern the workers most. This sort of strategy clearly reflects the radical pressures from the younger rank-and-file workers and the somewhat militant quality of some of the national union leadership. The trade unionists also were able to obtain some changes in the law. The 1979 Works Council Act in fact removed the manager from the chairmanship of as well as from membership on the council. Interestingly enough, there apparently already existed a prevailing practice for the worker members to caucus prior to official council meetings. This particular amendment might not produce significant change in the actual operation of the system.

The changes that may most radically affect the system are those that project extensive expansions in council jurisdiction. The council's right to information has been substantially extended to include the company's budget, semiannual investment plans, and annual reports on the company's social plan. Particularly unique is the right of councils to appeal management's substantive economic decisions, upon which the council must be consulted. Such appeals shall be made to the Companies Chamber of the Amsterdam Court of Justice.[25]

The plant-level union committees (*werkoverleg*) are supplemented by job stewards, who serve as union spokesmen in the plant and for whom the unions have been seeking increased facilities and privileges. These committees and stewards may prove to be successful trade-union strategies, partly because the workers seem to be only mildly satisfied with the works councils. Even a significant majority of those who are council members rate the effectiveness of their councils to be only moderate to poor. It has also become increasingly difficult to find workers who want to stand for election to the council.[26] What the FNV (the combination of the Social Democrat and the Roman Catholic labor federations) would like to see is for all works councils to become the apex of plant-level union organization. That is almost the case now in a number of firms.

Worker participation on company boards in the Netherlands is only indirect. Since 1973, nominations for membership on the supervisory boards (*Raad van Commissarissen*) of companies with one hundred or more employees and with a capital of at least ten million guilders are to be made by management stockholders and the firms' works councils. Each of these constituencies has the right to veto the other's nominations on the ground that such an appointment would result in an imbalance on the board. The supervisory board, which fills its own vacancies, may appeal to the national Social-Economic Council that such opposition is unwarranted and may thus be able to obtain a veto override.[27] Company employees and officials of trade unions in negotiating relationships with the firm are not eligible for board appointment. There is thus no direct worker participation in supervisory-board decisions, including the selection and supervision of the board of management (*Raad van Bestuur*).

Holding companies or parent companies with subsidiary operations outside the country and with more than half of their employees located abroad are exempt from the 1973 law. Altogether, some 325 companies are regulated by it. Opposition to the compromise form of Dutch codetermination has not come primarily from the employers since their ability to lead does not appear to have been undermined. This is partly because works councils have tended to leave the appointment initiative to management and have generally accepted management's nominations. They have reportedly done so because they have had some difficulty in finding qualified and acceptable candidates.[28] One other feature of its operation has been helpful to management: the system has stimulated a greater amount of dialogue between the council and management than would have been possible if the appointment power were not shared. Nomination discussions seem to have led to dialogue over a wider range of issues.[29]

Those who do not particularly like the system are the trade-union activists. While Protestant union leadership wants to see labor representation in the general form and style of Germany, the Catholic and socialist unionists do not really like board participation. Their position is related very logically to their desire to see management excluded from the works councils. They believe that workers' interests are compromised by participation. In their judgment, the contradictions between capital and labor are natural and inevitable, and thus really do not allow worker participation.[30]

Dutch trade unions have one power that could be potentially quite significant: the power to request an investigation in case of serious suspicion of company mismanagement. Such a request can be made after the union has informed management of its complaints and has asked the company's works council for its opinion. Such an inquiry is to be conducted by one or more court-appointed investigators and can result in a variety of degrees of government intervention in the corporation.

The trade-union proposal that really upset Dutch employers was first proposed as a government bill in June 1976. Its basic intent was to require firms to surrender a substantial portion of their excess profits (profits after taxes and after a certain compensation for equity capital and risk insurance). The original version of the proposal required that the funds be deposited in a central fund. Some of the fund would be distributed to workers employed by profit-making enterprises, and the larger part would be designated for the benefit of all the country's adult workers, possibly in the form of better pension benefits.[31]

Apparently, this proposal really tipped the scale. The chairmen of nine mostly multinational companies such as Shell, Philips, Unilever, and Akzo, in an unprecedented letter to the government and the Parliament, complained of the government's general posture toward business, particularly its failure to encourage investment.[32] The feature that probably aroused the greatest amount of fear was the provision that the central fund was to be administered by trade-union representatives. Even though several years have passed since the proposal was first submitted to the Parliament, it has not yet become the law of the land. The Labor-party-dominated administration that proposed the scheme has been replaced by several coalition cabinets which made suggestions for modification; however, nothing had come of these either to date.

Belgium

Worker participation in Belgium is limited to the shop floor and particularly takes the form of the works council, the safety and health committee, and the union delegation. The system is based on a mixture of legislation, government regulations, royal orders, and collective agreements.

Works councils (*conseil d'entreprise*, or *ondernemingsraad*) are required in enterprises employing one hundred or more people. Some two thousand firms are thus affected by the law. Before October 1978, the cutoff point was one hundred and fifty employees, but the National Labor Council would like to see it lowered to fifty.

The worker representatives are nominated by the most representative trade unions and are elected by secret ballot. The nominations must proportionally represent blue-collar and white-collar employees. Management is represented on the council by its chief officer and any other management representatives he would like to have on the council, provided that the management representatives do not outnumber the worker representatives. The plant manager serves as the chairman of the council. A works council must be introduced by management. They cannot be used, though, to exclude unions; councils can only be set up in shops where there already are unions.

The Belgian councils manage the company social services, the social-welfare program, and training activities. They must be consulted on hiring and firing policies and on any company policies that will affect working conditions, the firm's organizational structure, or company output. Information must be supplied to the councils on the company's economic and financial position and on the plans and the prospects of the firm and its parent company, if it has one. This requirement includes data on the firm's competitive position and its investment plans. The overall dualistic nature of the works councils in Belgium reflects the mixture of integrating and confrontationist features that also are the trademark of the country's industrial-relations system.

All firms with fifty or more employees are required to have advisory safety and health committees, which are composed in the same way as the enterprise councils.

Both wings of the Belgian trade-union movement are dissatisfied with the works-council structure.[33] Socialist unions would like to see them become workers councils, with management removed from the council. Others would prefer to see the councils become control structures rather than primarily consultative. The unions have therefore continued to maintain in-plant representation separate from both types of councils. In all plants with twenty or more employees, trade union representatives have the right to be individual as well as collective-bargaining agents. They are entitled by law to be supplied with economic and financial information relevant to their responsibilities.

Even though there is no worker representation on company boards required in the private sector, some state enterprises do observe the practice. Belgian railways, for instance, have three worker representatives sitting on their twenty-one-member board of directors. These have all been appointed by the minister of transport. A similar arrangement exists in Brussels's Public Transportation Company. In 1976, Parliament received a government proposal to require minority-employee representation on the boards of firms employing at least five hundred workers. It has not yet been enacted.

On this issue, Belgian unionists are divided as well. The General Confederation of Labor elements do not want to become part of the capitalist system; they will not really be satisfied until they have achieved "autogestion" (worker self-management). The Confederation of Christian Syndicalists prefers, instead, to extend the powers of the works council, which could include a right of veto for the council over economic and financial policy decisions by the company board.

Luxembourg

Luxembourg has worker representation both on the shop floor and in the boardroom. The former has existed since 1919; the latter, since 1974.

All firms employing fifteen or more persons must have personnel delegates (*délégués du personnel*). Where there are at least fifteen blue-collar workers, they have the right to elect from among themselves worker delegates (*délégués ouvrières*), whose number depends on the size of the firm's manual work force. If and where there are at least twelve white-collar workers, they will elect staff delegates (*délégués d'employés*). These delegations run plant welfare programs, are consulted on issues concerning worker health and safety, give advice on changes in work regulations, make proposals to management, and handle individual and group grievances. Their tasks are primarily affairs of day-to-day liaison.

Larger firms that employ one hundred and fifty or more persons are also required to have joint committees (*comités mixtes*). The employee representatives to these committees must be employees of the enterprise and are selected by the personnel delegates through a system of proportional representation. An equal number of management representatives on the committee is headed by the company's chief executive, who serves as chairman and is required to report twice a year on the economic and financial development of the firm. The committee is to be consulted on such social matters as changes in the work rules and production methods, and on such economic and financial questions that might have an effect on the level of company employment and organization.

The decision-making power of the committees includes determining general criteria for the hiring, promoting, dismissing, and transferring of personnel and company units. Health and safety and other welfare programs are also their concern.

Employee representation on company boards in Luxembourg is only required for corporations (*sociétés anonymes*) that are not closed family enterprises. Additional stipulations are a minimum of one thousand employees, state-ownership of at least 25 percent of the company stock, or being the substantial beneficiary of a state concession. Those in the first category are required to have a management board (*conseil d'administration*), one-third of which must be employee representatives. In the other two categories, there must be at least three employee representatives (with a ratio of 1:100), but they shall not constitute more than one-third of the board. Employee representation shall be proportionally composed of blue-collar and white-collar employees.

In the coal and steel sector, the representative trade unions can designate the employee representatives, who do not even have to be enterprise employees. In all other sectors, the employee representatives must be employees of the firm and must be elected by the personnel delegations. Both appointing organs can remove directors selected by them.

France

Worker participation in France is concentrated in the workplace, where it takes three forms: employee delegations; works councils, or enterprise committees; and trade-union delegations.

Employee delegates (*délégués du personnel*) are elected annually in enterprises with more than ten employees. Managerial, supervisory, and technical personnel select theirs; the other workers select theirs. Nominations are made by the trade unions that are most representative in each of these categories. However, if less than half of the employees in the respective constituencies participate in the vote, a second election will be held in which other groups can introduce slates of candidates as well. The size of the delegations is based on the number of employees.

The delegates present to the employer all requests or complaints on such issues as wage levels, job classifications, safety regulations, and possible infractions of labor laws. Apparently, this job-steward or employee-delegation system works well in the area of grievance representation. Macbeath reports that more workers participate in *délégué* elections than in those for the works councils.[34]

Works councils (*comités d'entreprise*) must be set up in all enterprises with more than fifty employees. Proportional representation is given to three constituencies: supervisory personnel, professional and executive staff, and the other employees. The exact formula for representation must be worked out between the firm's chief executive and the unions. Candidates are posed mainly by the unions, although nonunion candidates are allowed under the same circumstances as described for the selection of employee delegates. Each trade union that represents company workers is guaranteed at least one representative on the council; their role is consultative.

The councils, which are chaired by the employer, have decision-making and administrative responsibilities concerning the company's social activities and benefits, from arranging the Christmas parties to oversight of the sick fund; they also include proposing bonuses for workers who have made an outstanding contribution to the enterprise. They are to be consulted on all matters that will affect working conditions, levels of compensation, training programs, and worker layoffs. Information must be supplied them on major policy changes and on the firm's economic progress, including the presentation of an annual report. The company comptroller can be summoned to explain the financial data, and the committee can hire an independent accountant for this purpose. Since 1975, a company that anticipates laying off more than ninety persons in a thirty-day period must consult employee delegates and the works council before giving such notices.

There are some distinct features to the way the French system of works councils operate. Since the initiative to establish a council rests with management, only nine thousand of an estimated total of twenty-five thousand eligible enterprises appear to have actually organized them. Many French employers still see themselves as "patrons"; they assume they are entitled to have unchallenged and undivided authority in their enterprise. This attitude is particularly true in large enterprises. Smaller employers object to councils as unwarranted, cumbersome bureaucracy.[35]

Since French trade unions are fragmented, it is interesting to see what type of unions have been getting the largest support in works-council elections. Apparently, the General Confederation of Labor, the communist federation, has been getting the most substantial support. This is particularly true in the nationalized industries, but it is also the case in those enterprises in the private sector that employ more than one thousand persons.[36] One could safely assume, then, that a considerable number of councils in these sectors will be more confrontationist than integrating.

The third type of shop-floor structuring is the trade-union delegation (*section syndicale d'entreprise*). These delegations were not recognized by law until December 1968, as an aftermath of the worker uprisings of that year. The right to set up a delegation is reserved for unions in enterprises that employ more than fifty people. One power of the delegation is to appoint union delegates who will represent their union in contacts with the company manager. Since the functions of these delegates are quite similar to those of the personnel delegates as well as members of the works councils, the same persons can, and frequently do, hold all these assignments simultaneously. This feature contributes significantly to trade-union dominance of the entire system of participation. Employers, therefore, have become increasingly insistent that the grievance and works-council structures should be their domain. They would like to see the works council remain as a vehicle for integrating the workers into the workplace and as a vehicle of communication and consultation.

The government proposed in April 1976 that firms with more than two thousand employees should have an economic committee responsible to the works council. This committee, like its German counterpart, would be the prime channel for communication between management and the works council on the financial and economic condition of the company.

The Sudreau Committee for the Study of the Reform of the Enterprise, established in 1974, which suggested this and other changes, was quite concerned about the viability and representativeness of the works councils. Its intention was to increase the workers' entire sense of political efficacy in the enterprise. It, therefore, proposed new ways be found for employee participation at the company board level.

Corporations employing fifty or more people are presently required to admit two works-council delegates to the company board (*conseil d'administration*) meetings for the purpose of consultation. Two additional employee representatives must be admitted to represent supervisory technical and executive staff if there are at least twenty-five employees who fit into this particular category.

In state-owned enterprises, one-third of the voting members of the boards are to represent wage-earners. Both arrangements are derived from the preamble of the French Constitution, which projects the participation of employees in corporate decision making. A 1976 government bill, which sprang from the Sudreau Report, proposed the participation of worker representatives with full voting rights on company boards in the private sector. Under this proposal, which has not been approved yet, firms with at least two thousand employees would have the option of bringing such representatives into the boardrooms, provided that their number would not exceed one-third of the board's membership.[37] Compulsory worker participation has been opposed, not only by the *Patronat* (the employers), but also by the more radical trade-union leaders. The latter find all forms of participation short of autogestion (direct worker control of enterprises) a sellout to and an artificial support of capitalist economics.[38] The French trade unions are equally suspicious of the de Gaullist program of profit sharing. Under this program, a percentage of company profits is to be placed in a trust fund from which workers are to be paid cash dividends after five years. They view this merely as a legal gadget by which the French workers are being domesticated and deprived of their sense of class solidarity.

Italy

There are three structures on the shop floor of Italian enterprises through which workers are consulted and informed. The oldest and most prevalent of these are the internal committees (*commissione interne*). While some of these date back to 1943, they now operate under the general labor agreement that provides for them to be established in all companies employing forty or more persons. Blue-collar and white-collar representatives are elected separately and proportionally from slates of nominees presented by trade unions and independent groups. Proportional representation is applied as well to the allocation of committee seats among the unions and the independent slates.

The internal committees have frequently been compared to the German workers' councils. However, they differ considerably. The Italian committees are considerably weaker, and they are also of limited interest to the unions, who, like many of their French peers, tend to be rather antagonistic to management.

Even though the committees have some direct administrative responsibilities over the company's social programs, most of their other activities are concerned with monitoring the application of the labor contract and the safety and health regulations. They are basically consultative and advisory. Their task of submitting proposals to management on how production could be increased and work methods improved is somewhat striking. The committees have apparently been supplanted to a large extent by works councils and trade-union delegations.

Works councils (*consigli di fabbrica*) emerged after the turmoil of 1969. They are composed of worker-elected delegates, almost all of whom are trade-union members and activists.[39] Each delegate (shop steward) is expected to represent a homogeneous work unit, and the council's size and makeup therefore reflect the organizational simplicity or complexity of the firm. Some factories elect separate blue-collar and white-collar delegates. These works councils have become increasingly intertwined with plant-level trade-union organization and have, in fact, by their coalescing nature, facilitated the merging of unions.[40] They have frequently become the primary collective-bargaining structures; and it is through this process of negotiation and settlement that the workers have had their most distinct influence over the economic and financial decisions of their firms. Factory councils are reported to exist in ten thousand Italian enterprises. Sometimes (in 29 percent of the cases), they stand by themselves; but at other times, they are side by side with an internal committee.[41]

Under the 1970 Statute on Workers' Rights, trade unions obtained the right to organize trade-union delegations (*delegazioni sindicali*) in production units. It is left up to the unions to determine whether and how these delegations should be structured. They have turned out to be either union branch units, departmental committees, or co-optations of the works council. Such a diversity makes shop-floor organization in Italian enterprises appear rather confusing and somewhat haphazard. Garson suggests, though, that union militancy and the co-opting of so many works councils have made Italian participation come closer in reality to the German model than is generally alleged.[42] An interesting authority of the delegation is the power to hold referendums and to convene meetings of all plant employees. Union representatives who are not employees of the firm can participate in such meetings, provided that management has been notified.

Worker representation on company boards in Italy has been discussed from time to time. The idea has generally been opposed by the trade unions on the same grounds that they oppose the internal committees. The law provides for the presence of worker representatives on the boards of some state enterprises. Unions and management, however, have shown very little interest in making use of the provisions.

Ireland

There are no legal requirements for worker representation in Ireland, even though workers in factories have had the right to elect consultative safety committees or delegates since 1955. Where works councils exist, they are usually the product of joint action by management and union and they have combined consultative and bargaining functions.

A subcommittee of the national consultative organ, the Employer Labor Conference, drafted a national agreement on the establishment of works councils in 1973. Thus, it is possible that councils will eventually become mandatory. The Irish Congress of Trade Unions endorsed the idea and practice of works councils as projected by the European Commission in its proposed Company Statute, provided that employee representatives be elected through "the appropriate trade union machinery in each establishment."[43] It does not appear very eager to have works councils that will parallel or that could eventually supplant the union structures.

A few trade unionists have been appointed to the boards of some state-owned enterprises, even though they were not employees of the particular establishment. In July 1975, the Irish minister of labor proposed union-nominated, worker-elected directors on company boards for certain commercial enterprises, provided, again, that their proportion not exceed one-third of the board membership. The Irish Congress of Trade Unions expressed itself as willing to go along with worker directors on the boards of European companies if such an EEC statute were enacted. They are not yet willing, though, to endorse it for their own national economy.

Denmark

Denmark entered the worker-participation phase of industrial relations as late as 1964 for works councils and 1973 for board representation.[44] It stands out from the other EEC countries also in that its practices are based solely on collective agreements between the national trade-union confederations and the national confederation of employers rather than on statute law.

Danish cooperation committees, which are roughly comparable to works councils, have been obligatory in firms with at least fifty employees since October 1970, although they were made possible under an earlier collective agreement. The initiative for establishing such a committee is expected to be taken either by management or by a majority of the workers. The committee is to consist of two delegations of equal size: one represents management and the commercial and technical staffs; the other, the remaining workers. The elected shop stewards must be included within the representation of the workers. The manager will be chairman. By 1977, more than one thousand committees had been organized.[45]

The general purpose of the committees is, as their name implies, to encourage day-to-day cooperation between management and labor in order that job satisfaction may be increased, job security be improved, and productivity be heightened. Since the committees are frequently tied in with semiautonomous work groups in the factory, the committees are also to serve as channels for the exchange of ideas concerning production process and work planning. Guidance and review of charges of willful obstruction by either management or worker representatives will be provided by a national Cooperation Board.

Specifically, the committees have the right of joint decision in policy principles concerning work, welfare, and safety conditions in the plant. They are to be consulted on day-to-day production and work plans, as well as on major changes in company policy and organization. Management is obligated to supply the committee with information on the economic and financial condition and prospects of the firm. Great care is taken to distinguish between managerial prerogatives to make day-to-day decisions and the committee's right and responsibility to monitor whether such decisions conform to the agreed-upon principles. Participating job stewards and workers differ in their satisfaction with the committees and their operation.

Danish companies employing at least fifty persons have, since 1974, been required by law to include two worker representatives on their company boards. Whether or not there actually shall be such representation must be decided by a majority of the firm's workers. The exact size of the workers' representation may exceed two; it must never exceed the number of management representatives.

Worker representatives must be selected from those who have been with the firm more than one year prior to election. They shall serve on the board for two years and have full rights of participation, including the power to vote. Trade unions do not have a monopoly of nominations, but they have been willing to live with this fact for two reasons: first, their longstanding concentration on central collective bargaining and their strong interest in developing worker participation in corporate decision making through the Wage Earners' Investment and Profit Fund, a projected scheme for worker participation in company ownership that resembles the Dutch program described earlier; and, second, they have been very effective in their shop-floor activities and also somewhat in management offices through their shop stewards.

The United Kingdom

The most widespread vehicle through which worker representatives participate in shop-floor decision making in Britain is the so-called joint consultation committee, also known as the shop-stewards' committee. Its prevalence is partly due to the tremendous growth in the number of stewards. The number of shop stewards in British industry increased by more than 20 percent since 1970 to a total of about three hundred thousand. Some five thousand of these are now full-time employees (five times as many as ten years ago).[46] The importance of the committees has also increased in the private sector as a result of the greater decentralization of collective bargaining there.

The operation of these committees presents a variety of problems. Job stewards are primarily trade-union officials. Although they purport to represent the interests of all the workers, such representation is not as clear-cut as it may seem because there is so much fragmentation within the trade-union system, even at the shop level. The second problem is the weakness of or absence of companywide job-steward committees.

Consultation committees that more closely resemble continental works councils have operated effectively in a number of British firms. Some of the most frequently cited cases are those at Glacier Metals, Fairfield Glasgow Ltd., J. S. Fry and Sons, Richard Baxendale & Sons, and J. Newson & Son.[47] All of these have management sit with worker representatives, and their consultation has reportedly been instrumental in generating a spirit of co-operation in the enterprise. This effectiveness may result partly from the fact that the initiative for the councils has come from management, and that, in a number of these cases, unions had not yet made an inroad into the plant or consented to the arrangement.

What the exact prospects are for the popularization of works councils of the integrative variety is somewhat difficult to determine, partly because the Trade Union Congress, the British trade-union confederation, does not seem to want to become involved in requiring them statutorily. It did not even want to do so when the Labour government was in power. The door was left open, though, to require it of multinational companies, particularly of the projected European companies, if such an option would ever be provided by the European Assembly.[48]

The Conservatives have expressed strong interest in shop-floor consultation machinery over a number of years. Whether they did so out of pure conviction or as a tactical maneuver to offset TUC preoccupation with worker representation on company boards is not certain. The fact is they did so, and they could easily be accused of going back on their word if they ever were so inclined. The latter is somewhat open to question.

The Conservative party's September 1974 Manifesto suggested that it become a formal duty for all large- and medium-sized firms to consult with their workers' representatives on a range of subjects. Among these would be matters of shop-floor discipline, policies on layoffs, work methods, profit-sharing programs, and share-ownership schemes.[49] In May 1978, James Prior, then the Conservative spokesman for employment affairs, presented a twelve-point policy program to be the basis for the industrial-democracy platform in the next election. Among other things, he called for worker participation to start at the shop floor, for people to have a greater say and more responsibility over their jobs, and for the setting up of advisory committees to keep employees fully informed.[50] Mr. Prior did not change his tune after he became employment secretary. The Confederation of British Industries, the British Institute of Management, and *The Economist,* all three spokesmen for the British business community, have continued carrying the torch, although they have done it deliberately and with caution.

For several years in the middle seventies, all the talk about industrial democracy in Britain focused on the issue of worker representation on company boards. This emphasis resulted from the fact that the TUC General Council, in 1973, and the Labour party's subcommittee on industrial policy, in early 1974, had called for the establishment of a two-tiered structure of corporate organization (a supervisory and a management board) and for the inclusion of worker directors on the new supervisory boards. In August 1975, when the Labour government set up a committee of inquiry (the Bullock Committee) to study the implementation of its commitment to the trade unions, that committee was specifically instructed to deal only with worker representation on company boards.

On May 24, 1978, the Callaghan government finally issued its long-awaited white paper on industrial democracy.[51] In it, the government proposed that companies employing more than five hundred people be placed under legal obligation to discuss with worker representatives, before decisions are made, such issues as "investment plans, mergers, take-overs, expansion or contraction of establishments and major organizational changes." The shop-floor consultative structure was projected to be a joint representative committee, made up of the shop stewards and other "lay representatives of the various trade unions in the company." Legislation for this purpose was anticipated to be passed by the end of 1979, but Labour's defeat at the polls took care of that.

The scheme for worker participation projected in the white paper was clearly derived from the TUC proposals. The option would be created for companies to organize themselves on a two-tiered basis. Worker representatives would be incorporated as equal members of the supervisory (or policy) board in all enterprises employing two thousand or more workers. Although parity representation was its ultimate goal, the government suggested that a reasonable first step would be to elect worker representatives numbering up to one-third of the board's membership.

Another interesting compromise was the suggestion that the initiative for worker representation should be taken by the Joint Representative Committee, whose action would then be followed by a vote of the firm's workers to let them determine whether they would want to be so represented. Such a ballot would not be allowed until the JRC would have been in operation for several (3 or 4) years. The details of the actual selection of the worker representatives were not determined. Whatever they would be, one thing could be guaranteed: the trade unions would play a very significant, if not monopolistic, role in the nominating process. One other thing was generally presumed as well: all workers—union members and nonunion members—would participate in the selection process.

The nationalized industries were expected to set an example for the private sector, which they are already doing—at least, the British Steel Corporation, the National Coal Board, and British Leyland. At BSC, worker representatives have been appointed to the divisional boards since its onset in 1967. From a list of nominees supplied by the steel unions, the appointments are made by the corporation chairman. The Coal Board has consultative councils, composed of representatives of the board, the trade unions, and management associations, at the headquarters, division, area, and colliery levels of organization. The NUM (National Union of Miners) and TUC leaders have also been members of the Coal Board itself, and the industrial-relations member of the board has always been a trade unionist, although not an NUM official.[52]

Britain appears to be entering the age of participation, although with a great deal of deliberateness. It will be at least five or six years—if then—before worker-elected representatives will be on company boards. Joint representation committees, if they were to be established, will not soon have the power that resides in the integrative works councils of the northern continental countries.

THE EUROPEAN ECONOMIC COMMUNITY

An important stimulus to the entire worker-participation movement has been the European Commission. In consultation with the European Assembly and the EEC's Council of Ministers, the commission has dealt with worker participation in two main ways: through the proposal for a so-called Fifth Directive, and through the commission's proposed European Company Statute.

The Fifth Directive, which was proposed in 1972, sought to project principles to guide the organization of *sociétés anonymes* (limited-liability companies or corporations). It quickly ran into some difficulties, however, and was subjected to an array of detractions. The commission, therefore, decided to try focusing the public debate by issuing a green paper in 1975. Even though it has not gotten substantially past this stage, the 1972 proposal and the green paper have had their impact already, whether an actual directive will ever be issued or not.

Taking German and Dutch company law as a model, the green paper advocates that the community's public companies (companies whose stock is publicly traded) opt for a two-tiered board structure. In addition, it suggests that "not less than one-third of the members of the company's supervisory organ shall be appointed by the workers or their representatives or upon proposal by the workers or their representatives."

It also prescribes that "representatives should be truly representative of the employees of the enterprise in question, and that all employees should be able to participate in the selection process . . . in a way which will provide reasonable protection for minorities."[53] The possibility is left open that the employees in a firm will not want to be represented on the board.

The European Company Statute proposal is very specific in its content; it had to be since it is comparable to a legislative bill. If it is passed, it should be usable as law of the community. The proposal has been sharpened rather than softened since it was first proposed in 1970. The original, for example, called for two-thirds of the members of the supervisory board to be selected by the shareholders and one-third by the employees. The 1975 version reads: one-third by shareholders, one-third by the workers, and one-third co-opted by the first two groups. This third faction is to be independent of both shareholders and employees and is to represent "general interests." The worker representatives are to be elected indirectly by the firm's workers —that is, the workers elect electoral delegates and these, in turn, elect the employee representatives for the supervisory board.

European companies will also be required to have works councils that are directly elected by all employees. The 1975 proposal states that this council must "give its agreement to decisions planned by the board of management concerning the establishment of a social plan in the event of closure of a European Company or of parts thereof." Before a company makes any decision to close its doors or to merge, the council must be consulted as well. Trade-union interests have been protected by the statement that the council's jurisdiction is limited "to matters which do not involve the negotiation of ... collective agreements." The idea of firms being able to incorporate under European law will leave the option to the individual companies. It is not anticipated, therefore, that businesses will be required to incorporate in this fashion in order to be allowed to engage in transnational activity in the EEC. The prime question is not just whether the EEC's Council of Ministers will actually approve a Company Statute but, more importantly, whether European entrepreneurs will judge it beneficial to have their company so organized. For example, it will presumably greatly facilitate the creation of transnational mergers. That could be worthwhile enough so that management will be able to live with the ideological and operational discomforts they perceive as resulting from worker-participation practices and from the pre-scribed two-tiered structure of corporate organization. In addition, a number of the eligible firms are expected to have the sort of experience with both features that leaves them with no discomfort at all; they may, in fact, become models for others to follow for the mutual benefit of stockholders, managers, workers, and the general public.

CONCLUSIONS

There are clearly some distinct differences in how the law and the labor agreements of the several countries define the opportunities for workers to participate in corporate management. This chapter has outlined the differences as well as the similarities of the various national systems. Table 6 summarizes the differences. It ranks seven of the nine EE countries, Ireland and Luxembourg have been excluded, along three rather general variables. Even though three different ranking and indicating systems have been employed by Wilpert and his associates, the table presents the picture in a comprehensive, comparative manner.

It is widely concluded that the traditional distribution of power in the European business organization has been most directly affected by worker-participation schemes in which independent trade unions play a key role. The same appears to be true with regard to the degree of substance there is to the workers' participation in company decision making. Another general conclusion is that worker attitudes toward participatory opportunities have improved with experience and that the workers tend to develop an interest in having such opportunities expanded.[54] One can, therefore, only conclude that, even though the experience with worker participation in the several European countries may have different histories and be varied in form and scope, worker participation appears to be a distinct part of a progressive movement—a movement directed toward the attainment of greater dignity for the worker and improved labor stability and productivity for the employer.

TABLE 6   A Ranking of EEC Countries by Degree of Prescribed Worker
Participation in Management

	Direct Involvement of Workers	Involvement of Representative Bodies	Board Representation	Overall Standing
Germany	1	1	1	1
Netherlands	6	4	2	2
Belgium	2	3	3	2
France	4	2	2	2
Denmark	5	5	1	3
Italy	3	6	3	4
United Kingdom	7	7	3	4

Source: This is an adaption of the table presented by Bernhard Wilpert and Associates in a paper, "Participation and Its Consequences in Industry," presented to the Fifth World Congress of the International Industrial Relations Association in Paris, September 3-7, 1979.

Note: The ranking on the variables of "direct involvement of workers" and "involvement of representative bodies" are placed on a continuum that rates "relatively much involvement" as 1 and "practically no involvement" as 7.

The ranking on "board representation" suggests "workers having the right to elect at least a minority of board members" with a 1, "workers having no rights whatsoever to nominate and/or elect board members" with a 3, and "workers having either observers or having the right to veto the appointment of new members" with a 2.

NOTES

1. By Albert Gallatin, as quoted in Milton Derber's *The American Idea of Industrial Democracy, 1865-1965* (Urbana: University of Illinois Press, 1970), p. 6.

2. Campbell Balfour, *Industrial Relations in the Common Market* (London: Routledge and Kegan Paul, 1972), p. 103.

3. Walter Kolvenbach, *Employee Councils in European Companies* (Deventer, Netherlands: Kluwer/Metener, 1978) p. 109. This is an excellent, encyclopedic source on the subject.

4. Gerhard Leminsky, "Worker Participation: The German Experience," in Benjamin Martin and Everett Kassalow, eds., *Labor Relations in Advanced Industrial Societies: Issues and Problems* (Washington, D.C.: Carnegie Endowment for International Peace, 1980), p. 141. The Leminsky article reports that in a number of publicly owned enterprises, the executive director charged with the management of social and personnel questions was informally selected by the unions. This was a forerunner of another practice to be reinstituted after the war, a practice that the trade unionists failed to have included as a requirement for all enterprises employing more than two thousand persons.

5. Balfour, pp. 110 and 112.

6. Jozef Balcerek, "Participation Schemes in Different Socio-Economic Systems," in Bernhard Wilpert, Ayse Kudet, and Yilmar Ozkan, eds., *Workers' Participation in an Internationalized Economy* (Kent, Ohio: Comparative Administration Research Institute, Kent State University, 1978), p. 27.

7. Kolvenbach, p. 111.

8. See International Labour Organisation, *Participation of Workers in Decisions Within Undertakings* (documents of a technical meeting, Geneva, 20-29 November 1967) (Labour-Management Relations Series No. 33, 1969), pp. 2-3, and Robert W. Cox.

9. There are great varieties of sources that describe and/or summarize the legal provisions and practices in the various EC countries. Some of the more recent are: Kolvenbach, "Worker Participation in the European Community," *European Documentation*, no. 3, 1977 (published by Commission of the European Communities); Richard D. Lambert, ed., "Industrial Democracy in International Perspective," *Annals of the American Academy of Political and Social Science* 431(May 1977); *Employee Participation and Company Structure in the European Community* (Commission of the European Communities, Document COM (75) 570 final, 1975); J. Bautz Bonanno, "Employee Codetermination: Origins in Germany, Present Practice in Europe, and Applicability to the United States," *Harvard Journal on Legislation* 14 (1977): 947-1012; *Workers' Participation* (documents prepared for the International Management Seminar, convened by the Organization for Economic Cooperation and Development, Versailles, 5-8 March 1975); and Herbert Wiedemann, "Codetermination by Workers in German Enterprises," *American Journal of Comparative Law* 28 (Winter 1980): 79-92.

10. The overwhelming majority of councils in the metal and the chemical industries are elected jointly. Dorothea De Schweinitz, *Labor-Management Consultation in the Factory* (Honolulu: University of Hawaii, 1966).

11. James Ellenberger, "The Realities of Co-Determination," *The American Federationist* 10 (Oct. 1977): 12.

12. These are similar to the quarterly meetings of all plant employees the works council is to convene. Plant assemblies have not been successful in terms of frequency of such assemblies and in worker attendance. See Friedrich Fürstenberg, "West German Experience with Industrial Democracy," *Annals of the American Academy of Political and Social Science* 431 (May 1977): 48.

13. Data extracted from a study by the Deutsches Industrieinstitut, as cited in Ivor L. Roberts, "The Works Constitution Act and Industrial Relations in West Germany: Implications for the United Kingdom," *British Journal of Industrial Relations* 11 (Nov. 1973): 352. The differences among these sectors are clearly related to the varying levels of unionization.

14. Ivor Roberts, p. 355.

15. *The New York Times*, January 13, 1979.

16. This system of election is reminiscent of the complicated attempt to capture the best of both the single-member district plan and proportional representation in the method of electing members of the Bundestag (the directly elected, lower house of the German legislature).

17. Johannes Schregle, "Co-determination in the Federal Republic of Germany: A Comparative View," *International Labour Review* 117 (Jan.-Feb. 1978): 94.

18. *Mitbestimmung im Unternehmen* (Bundestags-Drucksache VI/334, 1970). The report was named after the chairman of a government commission charged with making a detailed study of the experiences with codetermination under the 1951 and 1952 laws. Professor Kurt Biedenkopf later became general secretary of the Christian Democratic Union party.

19. *The Economist*, December 15, 1979.

20. See Fürstenberg's analysis of the Biedenkopf Report in his "West German Experience," pp. 44-53. Also see Bonanno, pp. 959-62.

21. See Robert Ball, "The Hard Hats in Europe's Boardrooms," *Fortune* 93 (June 1976), pp. 187-89.

22. *The Times*, November 7, 1977.

23. Some enterprises use other constituency groups; some also conduct at-large elections—that is, all the workers (not just those in the particular category) select the category representatives.

24. B. W. M. Hovels and P. Nas, *Ondernemingsraad en Medezeggenschap* (Nijmegen, Netherlands: Sociological Institute of the Catholic University, 1976), p. 17.

25. Kolvenbach, pp. 210-11.

26. Hovels and Nas, pp. 19 and 71.

27. The Social-Economic Council is a tripartite consultative structure composed of equal numbers of representatives of management, labor, and government. Such councils exist in several West European countries, and they have been effective channels of communication and of pre-legislation consultation. Some even claim that their successful operation helped minimize labor unrest in the primary period of postwar reconstruction.

28. W. Albeda, "Between Harmony and Conflict: Industrial Democracy in the Netherlands," *Annals* of the American Academy of Political and Social Science 431 (May 1977): 77.

29. W. Albeda, "The Netherlands," in Benjamin C. Roberts, ed., *Toward Industrial Democracy: Europe, Japan and the United States* (Montclair, N.J.: Allenheld, Osmun, 1979), p. 121.

30. W. Albeda, "Changing Industrial Relations in The Netherlands," *Industrial*

Relations 16 (May 1977): 139-40.

31. *The Economist*, February 19, 1977, and March 11, 1978.

32. *The Economist*, May 29, 1976.

33. An excellent summary of the Belgian experience is contained in a paper by P. Gevers entitled "Works Councils in Belgium: A Greater Chance of Information Disclosure?" (Presented at the Fifth World Congress of the International Industrial Relations Association, Paris, September 3-7, 1979).

34. Innis Macbeath, *The European Approach to Worker-Management Relationships* (New York: British-North American Committee, 1973), p. 10.

35. Ibid.

36. François Sellier, "France," in John Dunlop, ed., *Labor in the Twentieth Century*, (New York: Academic Press, 1978), p. 211.

37. See Stephen Borstein and Kaitha Sapsin Fine, "Worker Participation and Self-Management in France: Recent Political Developments" (Paper presented at the 1976 Annual Meeting of the American Political Science Association, Chicago, September 2-5, 1976.)

38. Walter Kendall, "Industrial Democracy in Europe," *Personnel Management* 3 (Sept.1971): 34, and *Employee Participation and Company Structure in the European Community*, p. 121. Note that all the "reforms" discussed above have originated with the French government, and, interestingly enough, most of them came during the administrations of Charles de Gaulle and Valéry Giscard d'Estaing, both of which have been conservative in orientation.

39. Klaus Von Beyme, *Challenge to Power: Trade Unions and Industrial Relations in Capitalist Countries* (London: Sage Publications, 1980), p. 313.

40. Anthony Carew, "Shop-Floor Trade Unionism in Western Europe," *European Studies* 18 (1974): 5.

41. N. F. Dufty, *Changes in Labour-Management Relations in the Enterprise* (Paris: Organization for Economic Cooperation and Development, 1975), p. 40.

42. G. David Garson, "The Codetermination Model of Workers' Participation: Where Is It Leading!" *Sloan Management Review* 18 (Spring 1977): 71.

43. This is particularly striking since the 1947 national labor agreement had already provided that "employees must be given the opportunity to participate in the determination of their own work situation and to exert an influence on the decision-making in the company." Ann Westenholz, "Workers' Participation in Denmark," *Industrial Relations* 18 (Fall 1979): 376.

44. Ibid., p. 377.

45. *Employee Participation and Company Structure in the European Community*, pp. 88-89, and Bernt Schiller, "Industrial Democracy in Scandinavia," *Annals* 431 (May 1977): 69-73.

46. B. C. Roberts, "United Kingdom," in Roberts, ed., *Toward Industrial Democracy*, p. 170.

47. *Employee Participation and Company Structure in the European Community*, p. 167. Also Andrew W. J. Thomson, "New Focus on Industrial Democracy in Britain,"*Annals* 431 (May 1977): 136.

48. David Reid, "Pricking the German Bubble," *Management Today* (Jan. 1974): 85; J. Reynolds, "Employee Participation: A Trade Union View," in N. H. Cuthbert and K. H. Howlans, *Company Industrial Relations Policies* (London: Longmans, 1973), pp. 148-51; Pamela Pocock, "Participation in Preston," *Personnel Management* 5 (Dec. 1973): 31-33; and Gordon Prentice, "Participation at Fry's," *Personnel*

Management 6 (May 1974): 35-38.

49. *Employee Participation and Company Structure in the European Community,* p. 168, and *The Economist,* March 9, 1974.

50. *The Times,* May 15, 1978.

51. *The Times,* May 24, 1978.

52. George Graham, "Labour Participation in Management: A Study of the National Coal Board," *Political Quarterly* 38 (April-June, 1967): 184-99.

53. *Employee Participation and Company Structure* (Bulletin of the European Communities, Supplement 8/75).

54. Wilpert et al., *Workers' Participation in an International Economy,* pp. 11-12.

7

THE RESPONSE OF U.S. MULTINATIONALS TO EUROPEAN LAWS AND PRACTICES

Having reviewed the nature and dimensions of American multinational investment in the European Community, the manner in which American management perceives the roles and rights of managers and workers, the industrial-relations reputation of American multinationals, the kind of work-place reforms that have evolved in the United States, the type of labor and trade-union response experienced in Europe, and the array of legal requirements and customs concerning worker participation in European Community countries, the key question remains: How have American multi-nationals reacted?

The answer may appear to be obvious, particularly since American busi-nessmen are generally considered to be pragmatic and law abiding. On such grounds, one would logically assume that American multinational manage-ment would have simply adapted to local circumstances. Earlier chapters have shown, however, that American managers have distinct value commitments that make it difficult for them to remain strictly pragmatic at times. This cer-tainly has been the case when situations involved such basic issues as infringe-ments on management's prerogatives or the apparent possibility that trade unions would dominate their firms, the business community, or society at large.

Similarly, even though American firms have the habit of obeying the law and recognize that it is very bad business to become known as an outlaw or law breaker, their obedience does not indicate support for that law. Neither does it promise that these same firms will follow local custom where the force of law is not directly involved. Nor does compliance automatically promise that American multinationals will stay aloof from local legislative politics or from initiatives to alter existing practices when such opportunities appear promising. In one case, for example, American business interests found them-selves being told flatly to stay out of host-country politics. When the German government appeared to be on the verge of extending parity worker represen-tation on company boards to firms outside the coal and steel industries, the U.S. Chamber of Commerce in Germany was reprimanded for seeking to block the passage of such legislation. (More about that later.)

Questions such as "How have American multinationals reacted?" cannot be answered glibly for a variety of other reasons. First, there is too great a variety of firms, both in terms of their organizational characteristics and in their style of management. And corporate practices will also vary as a result of the differences in the legal requirements and customs of the various European Community countries.

This chapter will mainly be concerned with describing how American firms have behaved in the several European Community countries. But before we examine the situation country by country, we shall pose a number of caveats and later discuss some of the activities of European management and employer organizations that have been supported by a number of American firms. A brief attempt will also be made to determine whether West European worker-participation laws and trade unionism have played a major role in the acceleration of European direct investment in the United States—that is, whether there has been a certain degree of flight by European firms to escape worker participation in their home countries.

SOME CAVEATS ABOUT U.S. MNC RESPONSES

Before anything else, it should be understood that the American experience with worker representation on company boards, and to a somewhat lesser extent with works councils, is of fairly limited duration and scope. The German law requiring parity codetermination in firms outside the coal and steel industries was not enacted until March 1976 and did not go into force until July 1978. That particular experience is thus extremely limited. Similarly, the Dutch requirement that works councils be organized in all firms with more than one hundred employees only dates from 1971. Legal requirements for codetermination and works councils are not universal, either. The German Codetermination Act affects only some fifty American subsidiaries (those with more than two thousand employees) out of a total of about eleven hundred operating in that country.[1] Although the statutory base for requiring works councils is very stringent in Germany (firms with five or more employees), in other countries, the law is much more lenient. Therefore, there are a number of smaller subsidiaries operating in countries other than Germany that have never even experienced worker participation of the European variety.

It should also be established that American firms, including those operating in Europe, generally practice what is called a "democratic" style of management. When European managers were asked to characterize this method of operation, they identified its hallmarks to be sincerity and frankness in the expression of opinions, open communication from top to bottom, flexibility, consideration of individuals, and opportunities for advancement.[2] Others capsulize it in terms of the American propensity to use first names and to remove traditional class distinctions between managers and workers.

Within such "democratic" contexts, more consultation between superiors and subordinates probably occurs than was customary in the more traditional West European business firms, particularly as they operated prior to the democratization of European societies and the introduction of works councils and codetermination. Apologists for the American style of management are occasionally eager to point out that the younger, more energetic and ambitious European workers prefer to work for American firms for those reasons. These workers may have such a preference for a variety of reasons, however. Their tendency to seek employment with U.S. subsidiaries does not necessarily reflect only their dominant preference for the American style of labor-management consultation. American employers, for example, have tended to pay better than local firms. Their employees have also had to be less concerned about having to buck seniority. And, logically, white-collar employees perceive American multinational companies to be much more promising in personal advancement than are the smaller local enterprises. For whatever the reasons Europeans work for American subsidiaries, their employment preference does not prove that it is because the American "democratic" style of management gives the workers or their representatives as much influence over company decisions as has become possible through European works councils and codetermination. Neither does it establish that such an influence is or is not important to them. Trade unionists obviously have their own opinions on this issue.

The third observation relates to the internal communication practices of American firms. Especially important here is the extensive use of printed materials such as house organs (company newspapers or magazines) and company handbooks. These are the backbone of the elaborate communication system that many Stateside firms employ. Through them, managements hope to make their company employees feel that they are part of a team, as well as give them continuing education about company policies and activities. It is questionable, of course, whether these forms of communication are as effective as face-to-face contact is and are as satisfying as a give-and-take format of communication.

American firms that have developed viable procedures for upward communication in their Stateside operations also tend to use these in their European affiliates. IBM subsidiaries in Europe, for example, use the company's open-door grievance system (as described in Chapter 4), its Speak-Up program, and its general suggestion plan. [3] Other firms have been using employee surveys. Chevron Oil has gone one step further and has reportedly consulted its European workers before deciding to expand near Brussels rather than near Rotterdam.[4]

Because improved communication is unquestionably one of the prime benefits, (if not also one of the prime purposes), of worker participation, many American managers tend to question the need to formalize what to them appears an already existing practice. However, most companies do not really have a viable *upward* communication system. Neither can one consider a system of *downward* communication in written form to be an adequate substitute for participation in open discussion.

Neither are European governments and trade unionists enthralled by the occasional arguments that worker participation in particular firms should not be required until all firms have become convinced of the usefulness of such a method of communication and until they have decided to set up such a system voluntarily. What concerns trade unionists even more, of course, is the fact that even the most effective suggestion and grievance procedures do not guarantee that the interests of the workers will be heard or even considered when decisions are made about broader company policy. Therefore, European proponents of worker participation are not easily dissuaded from their concern that neither the American "democratic" style of management nor the usual intracompany practices are adequate substitutes for their works councils and for codetermination.

It seems justified to suggest a fourth caveat. Management of certain American multinationals tend to have reservations about West European worker-participation procedures because they could strengthen the influence trade unions have in the workplace. In Germany, as was suggested in Chapter 6, trade unions generally dominate worker representation on works councils, and worker representation on company boards include union leaders who appear to be far removed from the company's employees. One example of this is Chip Levinson, the general secretary of the worldwide International Federation of Chemical, Energy, and General Workers, headquartered in Geneva, Switzerland, who was elected to represent the workers of the German Du Pont subsidiary on that company's supervisory board.

Not all American subsidiary managers who prefer to work without trade unions are opposed to worker participation. In firms whose workers are not unionized, works councils and higher pay can help prevent workers from becoming unionized and union leaders from directly influencing company policy. Several subsidiary managers smilingly admit that to be a fact.

Finally, and probably most importantly, it should be remembered that variables have tended to affect the industrial-relations behavior of American multinationals in Europe. The same observations that were made in Chapter 3 are relevant here. Accordingly, American responses have varied in relation to the company's decision-making structure, particularly the degree of centralization in the company's decision making about industrial-relations questions. As markets become increasingly competitive and as recession or market saturation calls for headquarters decisions about such options as divestiture, relocation, or cutbacks, the managers of European subsidiaries have experienced greater pressures to conform to headquarters' priorities and perspectives, including those about such practices as worker participation.

Equally important is the longevity of a firm and especially the length of time its European subsidiaries have been in business. Younger firms and more recent entries into the European market have been apt to be more monocentric (centralized in decision making) and ethnocentric.[5] In the first phase of corporate development, subsidiaries have not been very inclined to adapt their decisions to local circumstances and values; neither have they been given much discretion outside a narrowly defined set of industrial-relations issues. Wilkins explains the next stage in the development of the multinational enterprise as polycentric, in which the firm's organizational structure can become a virtual labyrinth. She describes how some subsidiaries are managed in a monocentric way while headquarters' decisions regarding other subsidiaries of the same firm become polycentric, that is, local managers are free to adapt as trade-union or host-government pressures demand. A number of American firms exhibit the characteristics of this second stage of development. The behavior of such a company's subsidiary in England and/or France can be markedly different from that of its sister operations in Germany or Holland. Not only will the subsidiary managers in that type of company have been instructed to conform to different legal environments, they even tend to be different kinds of persons. They are either more or less ethnocentric than their colleagues in other countries or plants, and were selected for their specific posts precisely because they had those particular value commitments and/or leadership styles.

The most established American firms in Europe tend to reflect the same kind of flexibility and relative autonomy for their subsidiaries, even though such older firms have developed their own kind of corporate culture, which, where necessary, has superseded the value system of their home-country's business community. As long as the subsidiary's industrial-relations policies of the more established companies do not impede the global planning and bargaining position of the multinational enterprise, their flexibility and autonomy will tend to be maintained.

A third variable that has been most influential is the degree of continuity in the subsidiary's history. Subsidiaries that were autonomous host-country enterprises for a significant part of their history and that later were acquired by an American multinational have generally retained a considerable amount of autonomy. This is, of course, also a general trait of conglomerates, multinational or not and regardless of their nationality. This autonomy exists especially when the acquired firm was a profitable one and when its management was left essentially intact or was replaced by other host-country nationals.

Very influential in conditioning company responses to worker-participation practices has been the company's internal political culture. Thus, the Johnson & Johnson Company, whose company credo states that "executives must be persons of common sense and full understanding," is inclined to leave its subsidiary managers considerable discretion, as long as their operations meet company cost and earning goals and they do not pose problems and embarrassment for the parent firm. There are a number of other American firms that have placed high value on worker satisfaction, whether out of a sense of paternalistic moralism or out of a mindset that reasons that any forms of industrial-relations practices that promote a cooperative attitude on the side of the work force cannot help but promote greater productivity and quality of work performance. It is not uncommon, therefore, to meet subsidiary managers who have been "converted" to the merits of worker participation, although their liking for it is based on totally different considerations than those held by European trade unionists and government officials. Interestingly enough, such "conversions" have almost exclusively occurred as a result of the manager's participation in a seminar conducted under the auspices of an international management-consulting firm.

Subsidiary response also varies in correlation to the percentage of managerial positions filled by expatriates. Not only have many Americans failed to understand and appreciate local values, but they have also become aroused by such issues as codetermination and works councils. It is not necessarily true that local nationals favor codetermination; but they seem more able to deal with it pragmatically. What particularly compounds the problem is the fact that most American expatriates have been assigned overseas for a relatively short time. Thus, when compared with their British and Japanese counterparts, they are less apt to become culturally and organizationally integrated. A major part of the problem may be that most American companies do not give their expatriates preassignment orientation courses, except for an occasional handout about housing, schooling, and other family resettlement concerns.

The potential expatriate problem has been ameliorated by the fact that industrial relations and personnel positions are generally staffed by host-country nationals.[6] However, codetermination and many other industrial-relations issues do not involve just the personnel or industrial-relations executive. The kind of experience the subsidiary will have with worker participation is just as dependent, if not more, on the attitudes and behavior of the subsidiary's managing director and company executives who do not have industrial-relations assignments.

The use of expatriates varies among companies; it is heaviest among those that have had their subsidiary in place for a comparatively short period of time. They are also used extensively in the more ethnocentric and the more centralized companies. In contrast, subsidiaries that were bought by American interests as relatively profitable national enterprises have tended to keep their preacquisition management personnel in place and have allowed them to conduct affairs in their own way. Distinct changes in the use of American expatriates have apparently occurred since 1977, when the U.S. Congress made some drastic reductions in the income-tax provisions relating to expatriates. Now that fewer Americans want to work overseas, and MNC headquarters have begun to recognize the advantages of increased use of home- and third-country nationals, company industrial-relations practices are apt to stabilize as well.

THE EXPERIENCE IN THE SEVERAL EUROPEAN COMMUNITY COUNTRIES

Germany

In Germany, where worker participation has been the most widely introduced, American companies have a somewhat checkered reputation. The larger, older, and more sophisticated companies are obviously in the German market to stay, both to meet their international competitors head-on in their home market and to capitalize on the continuing growth potential of the European market. Many companies have recognized that works councils and codetermination are not so bad and that they can even be advantageous at times. In fact, a large number of these firms have developed very good relations with their works councils. Their fear that council members would be more loyal to their union than to their company has apparently proven to be unwarranted. Consequently, many managers acknowledge that works councils can be active and that their power can be quite significant. This has been particularly true since 1972, when the law enabled them to involve themselves in a large number of issues about which they were previously only to be informed. The extent of current works-council power is highlighted in the 1973 comments of Horst Bergemann, the former labor-relations director of Ford-Werke in Cologne, when he was quoted as having observed that "the council [has] veto power over all company initiatives affecting jobs." He suggested that they could deal with the questions of who shall be hired or fired, who shall be trained, who shall be hired to train them, and, certainly not least of all, whether overtime work shall be expected or not.[7] Heinz Allsup, chairman of Ford's general-works council is reported to have observed, at the same time, that, in such personnel questions, the council routinely consents to management's initiatives.[8]

Bergemann explained that the important thing was to keep the workers informed. When management explains the reasons for particular decisions, council members usually tend to go along with them. Various subsidiary managers have confirmed this same fact. They have also discovered that the works council can be very valuable as a vehicle to educate employees about company affairs. Management consultants have even suggested that active works councillors and worker representatives on the company board have improved management performance in that they make "seat-of-the-pants" management decisions less prevalent. They add that standards of staff work, analysis, and presentation also tend to improve.[9]

The favorable reports on the status and efficacy of works councils in American subsidiaries do not just come from management. A number of German trade unionists have been equally complimentary. In the petroleum industry, for example, works councils are fully organized in most firms, and the extent of information disclosed to them is described by trade unionists as generally favorable when compared with the information provided to councils in other industrial sectors. Petroleum MNCs in Germany are also reported to respect fully trade-union rights and to adhere fully to all relevant industrial-relations legislation.[10] In some American firms, the influence of trade unionists is said to extend even beyond the standards required by law. Ford Werke, for example, allows workers to be recruited into the union when they are newly hired.[11] It is not surprising, therefore, that the level of unionization at that plant and at other automobile- and farm-implement-manufacturer subsidiaries in Germany ranges from 78 to 95 percent, which is considerably higher than the average level of unionization for all German workers (40 percent).

One somewhat typical story about the level and type of influence that works councils can have in subsidiaries of U.S.-based companies was reported several years ago by Sydney Paulden in *The Times* of London. In confirming the extensive powers of the council at Schulke & Mayr and at Hinds-Turner (both subsidiaries of Sterling Drug), he told how Frau Meike Hinz, a bilingual secretary who also served as works-council chairman, made effective use of her power to call in experts of her own choosing to analyze what she perceived to be an industrial health problem. Frau Hinz had noticed a high-pitched noise (at a level not generally heard by human ears) coming from an ultrasonic welding machine, and she personally took the initiative that ultimately resulted in a soundproof enclosure for the machine.[12] Under the 1972 Works Constitution Act, works councils and their officers, like Frau Hinz, are unilaterally authorized to call in experts on any matter relating to the well-being of the company's workers.

Not all trade unionists have been happy with the kind of information management has provided the works councils. In 1976, for example, Richard Heller, the works-council chairman of Adam Opel's Rüsselsheim plant, complained that management's figures supplied as background data for investment-planning decisions were only global figures. He felt that those figures did not allow the council members to judge the impacts those programs would have on worker health and on the workplace. Management, in contrast, provided much more detailed data at the end of 1973, when the company experienced a sudden slump in sales and a rapid buildup in inventory. At that time, the works council was asked to agree to a thirteen-week period of short-time work and a limited number of separations with special layoff bonuses.[13] These facts do not imply that Opel's overall record is necessarily bad. The frustrations felt by German worker representatives is undoubtedly paralleled by those of American managers, who must remain alert to the German way of doing things and who find themselves delayed and restricted from the sort of freedom they have traditionally known and preferred.

Worker participation has brought about the most distinct reaction from American subsidiaries in Germany in the area of worker representation on the company supervisory board. As long as worker board membership was limited to one-third, things could be uncomfortable, but would not necessarily cause utter panic. Under those circumstances, even though worker representatives on the supervisory board would take positions that were sharply opposed to those of management, they were virtually never able to overrule the management-nominated, stockholder-elected two-thirds majority. The *Wall Street Journal* reported, for example, how the two worker-elected directors of Ford Werke in Cologne repeatedly called for cutting dividends and for investing the money in the business or putting it into higher wages and benefits for the worker. Every time they made the suggestion, however, they were outvoted 4 to 2.[14] Daniel Benedict reported parallel experiences at General Motors' Adam Opel plant. In both cases, the company's subsidiary board allegedly followed instructions from corporate headquarters to transfer the profits abroad rather than reinvest them locally, as the worker representatives had suggested.[15]

Just because worker representatives may have frequently failed to obtain board endorsement for some of their recommendations does not mean that their impact has always been negligible. Numerous management representatives have pointed out that worker directors can be and have been very influential. Their influence has been, of course, most directly related to the quality of their contributions—that is, how well their proposals were documented—and to the openmindedness of the other directors and the board chairman. Many corporate directors have said that they have become convinced that the increased exposure of worker directors to management data has made them more conservative than the management-nominated board members. It should be acknowledged, though, that most supervisory boards have been rubber-stamping management decisions and have left subsidiary chief executive officers plenty of room to run their businesses without much interference.[16]

The fact that codetermination has not proven to be an insurmountable hurdle for American multinationals is borne out by the very sizable, constantly increasing investments made since 1952, the year worker representatives began to appear on some American subsidiary boards.

The era of relatively good feelings between German management and labor as well as between American management and German labor seemed to come to a grinding halt, however, after the 1972 Bundestag election in which Willy

Brandt and the Social Democrats strengthened their power base and that of their SPD-FDP coalition government. The German Socialist party (SPD) leadership could be expected to honor its election promises to the trade-union movement to provide parity representation, even though it would naturally have to make some compromises with the Free Democratic party (FDP). The latter, for example, had insisted that parity of worker and management could only be discussed if junior executives were guaranteed to be part of the employee representation. FDP leadership also insisted that board chairmen would have to be acceptable to the shareholders.[17]

While the coalition partners were involved in delicate behind-closed-door negotiations, external pressure politics began to mount. The first initiative was taken by the DGB (trade-union federation), which urged Chancellor Brandt, in March 1973, to extend parity representation for workers beyond the basic industries of coal, iron, and steel to all large enterprises. Several weeks later, the president of the U.S. Chamber of Commerce in Germany, Dr. Milan F. Ondrus, entered the debate, an initiative that evolved into a story that received broad publicity in Germany as well as all over Europe.

The chamber president was not the only one who expressed management concerns about parity codetermination. The Federation of German Employers (*Bundesvereinigung der Deutsche Arbeitgeberverbände*) had presented its views in considerable detail to the Biedenkopf Commission. The federation chairman, Dr. Hanns-Martin Schleyer, had made repeated pronouncements on the subject.[18] Nevertheless, Dr. Ondrus's comments and the chamber's later activities presented an unusual twist.

What was so unusual was not that he suggested that, in drafting a law extending codetermination, attention should be paid to international agreements currently in force that were a part of German law.[19] What aroused so much public resentment was that a representative of foreign business interests tried to participate directly in the legislative debate. Trade unionists felt as if they had directly experienced the type of political interventionism by global companies that they had previously observed in Chile and in other parts of the Third World.

Action really picked up after the German government published the coalition compromise in January 1974. On March 12, the American Chamber of Commerce announced that its Executive Committee and its Supervisory Board had unanimously concluded that the proposed bill probably contradicted several international agreements to which the Federal Republic was a party. The chamber had reportedly also authorized a group of eminent experts to prepare a brief on the international aspects of the government proposal. When completed, this brief would be submitted to appropriate officials. The newspaper *Die Welt* revealed, later in the year, that the brief was partially financed by such German firms as Daimler-Benz, Hoechst, Robert Bosch, Hapag-Lloyd, and Gerling.[20]

On March 29, at a press conference on the occasion of his leaving the chamber presidency, Dr. Ondrus made several comments that were perceived by the advocates of parity codetermination as containing veiled threats. In the name of the American Chamber of Commerce in Germany, he welcomed the U.S. government's willingness to extend to German firms that invested Stateside the same standing and privileges as given to American firms. Dr. Ondrus then suggested that the commissioning of the legal brief did not indicate that U.S. firms wished to receive special treatment in Germany. He also observed that bilateral treaties cannot be unilaterally undercut in order to carry through national political programs but required prior accommodations from both partners. In closing, Dr. Ondrus expressed fear that "the more than $1.7 billion projected investments in West Germany for 1974 will, as a result of the planned codetermination, partially not materialize.[21] This release was soon followed by DGB charges of "massive mixing" by the chamber in the internal affairs of the German Federal Republic, charges that were promptly denied by the chamber.[22]

The commissioned brief was submitted by Professor Dr. Wilhelm Wengler, the director of the Institute for International and Foreign Law of the Free University, Berlin, on August 19.[23] After reviewing the relevant provisions of the German-American Treaty of Friendship, Commerce, and Navigation of 1954 and of corporation law of a number of industrialized societies, Professor Wengler concluded that the right of American investors to elect the members of supervisory boards was guaranteed under the 1954 treaty, particularly through its most-favored-nation clause, and under the investment treaties concluded by the Federal Republic. The second conclusion, therefore, was that instituting parity codetermination would be a limitation of the rights of American investors, a limitation that would be in violation of the treaty. The right to elect members of one's supervisory board was understood to be guaranteed under the clause dealing with the right to control and manage one's enterprise.

In early September, the brief was submitted to Chancellor Schmidt, to the U.S. Embassy in Bonn for referral to the Department of State, and to the parliamentary leadership of the four main German parties. The American Chamber of Commerce President Otto Schoeppler reportedly also sent a fiery letter to some fifty U.S. corporations. In the one to John Riccardo, the president of Chrysler Corporation, he urged Riccardo to do much more than he had done so far to prevent codetermination in the Federal Republic and to do so by contacting his congressman and senators and appropriate government officials. Schoeppler urged that pressure also be applied to the German government, and that it be suggested to them that future investment shall depend upon the legislative action. A chamber executive was said to have admitted that a six-figure amount of German marks had been appropriated for the lobbying campaign against the codetermination bill.[24]

The responses to these American Chamber initiatives were not long in coming. While the *Frankfurter Allgemeine Zeitung* wondered whether the German administration's reactions to the American Chamber's initiative was meant to avoid having to answer the legal points raised, DGB President Heinz Otto Vetter went on the offensive.[25] In Hamburg at a Printers and Paper-workers Union meeting, Vetter declared that Germany was not a "banana republic." He labeled the AmCham actions intervention in German domestic affairs "with almost unmitigated capitalistic chutzpah," and was warmly and loudly applauded when he concluded by stating that "colonialism in Europe is dead."[26] The next day, the official spokesman for the German government, Klaus Bölling, observed that Chancellor Schmidt had already noted that the chamber's action was not particularly fortunate. Bölling also commented that the German government would obviously observe treaty obligations.[27] In the meantime, Professor Hans Klein, a CDU member of the Bundestag and that party's codetermination expert, called Mr. Vetter's comments unjustified and observed that the chamber merely did its job. However, another CDU official, the chairman of the party's Committee on Social Affairs, Norbert Blum, supported Chancellor Schmidt's other allegation that it all amounted to unacceptable intervention.[28] The whole affair had taken on the proportions of an incident, with the State Department walking a very thin line, trying to stay out of the fracas as much as possible.

On November 25, a meeting was convened in Bonn to which leading German and American trade-union and business executives were invited. Chaired by Ernst-Wolf Mommsen, chairman of the executive board of Krupp, the meeting was held under the auspices of a foundation largely financed by Chancellor Schmidt's Social Democrat party and was conducted under exceptional secrecy. Speeches were apparently made by the chancellor, the finance minister, Dr. Apel, and the minister for overseas aid, Mr. Bahr.[29] The outcome of the meeting was never made known, which is understandable since it appeared to be called merely to inform and facilitate dialogue rather than to negotiate a compromise.

It should be emphasized again and again that the initiatives of the American Chamber did not stand alone. Neither were they necessarily the backbone of management's attacks on the administration's proposal, even though they were undoubtedly a crucial component and/or contributed to the emergence of a compromise law, as described in Chapter 6. There were other briefs, in particular, that presented some real problems for the Schmidt administration: one was by the Berlin jurist Rupert Scholtz; and the other was by the jurist Thomas Raiser. Both legal opinions raised questions about the constitutionality of the legislative proposal. Their objections were based on the basic law's Article 14, which guarantees the right of private property, and Article 9, which deals with organizational autonomy (in the sense that codetermination would make trade-union agents both collective-bargaining agents for the workers as well as partners in the management with whom the bargaining would be conducted).[30]

Several things have happened since the 1976 act went into effect in July 1978. For example, some American firms that were apparently growing to the two-thousand-employee level seem to have contained that growth. Other companies have reorganized in such a way that they are no longer covered by the law. There are also several cases where firms even changed their legal form from a limited-liability company to a general partnership, in which all partners are totally liable.[31]

A number of American firms have become involved in cumbersome disputes with their works councils about the classification of certain jobs for purposes of codetermination representation. Opel management attempted to list five hundred positions as junior executive—the special category from which at least one worker representative should be elected. The works council insisted that only one hundred and fifty jobs should be so classified. Ford, and undoubtedly others, have gone through the same process of classification bargaining.[32]

A more spectacular development has been the nomination and election of several prominent international trade unionists to membership of the supervisory boards of U.S. MNC subsidiaries. In January 1973, Herman Rebhan, the American general secretary of the International Metalworkers Federation, was elected as a representative of Ford Werke workers on that company's supervisory board. Du Pont acquired as one of its board members Charles Levinson, the Canadian general secretary of the International Federation of Chemical, Energy, and General Workers Union.[33] Levinson's election must have been particularly shocking to Du Pont since that firm had been most reluctant to welcome unions to their plants and had not become organized until just a few years earlier. Not only did the company have to learn to deal with a top international labor organizer, it would also be their fate to acquire as a member of the corporation's supervisory board one of the more aggressive critics of multinational enterprise.

A feature of the 1976 law that has caused organized labor a great deal of frustration are the provisions that deal with the *Arbeits Direktor* (the personnel director). In the coal, steel, and iron industries, this management official, who is a member of the management board or *Vorstand*, cannot be appointed unless he is acceptable to the labor representatives on the supervisory board. Trade unions strove to obtain the same guarantee for all codetermination firms; however, they failed to do so. Consequently, in March 1979, a real row occurred at Ford Werke when the representatives of the stockholders on the company's supervisory board insisted on nominating for the position of personnel director a man who had been explicitly identified by the worker representatives as unacceptable to them. Whether the judgment of the worker representatives (that he was arrogant and unable to relate to people) was correct or not, or whether management made the nomination because it felt it was important to curtail union power, the Ford contest turned out to be symbolically very significant. That controversy was not the only one of its kind. A similar situation developed at the General Motors subsidiary, Adam Opel.[34] That type of power testing may have been necessary, though, to get a clearer definition of the implications of the 1976 law until both sides can either obtain changes in the law or until they learn to live with it.

A second major disturbance was created in June 1977, when, only several weeks before the expiration of the constitutional deadline for raising questions of constitutionality, the Federation of German Employers' Associations initiated action in the Federal Constitutional Court. The suit, which was filed by the Federation and by nine individual firms, raised thirty-eight different constitutional questions, including those posed by Professors Scholtz and Raiser in the briefs mentioned earlier. Consequently, several American firms chose not to elect members to their supervisory boards until the court had declared whether or not the law was constitutional. Determination of that issue was finally made on March 1, 1979, when the 1976 Codetermination Law was upheld.[35] The Constitutional Court succinctly stated what it perceived to be the prime prerequisite for a productive codetermination era: "If there exists on both sides a readiness for loyal cooperation, codetermination will have a different result than if the atmosphere in the company is dominated by mutual distrust or hostility."[36] And what the court repeatedly stated was that the special tie-breaking double-vote privilege of the board chairman (ultimately electable by the shareholder representatives) gives the management-shareholder side of the board a guaranteed majority anyway. Thus, parity representation had not really come about.

The greatest frustrations with the codetermination law undoubtedly have been felt by labor and not by management. Management has really won the first phase of the battle, even though it has lost some of its autonomy. After all, management appeared to be on the verge of losing considerably more than it actually did. Although trade unionists have acquired the opportunity to insert some of their top talents into the corporate boardroom, they find themselves simultaneously being divided between blue-collar, white-collar, and managerial employees. They cannot help see the managerial employees' representative as actually a representative of management rather than of the general work force. And with the stockholder-representative board chairman having a double vote in case of a tie, and the possibility that the stockholder majority can appoint an antiunion personnel director, trade unionists wonder who really won the war.

The Netherlands

The American experience in the Netherlands has been somewhat different from that in Germany. That fact was clearly reflected in the findings of a McKinsey and Associates study conducted in 1978. When the Dutch government saw already-eroding foreign investments plummet sharply in 1975 and 1976, it contracted with the American consulting firm to poll some two hundred foreign businessmen to determine their attitudes about doing business in Holland.

McKinsey found that American respondents to their survey were quite critical of the Dutch business environment. Not only did they indicate that the country had a limited market, they also expressed concern about the lengthy bureaucratic procedures of Dutch officials, the behavior and attitudes of Dutch workers, and the extensive social policies protecting the workers. Their main complaints were that high wage and social-insurance costs were coupled with relatively unimpressive productivity and high absenteeism. What appeared to antagonize foreign investors most distinctively was the excess-profits tax proposed by organized labor (see Chapter 6). It seemed as if foreign investors perceived this particular proposal as the most clear-cut manifestation of the increasing assertiveness of Dutch trade unionists. In another survey, taken a year earlier, 40 percent of the foreign investors said they would cut their present investment or quit Holland if the proposal were enacted into law. Sixty percent said they would expand no further under such circumstances.[37]

The combativeness of the Dutch trade unions has also definitely left its imprint on the manner in which the works councils have operated in that country. Most striking is the way in which the councils have become virtually duplicated by plant-level union committees. Thus, in firms whose workers are organized (and that includes a number of American companies), a fair amount of confusion has developed over the respective jurisdictions and postures of these two bodies. Statutorily, the works councils should be supreme; in fact, the union consultative committees have turned out to be the more assertive entities.

In contrast, the works councils have frequently been very effective in nonunionized plants, where they have developed into important channels of communication and have become valuable ways of obtaining worker support for company policies and/or of handling worker grievances. Accordingly, most American managers, both in unionized and in nonunionized plants, did not consider the councils to be very objectionable, provided the plant manager maintained his right to chair the works council and the right to nominate candidates does not become limited to just trade unions. They know that such changes in the system could eliminate management's opportunity to use the works council as a device to prevent worker unionization, a purpose the current council can and does serve, whether one likes it or not.

There are, of course, always exceptions to the generally positive attitude of American managers. A significant number of managers of younger firms, of firms that are labor-intensive, and those managers who work for the more ethnocentric companies have not always been very supportive of the works-council structure. Many of them find the councils to be time-consuming and not very productive. A number of them complain that they have to spend great amounts of time on trivia. Others are concerned that worker representatives are not able to understand the financial and economic data supplied them.

Firms like IBM have tried to deal with this problem by setting up training programs for works councillors. The Dutch government encourages such training programs by helping to defray their costs. Funds for these purposes are made possible through a levy imposed on employers with works councils, and they are extended to firms, unions, and other agencies that conduct training programs approved by the staff of the Social-Economic Council, a tripartite national structure composed of representatives of government, labor, and employers.

In spite of everything, including such remedial training programs, managers who see themselves above all as professionals (as American expatriates are especially apt to do because they have frequently attended professional management schools) still seem to prefer being free of the works councils. At the same time, as was the case with certain subsidiaries in Germany, a number of these professionals tend to admit that some of their own decisions are now made with considerably more care and forethought than when they were not expected to give continuous and thorough accounting to the works council. In addition, some recognize that the council structure has given the charismatic manager an excellent chance of projecting himself and his decisions—a much better opportunity than would have been possible if he had to rely only on his subordinates, on written materials, on an occasional shop-floor conversation, or on a not-always-impartial trade-union official.

Worker representation on supervisory boards in Holland is not really much of a problem for American subsidiaries for two reasons. First, the law is really very limited in its application. Basically, it only provides for a works-council veto in cases where management nominates someone who will bring the board into noticeable imbalance. Works councils have rarely exercised this right, particularly since the supervisory board can appeal their objection, and also because management appears to have exercised considerable care not to create unnecessary conflict situations. The second reason Americans have not been extremely concerned about this veto power is the special status the law gives to subsidiaries of foreign multinational corporations. The Dutch have, in effect, placed more weight on the efficient operation of a multinational enterprise than on the capacity of workers to influence board decisions.[38] Thus, the jurisdiction of the supervisory boards of subsidiaries is limited by their being allowed to defer the appointment of the subsidiary's managing board and the approval of the subsidiary's budget to the supervisory board of the parent company. All this makes the effects of so-called worker participation on the company board severely limited insofar as American companies are concerned. It is, therefore, not surprising that foreign firms, including those headquartered in the States, have fewer works-council-approved board members than do the Dutch companies.

The difference between the American experience in the Netherlands and that in Germany is partly the result of the differences in the political profiles of the American business communities in the two countries. The American Chamber of Commerce in the Netherlands has maintained a much lower profile. Some of this is undoubtedly due to the different styles of the respective AmCham general managers. While Paul C. Baudler served for more than twenty-five years as chief executive in Frankfurt, the American Chamber in Holland was not even organized until 1962. In addition, the organization's office in The Hague has had at least two managers since its inception, and both of these have defined the chamber's and their personal political roles in much less vigorous terms than was the case with Mr. Baudler. While some may argue that the business community in Holland did not experience the sort of frontal attack as occurred with the German Codetermination Act, others would point out that the 1976 excess-profit-taxation proposal amounted to an equally obnoxious deprivation of the right to enjoy the fruits of one's private property. Regardless of whether the issues facing the two communities were equally challenging or not, American business leadership in the Netherlands has tended to act politically on an individual basis or through such organizations as the Association of Dutch Employers rather than the American Chamber. As mentioned earlier, American businessmen appear to have responded to Dutch policy issues primarily through their investment decisions rather than through direct lobbying activities.

One of the few times the American business community in Holland engaged in political action was in 1976, when the Dutch government announced its intention to legislate that management could no longer be part of the works council (only when the council convened a consultative meeting). It was simultaneously suggested that, in the future, works councils would be able to avail themselves of both the personnel and the resources of the trade unions. Immediately after these proposals were aired, employer organizations and individual American subsidiary managers were activated to use all available channels of indirect and informal communication to inform appropriate government officials of their objections. Another rather subtle tactic, initiated and executed by individual subsidiary managers, was to push for the early release of a preliminary report of a study commissioned to a leading academic research institute that was expected to, and did, show that most Dutch workers were satisfied with the prevailing methods of operation of the works councils. Worker satisfaction was reported to include both features that the government's reforms were designed to alter: the council's composition and its jurisdiction.[39] The campaign against the government proposal also included a number of well-placed newspaper stories showing how American investments in Western Europe, and Holland in particular, were on the decrease, and how the Dutch seemed to be pricing themselves out of the foreign-investment market.

The subtlety and low profile of AmCham The Netherlands is partly reflected in the sort of workshops they have organized. In March 1976, for example, the chamber contracted with Dialog, the public-communications division of the J. Walter Thompson organization, to conduct a workshop in the art of communicating with press, government, employees, consumer groups, and TV commentators. The program's prime objective was to facilitate a more effective corporate-management response to public criticisms of multinational business. The instructional program, therefore, included taped interviews both "before and after" so that a participant's progress could be measured. Thus, helpful hints were given on how one might want to respond to difficult and hostile questions.

Comments about the American experience with worker participation in the Netherlands made by American subsidiary managers and officials of the Dutch government, trade unions, and employer organizations are fairly parallel with those made about their experience with works councils in Germany. The main difference seemed to be that American managers were clearly appreciative of the fact that, in Holland, trade unions had not been able to monopolize works-council nominations, and that the Dutch works-council structure could be used to keep unions out of the shop or refinery. Trade unionists were apt to underscore their perception that certain American firms had obviously made optimum use of that latter possibility.

Belgium

The fact that the American experience with worker participation has not been nearly as substantive in Belgium as it has been in Germany and the Netherlands is reflected in a variety of ways. For instance, opinion surveys of Americans working there do not even include questions about the worker-participation issue. In one survey conducted in the mid-seventies, American managers were asked a series of questions regarding their expectations about possible Belgian government actions. The list of possibilities included the requirement of more financial disclosure, the repeal of the financial and fiscal benefits available to multinational corporations, a limit on the amount of earnings that can be returned to the parent firm, and the requirement to increase R & D expenditures in Belgium. Nothing was asked about managerial expectations concerning changes in worker-participation requirements.[40] Surveys of this kind obviously focus on issues that are of current concern to the business community. The Belgian government and trade unions simply have not shown much interest in making substantive alterations in the nation's worker-participation scheme. Thus, there was not really any need to measure the American reaction to an impending threat. The absence of such questions also indicates, however, that there does not appear to be any substantial discontent about the existing requirements and practices.

American firms have been more concerned about such manifestations of worker radicalism as plant occupations and demands for autogestion (total worker control of factories) than about such relatively moderate and innocuous forms of worker activism as works councils and safety and health committees. Even though calls for worker self-government have been anything but unanimous and far from viable, the same thing cannot be said about the phenomenon of worker occupations.

The two most publicized cases are those of Prestige and Badger. In 1976, Prestige, a subsidiary of American Home Products, wanted to close a plant with a work force of about three hundred. Trade unionists responded to the initiative by conducting a lengthy sit-in. The company, nevertheless, held out, closed the plant, and pulled out of the country. The Badger case, which occurred two years later, was almost identical. The main difference was that this Raytheon subsidiary was not only severely criticized in the Belgian and West European media for its plant closing, it was also reported to the Committee on Multinational Corporations of the OECD (Organization for Economic Cooperation and Development). It was reported as a violation of the OECD's 1976 Code of Conduct for Multinational Corporations. It seems logical to suggest that the type of confrontations Prestige and Badger experienced might have been avoided if the communications through the Prestige and Badger works councils could have been more effective. Kassalow, in his ILO report on the industrial-relations behavior of multinational corporations in the food and metal industries, concluded that such seems to be the case in most incidents of severe deterioration of industrial relations.[41]

The experience of American enterprises in Belgium has also been affected by the fact that most of them have been rather heavily unionized, and that the nation's union system is ideologically fragmented. As such, they have been subjected to a variety of cross-pressures. First, most trade unionists are not very interested in works councils and even less in codetermination. Socialist trade unionists are particularly inclined to consider them capitalist ruses, especially as long as management can make up as much as 49 percent of the works-council membership. They would rather reform the total political-economic system than become integrated into it. The only form of worker participation that socialists could live with is autogestion, and Belgian and

American entrepreneurs certainly would not tolerate that. Worker self-government of the workplace will only occur if and when the entire social, economic, and political order of Belgium were to be altered. That does not seem to be a significant probability in the foreseeable future.

Most members of the American business community in Belgium have quietly adapted to local worker-participation practices. They have focused their political activities on issues that are more important to them, and such activities have tended to be amiable, behind-the-scenes interactions rather than those that are confrontationist in nature. That general posture is clearly reflected in the low profile of the American Chamber of Commerce in Brussels. However, AmCham's Legislative Affairs Committee has definitely been active; it has prepared position papers and organized and conducted informal consultations with appropriate officials. All this activity has been highly rational, and, although its message may have been forceful at times, it does not appear to have ever become threatening or confrontational. The Brussels office, which would have been in a natural position to become the rallying point for lobbying activity by American business on the European Commission, has adamantly refused to be part of any united-front position taken by the American Chambers in Europe. Mr. Baudler, manager of the AmCham Frankfurt office, has been hoping that it would change its mind.

France

Not much more can be said about the American experience with worker participation in France than was said about the experience in Belgium. Since French trade unions have placed much more emphasis on their employee delegates than on effective participation in the works councils, and have generally been opposed to participatory opportunities, American managers have had mixed experiences. A number of them speak rather patronizingly about the worker representatives in their plants. Having had to deal with harassment and confrontations, they almost make it seem as if they tolerate the playful and tantrum-like behavior of the works councillors rather than that they consider them to be viable elements in managerial decision making.

Most American companies have, nevertheless, established the legally required structures, which was borne out in the ILO study of multinationals in the petroleum industry.[42] It should be underscored, however, that in France, the company-level works councils meet only twice a year: there is a meeting in the spring to discuss the annual report and a meeting in the fall to discuss the company's prospects. It is understandable, then, that the evaluation by union officials at the John Deere subsidiary was rather negative; their conclusion was that the unions have no real participation in company decision making. For those companies where works-council members sit on the company board, the verdict was not different. Again, the general consensus was that they had very little real impact, and that management felt very few obligations toward worker representatives.

The more viable worker-participation procedures used by American companies in France are not the ones generally described under that rubric. One of these "other vehicles" is the employee survey, which Esso-Standard S.A. France, an Exxon subsidiary, has been administering since 1968.[43] The first survey resulted in a variety of new company practices, particularly in some significant changes in the company's internal communication patterns. One of these was the decision to disseminate information regarding works-council meetings more quickly. Another American subsidiary that began using the survey method at the same time is IBM France. Each year, one or several divisions of all IBM European subsidiaries are surveyed. The company then publishes for its employees the global results, with comparative data broken out for the various subsidiary locations. The surveys are used to identify problems in the organization. Similar processes have been followed at Minnesota de France, Rank Xerox (the European subsidiary of Xerox), Singer, Pfizer, and Bull-General Electric, to name a few. The introduction of employee surveys appears to confirm that there are distinct deficiencies in the communication that takes place through the works councils and the works councillors on the company boards, and it certainly suggests that corporate management does not seem to benefit from two-way communication through the formal participation structures. The gnawing question remains: What might be to blame for this—union and/or managerial obstinacy or a lack of patience and tact on both sides?

An interesting twist to the worker-participation scheme for multinational corporations was suggested in the previously mentioned Sudreau Report. It recommended that such companies send a representative from corporate headquarters to their French subsidiaries. That person's job would be to establish a direct communication link between the firm's works council(s) in France and the company's global managers.[44] Action on the proposal was first postponed until after the 1978 elections; it has not yet been enacted. It has been very difficult to determine whether any American firm has put the suggestion into practice.

United Kingdom

The industrial-relations experience of American subsidiaries in the United Kingdom has been earmarked by both cooperation and confrontation. There are, accordingly, a number of firms that have developed machinery for labor-management consultation that has proven to be very successful. Other companies have histories of virtually endless labor disputes and of dismal worker productivity. Contrasts not only exist between individual companies, but there are regions and industrial sectors where things have been quite stable and others where the description "chaotic" seems most appropriate. It is, in fact, more risky to generalize about the state of American industrial relations in the United Kingdom than it is for virtually any other West European country. This is partly because industrial relations in Britain were unregulated for so long and then became regulated only in a limited way.

One sector that shows some rather interesting differences among firms is the automobile industry. General Motors is the prototype of a firm with a very stable industrial-relations record in Britain. Trade unionists have repeatedly reported that they feel considerably involved in consultative and negotiating machinery at GM's Vauxhall plant, even though they recognize that their influence is mainly limited to questions of industrial relations. The same favorable comments are not generally heard about Ford and Chrysler.

The Ford Motor Company has been experiencing serious labor-relations problems in the United Kingdom since the early sixties. A number of people have even suggested that the Ford plant at Dagenham has had the worst labor-relations record of any U.S.-owned factory in Europe.[45] Somewhat typical of the confrontations that occur from time to time at Dagenham is the three-week strike that took place at the end of June 1977. That strike began when a production-line worker, who was operating an automatic welding machine, refused to change his way of doing his job on the grounds that following company job prescriptions would hurt his wrist. He was suspended for three days. Immediately, some seventy fellow workers walked out and observed a three-day sympathy strike. Management responded by laying off a number of these people. As a result, things got out of hand. What really seemed to become the symbolic core of the problem was the fact that not one of the laid-off workers or the sixteen thousand other Ford workers who were idled as a consequence of the row was paid any compensation. Feelings grew more bitter each day, and the strike turned into a virtual catastrophe. All this seemed to be an unpleasant aftereffect of the September 1976 "riot" when Dagenham body workers did more than $30,000 damage to the managers' dining room.[46]

While conditions have generally been most unpleasant for Ford in Dagenham, the same has not been true in the company's plants in Wales, particularly in the transmission plant at Swansea. Henry Ford seemed to suggest that the labor peace at Swansea was mostly the result of the excellent work of Brian Phillips and Terry Bennett, the two main shop stewards at the plant. Mr. Ford is also rumored to have said that Welsh workers are more intelligent than those in England.[47] The company's relatively good experience in Wales must have contributed significantly to the decision, in September 1977, to build a new engine plant there, with the recognized intention of having that plant's production replace a substantial proportion of the output of the

Dagenham engine plant. The company's estimate of what sort of labor trouble it might possibly experience, even in Wales, is evident from the plant's design. Production and quality control at the new plant were designed to become so automated that the plant would be virtually immune from the sort of disruptions that have been experienced at other company assembly plants.

Chrysler-U.K.'s story was somewhat different, although not much. While Ford's Escort, Cortina, and Fiesta turned out to be smash hits and while Ford dominated the U.K. truck market, Chrysler was not able to find the right product formula. At the same time, their labor problems were not much different from those at Ford's Dagenham plant.

It is true that Chrysler became involved in Britain much later than the other American car makers. The company also became somewhat obligated to the British government, primarily because of the conditions imposed by the government when Chrysler bought into the Rootes firm. This latter condition did not enable the firm to have the flexibility it needed to reach its potential. Whatever the various complications were, though, the company did not serve its own good interests by the way it related to its workers and the general public. Young and Hood are not the only analysts who have observed that Chrysler "seemed to overreact in its handling of disputes," and was guilty of having committed "a series of heavy-handed and ill-considered actions."[48]

What is so interesting about the Chrysler story, though, is not what happened in those early years, but rather how things have gone since 1973. First, in 1973, after the so-called shoddy-work strike at Ryon, the company established a joint union-management committee charged with monitoring plant output quality and quantity. When this turned out to be successful, the company surveyed all their U.K. employees to determine the extent to which they were interested in further participation opportunities. They found, to their surprise, that in several plants, *all* the workers expressed such an interest. The company was again hit by severe strikes in May 1975, which seemed to be the right time to take the next step. That summer the company offered to introduce an elaborate worker-participation scheme if the unions would agree to synchronized, centralized collective bargaining. They would also have to agree that all future strikes would be subject to settlement by arbitration. It was quite a package, although cynics readily suggested that it was merely a part of the company's diplomatic prelude to the dance that would finally result in the Labour government's bailing out of Chrysler.[49]

Chrysler's proposal to the workers was to set up plant-level employee committees, which, in turn, would select members for a central company-wide council of twenty-five people. One member of the council, and its chairman, would be Don Lander, Chrysler-U.K.'s managing director. The companywide council, in turn, would appoint two directors to the company's thirteen-member board. It also provided that the unions would fill the committee positions and that white-collar workers would be provided separate representation. The company tried to entice the workers to support the proposal by offering to pay each worker fifty pounds if they consented to the general idea by September 1975 and another fifty pounds if they accepted the details by December.[50]

Another American firm that has done some interesting things in Britain is Albright & Wilson, a chemical subsidiary of Tenneco. In 1975, it followed the example of the British chemical giant, Imperial Chemical Industries, Ltd., by working out an arrangement in which union leaders would be members of a top management committee and of liaison committees for the company's fourteen divisions.[51] Thus, A & W worker representatives have become involved in making a variety of decisions, some of which extend beyond the traditional realm of industrial-relations questions such as pay, safety, work organization, and training.

It could be rather coincidental, of course, that these and other work reforms were introduced by a number of firms during the same summer in which the Bullock Committee was established. The rhetorical and political value of the reforms became somewhat obvious when the Confederation of British Industry (CBI) made several pronouncements that summer to the effect that codetermination may well have to be considered if Britain wanted to regain its competitive position in world markets. A number of companies found these remarks inspiring, leading them to try some forms of worker participation that would be more acceptable to them. Their interest in reform could also have been linked to the Labour government's determination to legislate worker representation on company boards. It was time for the companies to preempt the government's plans and prove their goodwill by instituting some workplace reforms.

Indirect evidence that a number of other American subsidiaries must have labor-management consultation structures and procedures is derived from a 1977 survey by CBI, which found that 80 percent of the responding firms said that they consulted workers regularly before making changes in working conditions. Seventy percent said they did so before implementing decisions on production and work methods. It was also found that three-fourths of the companies with two thousand or more employees operated formal methods of joint consultation. In addition, 65 percent said they held regular information meetings between supervisors and staff.[52] Although these data do not suggest structures and processes that even resemble German and Dutch works councils, they do reflect a growing tendency among managers to disseminate information to their workers as well as to improve the plant's upward communication system, whether through shop stewards or in some other way.

American subsidiaries have also done a variety of interesting things in the area of employee training. Rank Xerox and Vauxhall, along with a number of strictly independent British companies, have acquired the services of consulting firms that specialize in preparing employee training programs that combine briefings about company affairs with basic education in elementary economics. Ernest Jones, of Mobile Training, describes, for example, that each of their prepared briefings about money and business brings out three main considerations: where employees fit in, why the topic concerns them, and how they could participate. He legitimizes his work by suggesting that it creates "a first vital state of understanding to any scheme of participation," which he presumably expects to develop increasingly in the United Kingdom.[53]

As suggested before, certain industrial sectors in Britain appear to have been more inclined to consult with worker representatives than have others. We have already mentioned Albright & Wilson and ICI, whose participation innovations are representative of what is happening in a number of other labor-intensive chemical companies. Fairly good interaction exists also in a number of metalworking industries. At Caterpillar and at Otis, for example, trade unionists have observed that the shop-steward committees have been able to exert a fair amount of influence over plant-level decisions.[54] In the petroleum industry, trade unions report having influence on company decisions at the refineries at all levels, from shop floor to boardroom. The same thing is not being said about conditions at exploration and production operations. There appear to be some real communication problems, for instance, at off-shore oil rigs, particularly those of foreign-owned oil companies.[55]

We should remember that a considerable segment of British trade unionists have a lot more in common with their French and Italian peers than with their northern European peers. They perceive these consultation structures and procedures to be mostly management-initiated. To them, they are clever devices to divert the attention of the workers and society at large away from the basic problems of management selfishness and callousness. As Marxists, they consider nationalization to be the only acceptable answer to the malaise of the working class. And, what actually may be more important to emphasize is the fact that British workers feel a far greater degree of alienation from and distrust for management than is found in most other northern European countries. To the alienated, embittered Marxists, American subsidiaries are especially irritating; they see them as prototypes of the capitalist economic system that they feel has exploited them. Some are even convinced that so much American direct investment has come to Britain because labor costs are much lower there than on the Continent, and because companies have been able to get by with considerably more questionable practices there.

ORGANIZATIONAL RESPONSES TO THE WORKER-PARTICIPATION MOVEMENT

The concerns of the American business community in Europe are not limited to compliance with the local worker-participation laws as they apply to their workplaces and their boardrooms. Many companies have already learned to live with them, although some have done so grudgingly. What worries many American expatriates and corporate headquarters of U.S.-based multinational corporations are the various proposals for expanding earlier amending the current participation requirements. The incident described above, involving the American Chamber of Commerce in Germany, illustrates what sort of response is engendered by such demands for reform. There are, however, a variety of other ways in which companies and business organizations have reacted to work initiatives.

Many multinational firms have realized that they must first put their own houses in order. That discovery, in turn, has frequently included the realization that the company's interests require that it develop and maintain the best possible relations with the variety of entities that impact upon it. Several of them, therefore, have established in-house staffs for conducting external affairs—that is, rough equivalents of a ministry of foreign affairs or a state department. It is interesting that much of this type of organizing has occurred in Europe, and a fair amount of it has been by subsidiaries of American multinationals.

Such external-affairs staffs are given a variety of responsibilities: most basic is their intelligence function. They are generally expected to have a detailed awareness of all those economic, social, and political conditions and anticipated changes that impact on their company, and to transmit such information to appropriate corporate officials. Their second task is to define what some have called "the area of good corporate citizenship" in each country where they operate. This is done to enable the company to develop, on the basis of that profile, a set of company policies and programs that allow it to exist in harmony with its environment. Monsanto Europe has gone one step further in this area: its director of corporate affairs has developed a book showing Monsanto's contributions to the various locales where it operates. This serves as a convenient tool for company executives in projecting a more accurate image to national authorities, EEC officials, and others.[56]

The third function of external-affairs staffs is to develop and make top-level contacts with other companies whose interest is related to that of their firm, with relevant public officials, with trade associations, and with business organizations. Not least of its tasks is to present the company's views wherever that seems appropriate. The general admonition that management consultants have given about these latter two tasks is to avoid adversary attitudes as much as possible, to seek the opportunities in every challenge, and to anticipate or preact rather than to defend and react.[57]

External-affairs staffs are certainly not maintained by all U.S. corporations doing business in Europe. Their presence or absence is clearly related to the size of the operation, the nature of its product or service, and the degree of impact that external entities have on the business. In cases where there are external-affairs staffs, they are apt to be of fairly good size, though. The French subsidiary of a major U.S. oil company, for instance, has a staff of about thirty people, and this unit is only one of several responsible to the external-relations director for the European region.[58]

It is not surprising that a corps of consulting firms has emerged to provide support services for external-affairs staffs and/or to substitute for such a staff for those companies that have not established one. One of these organizations is International Business-Government Counsellors, Inc. Founded in 1972, this firm originally focused on Washington, but it has now also established a European regional office in Brussels and representative offices in Geneva and Paris.[59] The firm not only counsels, it also publishes biweekly reports. One of these is the *Brussels Report*, which reports on European Economic Community activities, including its initiatives on worker participation. Each newsletter has a supplement, which provides guidance about how the EEC is organized, announcements about personnel changes at the commission, reports on specific EEC policies, and exclusive interviews with top EEC officials. The firm's other newsletter is the *Washington International Business Report*, which does basically the same thing with regard to the U.S. government. Also relevant is IBGC's MNC monitoring service, which provides a complete tracing of the regulatory intentions and activities of all relevant international organizations, including the EEC. Thus, there are very few reasons why a company that is interested in more effective participation in local and regional communities, as a strategy toward continued business success, cannot improve its external relations.

Some of the American firms that are reputed to have the most sophisticated EEC-monitoring operations in Brussels are Ford, Union Carbide, IBM, and Goodyear.[60] Other companies are not idle, but they probably have such activities submerged in their European headquarters in Brussels (such as ITT and Monsanto) or they have their executives or external-affairs representatives make frequent calls on EEC officials.

There is a third organizational response American businessmen have made: participation in employer organizations and/or trade associations. Several of these organizations, many of which came into being at the turn of the century as responses to the growing strength of trade unions, have a considerable amount of political power. One of the most legendary and most powerful of the national employer organizations is the Patronat (Conseil National du Patronat Français). It was the Patronat that apparently kept the Giscard d'Estaing government from enacting some of its worker-participation programs. It certainly was successful in keeping the government out of the collective-bargaining process.[61] Equally aggressive and successful have been the BDI (the Federation of German Industry) and the BDA (the Federation of German Employers), particularly under the leadership of the assassinated Dr. Hanns-Martin Schleyer, who, until his death, was simultaneously the president of both organizations.

Some observers have suggested that European employer associations have become the vanguard of an increasingly determined managerial backlash to government intervention. The case of the Confederation of British Industries exemplifies this possibility. This organization of some eight hundred companies and eighty affiliated trade associations really changed in the middle seventies. It has not only stepped up its membership-recruitment activities and expanded its staff and its databank, but it has also abandoned its strictly ideological rhetoric and become more sophisticated in its positions. CBI's decision in 1977 to begin convening annual conferences was an interesting strategy. It calculated that, in this way, employers might eventually obtain the same degree of publicity that, until then, was received only by the annual conferences of the Trade Union Congress, the Labour party, and the Conservative party. The annual conferences were judged to be important also as stimulators of heightened employer solidarity.

The managerial counteroffensive has taken a variety of other forms. The British Institute of Management, for instance, decided it was time to abandon its status as a charitable organization; such a conversion would allow it to engage in overt political activity. Another interesting move in Britain was the establishment of such entities as the Industry and Parliament Trust. Established in 1977, the trust arranges a kind of cultural-exchange program between businessmen and members of Parliament. Businessmen are brought to Westminster for detailed instruction in the workings of the British government and public policymaking. MPs are given twenty-five-day internships in business firms, where, among other things, they participate in simulations of business decision making.

Membership in employer and industrial associations has not been taken out by all American firms in Europe. The rate of affiliation appears to be related to a variety of factors. Which firms affiliate depends, first, on the customs and the industrial-relations systems of the host countries. Almost equally important is the industrial sector of which the firm is a part. In Germany, for example, the proportion of industrial firms, banks, and insurance companies (domestic and foreign) that are affiliated with employer associations is estimated to be higher than 80 percent. The company's general posture is another important variable. General Motors, for example, is typical of the relatively few firms that are members of employer associations in all countries where they have plants. Ford is much more selective.

It should be understood that even though some firms do affiliate with associations, they do not necessarily play active roles. There are some executives, however, who are active. Once in a while, an executive of an American firm shows up as the chairman of an employer association's working group on multinational corporations, as chairman of a national industrial association, or as a leader of a task force on a particular policy question. Such activism may well be a function of the length of time the person or the firm has been operative in a location. Many of the associations have traditionally been dominated by old local elites.

Occasionally, U.S. subsidiaries couple their indirect political action through industrial and employer associations with direct personal communication. In October 1978, for example, Ford, Esso, Kodak, Rank Xerox, and five other firms cosigned a memorandum to the British Department of Trade, predicting a deterioration of the investment climate in that country if Parliament were to enact the recommendations contained in the government's white paper on industrial democracy.[62]

A structure that has played an important role in the European business community's efforts to moderate union demands for worker participation is UNICE, the Union of Industries of the European Community. This union of national employers and industrial associations is committed to the strengthening of solidarity within the European industrial community and seeks to stimulate the development of an acceptable industrial policy for the European Community. Its major task is obviously to attain these goals through pronouncements and educational programming, whenever and wherever they are deemed advisable. One of the union's pronouncements took the form of a 1975 resolution by UNICE's Council of Presidents on the subject of worker participation. In this action, the council urged businessmen in the several European Community countries to oppose the adoption of any new far-reaching measures that would bring that country's worker-participation practices out of line with those practiced in the other EEC countries. This action was clearly meant to support BDI's and BDA's opposition to their national government's proposed codetermination law. UNICE has also made several statements outlining its reservations about the European Company Statute proposal and the worker-participation provisions contained in it.

There has been another organizational response to the growing power of European trade unionism and the worker-participation movement. Billed as a service organization to "enhance the competitive strength of European industry," it purports to offer "business leaders a wide range of opportunities to work together in a spirit of cooperation to find innovative solutions to their problems and to develop new organizational problems for the future." The European Management Forum claims that, in the first six years of its operation, more than nine thousand business leaders participated in its activities.[63] The forum's annual Davos Symposium draws as many as 450 captains of industry and is now frequently said to be the most prestigious European business conference.[64] In February 1980, it heard presentations by such divergent personalities as Henry Kissinger, Luciano Lama, an Italian Communist trade-union leader, and a Chinese trade delegation. The 1978 forum theme was "Successful Enterprise in an Adverse Environment: The Challenge for Innovative Management." These samples make it clear that the forum, its programs, and its publications have come to play an important part in the European business community's counteroffensive against its challengers.

ARE EUROPEANS FLEEING?

Several years ago, *The Economist* ran a story entitled "Let's Go Where the Unions Aren't." It reported that foreign investment appeared to be shifting from the mideastern region of the United States to the southern states. References were made to a "business climate" study prepared by the industrial consulting division of Dun and Bradstreet, which rated the states of the Union. Rated least attractive were New York, California, Massachusetts, and Delaware. Most attractive were Texas, Alabama, Virginia, South Dakota, South Carolina, North Carolina, Florida, and Arkansas. All of these latter states have right-to-work laws, and their rates of unionization range from 7 to 19 percent. South Carolina, which, at that time, seemed to be the most successful Pied Piper, had already acquired some seventy firms; among these were Hoechst (Germany), Sandoz (Switzerland), Michelin (France), and ICI (United Kingdom). Robert Will, a site-selection consultant from Cleveland, was quoted as having observed that "foreigners are terrified about being unionized."[65] All this does not prove that European entrepreneurs make the escape from European worker participation a primary consideration in their decision to invest in the United States. What it suggests, nevertheless, is that European entrepreneurs very much appreciate the lower rates of unionization. It could also indicate that they really might not want to deal with the type of industrial relations that American trade unions tend to bring about. It might even be possible that the drift to the southern states signifies an appreciation for that region's more conservative culture, where the advocacy of free enterprise is not as readily undermined by ridicule from progressive academics and journalists.

Any inferences made about the influence U.S. industrial-relations practices and labor costs have had on the decisions by European firms to invest in the

States need to be qualified by the realization that a considerable number of such investments have been acquisitions. These have happened because the dollar has been weak, the stock market depressed, and American investors easily tempted. A number of owners who were accustomed to maximizing their profits just could not believe the prices they were being offered. Neither did they understand why they should turn down such offers when it would take them some time and a lot of hard work to make that much money. European investors have generally taken a more long-range perspective. Many of them have not made much profit in their first years of operating in the States; they have generally been content to establish a presence, to lay a solid base, and to wait for the eventual big payoff. They know the American market is strong, despite recessions, and they consider the political climate much safer. In other words, a number of them undoubtedly welcome the opportunity to get into the manufacturing business here because they believe that the risk of eventual nationalization is smaller than it is anywhere else. They do not foresee any significant leftist movement in America's future, either, at least nothing comparable to what they have experienced in Europe.

Some choice quotes have been used to prove that many European firms are fleeing to the United States. Critics of European worker-participation practices find considerable satisfaction, therefore, from statements such as the following one made in 1976 by Herbert Hergeth. The president of Hergeth KG, a German manufacturer of textile machinery, one of the first foreign businesses to establish a subsidiary plant in South Carolina, reportedly said: "The right of the worker to interfere in Germany makes it nearly impossible for good management to handle a company. According to law, the worker can decide who gets the job, who gets fired; they can look at the financial statements and even tell us what machine to buy."[66] Undoubtedly, some will suggest that Herr Hergeth's observation was somewhat prejudiced and should be seen as part of the rhetoric that was so strident in Germany in the middle sixties. A recent study also mentioned, though, that European investors considered American trade unionists more flexible and less interested in participating in management decisions than were their peers in Europe. This consideration ranked closely behind a liking for the large American market, the healthier free-enterprise system, the desire to diversify geographically, and the realization that U.S. labor costs were no longer unfavorable.[67]

Basically, European investments in the United States may not signify a flight from worker participation. It cannot be denied, however, that European companies have seen greater long-range profitability in the U.S. market than at home, and that such a calculation is partly derived from their view of the American political-economic system. That view includes a judgment about the trade-union culture and the possibility that one can do business on this side of the Atlantic without trade-union interference and/or presence.

CONCLUSIONS

Even though not all American multinationals have reacted in the same way, many of them have experienced virtual culture shock on finding themselves having to adjust their management practices to the local laws and practices of worker participation. Most companies have learned to live with it, though. In a few cases, in fact, they have found works councils to be a vehicle that enabled them to block out or circumvent trade unions. A considerable number of firms will even admit that the communication and consultation patterns imposed on them may well have raised the quality of plant and office management.

The general composure that American firms have maintained on the subject (possibly excluding the American Chamber of Commerce in Germany) has tended to crumble, however, when worker participation becomes trade-union controlled and when worker presence on the company board edges to the point of parity between shareholder-management and worker representatives. The general attitude of most American expatriates undoubtedly involves some latent animosity, particularly if they perceive the European practices to be mere stepping-stones to the eventual nationalization of their enterprises. To many of them, European forms of worker participation in management are basically un-American.

NOTES

1. The total number of German and foreign firms affected by the law is only around 650.
2. Herbert J. Chruden and Arthur W. Sherman, Jr., *Personnel Practices of American Companies in Europe* (Washington, D.C.: American Management Association, 1972), pp. 79-80.
3. Ibid., p. 85.
4. *The Economist*, September 10, 1977, survey p. 25.
5. Mira Wilkins, *The Maturing of the Multinational Enterprise: American Business Abroad from 1914 to 1970* (Cambridge: Harvard University Press, 1974), pp. 416 ff., and Howard V. Perlmutter, "Towards Research on the Development of Nations, Unions and Firms as Worldwide Institutions," in Hans Günter, *Transnational Industrial Relations* (London: Macmillan-St. Martin's Press, 1972), pp. 28 ff. Wilkins calls the first stage "monocentric"; Perlmutter, "ethnocentric."
6. Somewhat typical of the use of home-country nationals are the following figures about the managerial staffs of MNC subsidiaries located in Belgium. Ninety percent of personnel and research managers were Belgian, 60 percent of general managers or controllers and 40 percent of managing directors were also Belgian. See Commission of the European Communities, *Multinational Undertakings and Community Regulations*, Bulletin of the European Communities, Supplement 15/73, p. 24. At about the same time, the Ford Motor Company reported that only two of its thirty national companies have U.S. expatriates in the employee-relations position.

Robert Copp, "Ford Motor Company as a Multinational Employer," *Monthly Labor Review* 96 (Aug. 1973): 455.

7. Quoted in "The Worker's Voice," *The Wall Street Journal*, January 23, 1977, p. 21.

8. James Furlong, *Labor in the Boardroom: The Peaceful Revolution* (Princeton, N.J.: Dow Jones Books, 1977), p. 120.

9. These observations were also made to the author by various subsidiary managers. They have been reported as well by George S. McIsaac and Herbert Henzler in "Codetermination: A Hidden Noose for MNCs," *Columbia Journal of World Business* 9 (Winter 1974): 73, and *The Economist*, September 10, 1977, survey pp. 27 and 28.

10. International Labour Organisation, *Social and Labour Practices of Multinational Enterprises in the Petroleum Industry* (Geneva: ILO, 1977), pp. 26, 27, and 88.

11. International Labour Organisation, *Social and Labour Practices of Some U.S.-Based Multinational Corporations in the Metal Trades* (Geneva: ILO, 1977), p. 85.

12. Sydney Paulden, "Industrial Democracy at Work in Germany," *The Times*, May 30, 1977, p. 22. For the statutory provisions, see *Co-determination in the Federal Republic of Germany* (Bonn: The Federal Minister of Labour and Social Affairs, 1978).

13. Robert Ball, "The Hard Hats in Europe's Boardrooms," *Fortune* 93 (June 1976): 183.

14. *Wall Street Journal*, February 23, 1973, p. 21.

15. Daniel Benedict, "Labour and the Multinationals" (Paper presented at the International Conference on Trends in Industrial and Labour Relations, Montreal, 24-28 May 1976), p. 14.

16. McIsaac and Henzler, p. 69.

17. An interesting and detailed history of these developments is contained in David T. Fisher's "Worker Participation in West German Industry," *Monthly Labor Review* 101 (May 1978): 59-63.

18. See Bundesvereinigung der deutschen Arbeitsgeberverbände, *Stellungsnahme des Arbeitskreises Mitbestimmung zum Bericht der Sachverständigenkommission: Mitbestimmung im Unternehmen* (Bundestagsrucksache VI/334).

19. Press release from the American Chamber of Commerce, Frankfurt, March 29, 1973.

20. *Die Welt*, October 15, 1974 (as cited in Uda Mayer, "Paritätische Mitbestimmung und Völkerrecht, December 1974, p. 772).

21. "Amerikanische Handelskammer weist DGB-Polemik zurück," *AAC Information*, April 10, 1974.

22. Ibid.

23. *Völkerrechtliche Zulassigkeit der Anwendung des geplanten Mitbestimmungsgesetzes auf Amerikanischen Beteiligungen in der Bundesrepublik Deutschland*, August 19, 1974.

24. *Der Spiegel*, October 14, 1974. The campaign budget figure was confirmed also by *The New York Times* on October 19, 1974.

25. *Frankfurter Allgemeine Zeitung*, October 15, 1974.

26. *The New York Times*, October 19, 1974.

27. *Deutsche Press Agenz*, October 16, 1974, 4:10 P.M.

28. Ibid., 5:14 P.M.

29. *The Times*, November 26 and 28, 1974.

30. The most important passages of the briefs are cited in the November 8, 1974, issue of *Wirtschaftswoche*.

31. Furlong, p. 78.

32. Ibid., p. 69.

33. "Two Leading International Trade Unionists Elected to Supervisory Boards," *Social and Labour Bulletin*, no. 2 (1976): 121.

34. *Die Zeit*, March 9, 1979, p. 7.

35. *The Bulletin* (of the Press and Information Office of the Government of the Federal Republic of Germany) 27, no. 7 (March 28, 1979): 44-45. Also see *Die Quelle*, March 1979, pp. 131-36.

36. Quoted in *Wall Street Journal*, March 12, 1979.

37. *The Economist*, December 9, 1978, pp. 86-87, and September 10, 1977, survey p. 28.

38. P. I. Davies, "European Experience with Worker Representation on the Board," in the Industrial Democracy Committee's *Industrial Democracy: The European Experience* (London: H. M. Stationery Office, 1976), p. 72.

39. B. W. M. Hovels and P. Nas, *Ondernemingsraad en Medezeggenschap* (Nijmegen, Netherlands: Institute for Applied Sociology of the University of Nijmegen, 1976).

40. Frederick T. Bent, Etienne Gracco, and Raymond Vuerings, "The Belgian Environment for Multinational Business: Conflicting Perspectives," *Columbia Journal of World Business* 10 (Fall 1975): 128.

41. International Labour Organisation, *Multinationals in Western Europe: The Industrial Relations Experience* (Geneva: ILO, 1975), p. 17.

42. International Labour Organisation, *Social and Labour Practices of Multinational Enterprises in the Petroleum Industry*, p. 77.

43. C. R. Robert, "Opinie-onderzoek by Esso-Standard S.S., France: een vorm van participatie," in Hubert Buntix, *Geengageerde Bedrijfsstructuur* (Den Haag: Nederlandse Vereniging voor Management, 1973), pp. 87-107.

44. *The New York Times*, April 26, 1976. Action on the 1976 proposals has been postponed several times. See also: *Social and Labour Practices of Some U.S.-Based Multinational Corporations in the Metal Trades*, p. 87.

45. See, for example, David E. Ricks, Marilyn Y. C. Yu, and Jeffrey S. Arpan, *International Business Blunders* (Columbus, Ohio: Grid, Inc., 1974), p. 42.

46. Two accounts of the 1977 incidents were in *The Times*, June 18, 1977, and *The Economist*, July 2, 1977.

47. These opinions are attributed to him by Stephen Aris in his most interesting account of the Ford decision to build a new $400-million engine plant at Bridgend in South Wales. "The Battle of Henry's Ear," in *The Sunday Times*, October 9, 1977, p. 17. The Japanese, and Sony in particular, have many good things to say about Welsh workers. Sony has a strike-free record there as well.

48. Stephen Young and Neil Hood, "Multinational and Host Governments: Lessons from the Case of Chrysler UK," *Columbia Journal of World Business* 12 (Summer 1977): 99.

49. On December 16, 1975, it was announced that the British government agreed to underwrite a 72.5 million-pound loss and to loan Chrysler 55 million pounds for

capital investments, and that several leading banks would extend an additional guaranteed loan of 35 million pounds. See John Starrels, "The Dilemmas of Planning: Chrysler and the Wilson Government: Or How Labour Came to Love the Automobile" (Paper presented at the Annual Meeting of the American Political Science Association, Chicago, 1976). Chrysler-U.K. ended up selling out all of the European operations to Peugeot-Citroën in late 1978.

50. *The Economist*, August 30, 1975, p. 66.

51. See *Business Week*, July 14, 1975, pp. 133-34, and *Chemical Week*, July 2, 1975, pp. 30-31.

52. Summarized in the *Social and Labour Bulletin*, no. 1/78, p. 23.

53. *The Times*, November 6, 1978.

54. International Labour Organisation, *Social and Labour Practices of Some U.S.-Based Multinational Corporations in the Metal Trades*, pp. 85, 87, and 88.

55. International Labour Organisation, *Social and Labour Practices of Multinational Enterprises in the Petroleum Industry*, pp. 28-29 and 88-89.

56. J. J. Boddewyn, *Corporate External Affairs* (Geneva: Business International, 1975), p. 89.

57. Ibid., p. 9.

58. Ibid., p. 105.

59. *Multinational Government Relations: An Action Guide for Corporate Management* (Washington, D.C.: International Business-Government Counsellors, Inc., 1977).

60. John Robinson, "MNC's and the EC," *Europe*, no. 216 (Nov.-Dec. 1979): 10.

61. *The Economist*, February 25, 1978, p. 87.

62. *The Sunday Times*, November 5, 1978.

63. European Management Forum's advertisement in *The Economist*, January 21, 1978.

64. *The Economist*, February 9, 1980.

65. *The Economist*, June 4, 1977.

66. *The New York Times*, July 26, 1976.

67. U.S. Senate, Committee on Government Operations, *The Operations of Federal Agencies in Monitoring, Reporting on, and Analyzing Foreign Investments in the United States*, a report, July 30, 1979, p. 211.

8

THE IMPACT ON THE AMERICAN SYSTEM

Since a number of American companies and expatriates have been exposed to, and/or have had to work with, forms of labor-management relations that differ significantly from those practiced in the United States, several questions arise. For example, has there been, or will there likely be, any impact from these experiences on the American industrial-relations system? What, specifically, has this impact been or will it be? Will the impact increase or wane over time? How does the impact relate to the larger area of variables that have been affecting U.S. labor-relations practices and organizational life?

Before such questions can be answered, it should first be reemphasized that those Americans who have worked in Europe have had different worker-participation experiences. Accordingly, those who were assigned to operations in France or Italy have different perceptions of works councils than do those who worked in Germany or Holland. The more striking differences between these two groups concern their awareness of what it means to have worker representatives on the subsidiary's board. Perceptions will vary according to where one works and when one was assigned there. This is especially true of those who were in Germany before 1978 — before "parity" codetermination went into effect — and those who came more recently. We should not ignore, either, the reality that the perceptions of European worker-participation schemes are conditioned to a considerable extent by the socio-political values and personalities of the different expatriates before they ever arrived there. Assuming that there are significant variations in the values and personality types among those who have made corporate management their career, dogmatic advocates of free enterprise would probably consider worker representation on company boards to be undeniable features of revolutionary socialism, while open-minded admirers of alternative life-styles and societal organization might find them interesting avenues to greater human fulfillment. Differences in impact on the expatriates will clearly result also from variations in the political cultures and organizational adaptiveness of the corporations for which they work. The basic point is, therefore, that the experiences of the American expatriates and their impact are far from homogeneous.

The probability that the experiences will not have any Stateside impact whatsoever is extremely low. It is true that of the total pool of managerial manpower in American-based multinationals, only a few have ever worked in Europe; therefore, the number who have had experience with works councils and worker directors is statistically very insignificant. In addition, many who worked in Germany or Holland, the countries that could provide one with the more substantive worker-participation experiences, had no direct involvement at all themselves. Such direct experience has generally been limited to the industrial-relations executives and the plant managers, and American expatriates have only been predominant among plant managers. Specialists such as engineers, geologists, marketing specialists, and financial managers only heard or read about worker participation, and much of that exposure seemed to be somewhat remote. The perceptions of these specialists have tended to be much more negative than those of the persons who had direct personal experience, even though most of these did not necessarily become ardent converts. One might be tempted to suggest that the more detached and objective evaluations of those not directly involved would be more accurate and therefore more valuable. However, careful attention should be paid to the probabililty that the more technical, specialist personnel often seem to be the ones who tend to be conservative, more individualistic, and more adversarial than either the industrial-relations specialists or the general managers.

THE QUESTION OF IMPACT

It should also be established that a certain number of American expatriates, who originally expected to serve overseas for the usual expatriate term of three or four years, have opted to remain overseas and forego promotions for the sake of working in a job or an environment that they have come to enjoy. It is interesting that most of these longer-term American expatriates have begun to like, if not almost prefer, European worker-participation procedures, and their perceptions differ substantially from those of the shorter-term expatriates. Their impact on corporate-headquarters practices and on labor-management relations in the U.S. economy is distinctly limited, however. They seem to be considered somewhat eccentric by their Stateside superiors and peers, as persons who have exchanged some of their American values for those of their country of assignment. Recent patterns of overseas assignments suggest that the number of Americans being assigned to Europe has been decreasing sharply. The jobs that were previously performed by short-term-assignment expatriates are increasingly performed by the few who preferred to stay overseas, by local nationals, and by third-country nationals. The impact of direct experience with European practices of worker participation in management is, therefore, limited to the number whose experience was extensive enough to become somewhat acculturated, and by the fact that the number of such people has been decreasing sharply.

Granted, then, that the number of Americans who have had direct experience with the more viable forms of European worker participation is rather small, and that many of those who have become favorably disposed have remained in Europe, thus rather removed from where policy decisions are made about labor-management reforms in the United States. This does not mean, however, that there are not at least several high-ranking executives in corporate headquarters and in Stateside operations who have had direct experience with worker participation and could thus have an impact on American practices if they so choose.

THE NATURE OF THE IMPACT

Presuming that some impact has occurred, or will occur, as a result of the direct experience of American expatriates, the question remains: what is the nature of the impact? It is to be expected that very few of those who have had direct experience would favor transferring these practices in their exact European forms. It is, of course, recognized that the practices of the several countries are, first of all, products of local cultures and experiences. The German system of codetermination, for example, is unique in form and content when compared to that of other European countries. It is also the product of a unique national history, and is thus related to the existing balance of political power between business and labor, Germany's highly centralized trade-union system, and the underdeveloped structuring of trade unions at the factory and office level. Also essential were the defeat of nazism, with the concomitant determination by the occupation powers and trade unionists to prevent the resurgence of fascism, and numerous other variables that are distinctive of Germany's history of worker participation. Similar observations can obviously be made about the practices in the other nations. None of these could simply be grafted on or substituted for American practices because those, too, have been derived from their own singular heritage.

Part of the reason that the championing and adoption of European practices is highly unlikely is the parochialist orientation of most Americans. Many Americans are convinced, for example, that their nation is more than a melting pot of the cultural heritages of its immigrant population. In fact, many tend to see the American way of life as the ultimate hybrid or the purest distillate of all that is good and noble in human existence. Any assertion, therefore, that Western Europe may have evolved socioeconomic patterns that are worthy of being grafted on the body economic of the United States is sharply resented. Many American business managers also remember how their managerial know-how became the model for the modernization of business firms all over the world. They distinctly recall that this was the case in Western Europe immediately after World War II. What they have forgotten is that advantages can be temporary. This same American failure to recognize the merits of socioeconomic innovation from abroad has made them unaware of how Europeans have been considerably ahead of Americans in making their cities pleasant places to live (most of them with urban transportation systems that are far more advanced than those of most American cities). Europe has also learned that societal planning does not automatically signify a Soviet-style command economy and that such planning can be done democratically. Goal-planning does not have to be followed by the total centralization of all economic decisions, but merely by a system of mutually agreed-upon incentives and commitments.

Another obstacle to the complete adoption of European worker-participation practices is the fact that a considerable number of American corporate managers would at least prefer to see them modified so that the system would not be trade-union dominated. Another group would undoubtedly like to see works councils instituted if they would assume some of the rights and responsibilities of union locals. Similar feelings undoubtedly exist about possible domination of worker directors by unions. The endorsement by managers of the appointment of worker directors in American companies is a totally different issue. While certain people might see the benefit in some sort of labor-management committees for their plants and offices, there will be very few who could accept worker participation at the board level. Just as much as the outright transfer of European practices seems highly improbable, so, too, are the chances of their being totally rejected. It is highly likely that a considerable number of expatriates have returned to the States with negative feelings toward European practices because, as suggested above, most expatriates will not have had direct personal experience, and a number of those who did will not have worked with it long enough to overcome the understandable culture shock that accompanies an introduction to such totally un-American procedures.

Relevant here as well are the observations made about the prevalent experience of the specialists and their tendency toward total rejection of worker participation. Not only are they more prone as a group to have negative feelings toward power-sharing, but their number has obviously been larger than those who worked overseas as general managers or as industrial-relations directors. Accordingly, most expatriates have probably returned with negative inclinations and are relieved to be home, where labor-management relations can be handled in the "right" way. Thus, most expatriates who are thoroughly committed to American management's traditional values of individualism, competition, and confrontation, will still tend to be highly uncomfortable with the more consensual labor-management arrangements.

The discussion of the predominance of negative reactions to European worker-participation practices by American expatriates does not negate the conclusions in Chapter 7. Most expatriates who served as general managers and industrial-relations directors obeyed local laws and generally also conformed to local customs. Compliance with local practices, nevertheless, did not necessarily produce the conviction that all or even part of those practices would be desirable or practicable in Stateside operations. It seems likely, though, that some of those who became converts restrained their enthusiasm for a more propitious time when the corporate hierarchy might become interested or when they would have reached a position from which to initiate such desired reforms. No systematic survey has been taken of a truly representative sample of expatriates who have had direct worker-participation experience and who would also be likely to return to the States. There is, however, an overwhelming impression that only a few are apt to return to the States with the determination to initiate a holy crusade for worker participation, whatever the personal costs might be.

It seems valid to conclude that there has been some impact from the experience of American expatriates, and that the majority of them may only have had their preference for the American way of doing things reinforced. That does not mean, though, that worker participation will not increase significantly in the United States. Nor does it indicate that such changes in American corporate management, if they occur, will not, to some extent, have been stimulated by the fact that Americans gained relevant experience in Western Europe. Some of that impact will be indirect—through vehicles other than the expatriates who worked there; it will also be part and parcel of a much larger array of stimulants for change.

A fair amount of the stimulus toward labor-management reforms has come from the publicity given to German and Japanese practices. A number of the articles and television documentaries about the German and other European practices have generally referred to the fact that certain American firms have learned to work with such processes. Some have raised the same question that stimulated the writing of this book: what are the probabilities that such practices will be adopted in the United States? Until recently, the answers have not been very satisfying. It is the considered judgment of this author that much more serious attention needs to be given to the subject.

European practices have also attracted some notice by the continuing search for better forms of work organization by those academics and managers who are committed to the human-relations school of management and by those who have become involved in the quality-of-work-life movement. Additional publicity has resulted from the work of those who are committed to the democratization of American society and its workplaces. The European experiences are so noteworthy because they offer tangible evidence to be studied, even though they are not directly transferable and even though they have their distinct shortcomings. They are more useful as proof than as the mere speculations of wishful idealist thinking. The fact that fellow Americans have actually experienced the European structures and procedures makes their feedback even more useful when compared to the testimony of Germans and other nationals whose judgments might be distorted by their patriotism.

PRESSURES FOR REFORM

It is becoming more evident every day that the pressures for workplace- and corporate-governance reform are beginning to mushroom in American society. What is interesting and promising to those who desire such changes is that such pressures seem to come from a variety of sources: some of these stimuli originate in American society; others are external. Even though the voices for workplace reform from within the corporate world may have been limited, there are some who have practiced what they preached. Chapter 4 testifies to that. The same attitude is true among American trade unionists. While many of them used to consider labor-management com- mittees as disguises for speedups or planned cutbacks, an increasing number of local and even some national labor leaders have begun to recognize them as a useful device for salvaging an employer in trouble. This, after all, could mean greater job security and possibly even financial payoff for the workers. Reform is also being promoted by such governmental agencies as the Federal Conciliation and Mediation Service and the Department of Commerce.

The most significant catalysts for reform are not institutional, and some of these even have their origins outside the United States. The 1980 recession has dramatically increased the number of unemployed and has heightened the probability that there will be considerably more layoffs and plant closings. It is inevitable that all parties concerned in such tragic circumstances become increasingly aware of the moral and the financial costs of having so many fellow citizens experience such hardships that seem beyond their control. Historically, most changes in work organization in American factories have been initiated in times of trouble and distress. In some cases, they are, in fact, actions of last resort. If the 1980 recession becomes a depression or if it is combined with a series of inner-city eruptions such as occurred in 1968 and again in 1980 in Miami, the pressures for change would become undeniable. Even though workplace reform would not provide the direct solution to the problems of the American ghettos and barrios, a national surge of reform could logically include alterations in the authority structures of the workplace.

The projection of the worst-possible scenario introduces an even more important justification for seriously considering workplace reform. Limited worker participation in corporate management may well be preferable for management as well as for all other elements of the American economy compared to the alternative reforms that might be generated by the massive infusions of popular suspicions about corporate management that have already begun to occur. The talk about nationalization of the oil industry might appear spurious to some; it is dangerous to dismiss it too lightly. The possibility of always being able to bank on political clout and on the American political system's susceptibility to well-placed political pressure may be much too risky. Neither can the American people be expected to give knee-jerk endorsements continually to free-enterprise rhetoric. Rampant inflation, a distorted tax system, consistently rising corporate profits, and high managerial compensation and perks have already produced a considerable amount of alienation within the American public. Buildups of this nature almost inevitably lead to a confrontation, and it is quite possible that managerial prerogatives might become much more drastically curtailed than they already are. All these possibilities may have made genuine work reform a matter of enlightened self-interest for management as well as for workers.

The need for reform—short of the crisis circumstances painted above— is derived also from the increasing educational level of today's workers and from the simultaneous blossoming of the human-rights movement. This movement was described in Chapter 2, insofar as it has expressed itself in the workers'-rights movement. Not only are better-educated workers apt to have greater analytical abilities than did their less-educated forefathers, but they are also less inclined to appreciate or tolerate the inegalitarianism that comes with the hierarchical authority structure of the traditional workplace. Today's workers are undeniably aware of their own expertise and of the comparative ignorance about many work processes by those in corporate offices. If today's workers seem only interested in collecting their paychecks and getting out of the shop, the cause of that rejection might well be management's denial of their expertise, inventiveness, and common sense. To many of today's workers, work has become a degrading activity, a necessary evil, a way to a paycheck, and a way to more leisure-time escapism.

It may be true that much of the work that needs to be done in an industrialized society must be drudgery. This will be true as long as workers' intelligence and automation are not given an opportunity to make the work more self-fulfilling by letting the workers use their brains rather than just their brawn. Would it not be a better situation if companies invested in training their workers for more sophisticated assignments and had cybernetics take care of some of the routine tasks? Such a combination of job security and visible progress would certainly make an impact on the productivity crisis that has been haunting American industry. If such a strategy were followed, numerous existing jobs might be lost to automation, but workers would not feel threatened because enterprises would acquire the kind of flexibility and ingenuity in production and training that would create new product lines and make American products competitive again.

The most promising basis for enlarging worker participation in American management may well be the determination to solve the production crisis. Labor-management cooperation is, of course, not the only method to increase productivity, but it can play a very significant role. This certainly has been the case with quality-control groups in Japan and in the Stateside operations of such firms as Texas Instruments and General Motors' Tarrytown plant. These and other examples have been described in Chapter 4. Research has explicitly shown that an increase in the level and content of labor-management cooperation is definitely associated with an increase in group productivity.[1] While the same research showed that a productivity-related financial-reward system tends to enhance that effect, group-participation activity was the principal indicator in productivity gain.

As mentioned before, labor-management cooperation will not solve the American productivity crisis by itself. There must also be willingness by both labor and management to make better use of automation and cybernetics. In addition, management must be satisfied with longer-term payoffs rather than demanding optimum short-term profit maximization. Everyone in American society will have to become conscious of the nation's need to generate more capital by increased personal savings, or the modernization of capital equipment and factories that is so badly needed will never be possible. The prevailing urge for instant gratification through immediate consumption may be difficult to overcome, however. It may be that such hedonism is mainly compensatory and escapist behavior, a way by which all of us titillate our senses while we know that a depression is inevitable or that prolonged inflation makes delayed consumption highly unadvisable. It might be quite surprising to see the kind of lifestyle changes that could result from the infusion of a healthy dose of hope and expectation.

One of the greatest mistakes that American management could make is to use worker-participation schemes to undermine the viability of the nation's unions, and to institute workplace reforms unilaterally without the involvement and agreement of unions where they are already organized. The longevity and success of workplace reform can only be guaranteed if and when unions and management recognize reciprocal advantages. If, at any time, the unions or the workers get the impression that reforms are being used to achieve one-sided benefits, then such projects will be inextricably doomed. The adversarial system, so prevalent in our culture, has already erected an almost-insurmountable barrier of distrust and cynicism. It should not really be necessary to hold back with reform until American values have changed radically. The move from individualism to holism can only occur, though, when confidence and dignity are extended to all parties in the human organizations, including business firms.

It has been suggested by some that the introduction of worker-participation procedures could alleviate some burdensome governmental regulations of the American economy. This could certainly be the case with the much-maligned Occupational Safety and Health Administration (OSHA). American management needs to recognize that the rate of worker injuries in U.S. industry is double that of such countries as Sweden, where shop-floor safety committees have far-reaching powers to solve the particular safety problems in their plant. Since so many American workers are not unionized and therefore not protected by their union grievance procedures, it seems much more practical for management and workers to solve their safety problems together in their own shop rather than leave that job to a governmental agency. Bureaucrats must strive for uniformity and consistency in their regulations and enforcement, which, nevertheless, creates a mountain of problems. After all, who knows better what the special problems of the individual workshops are—the people who work there or the inspectors who have to deal with a great variety of operations?[2]

It is equally important for everyone to recognize that the bulk of governmental regulation was not born out of the evil conspiracy of those who wanted to destroy free enterprise. Rather, it comes from the well-meaning minds of those who were no longer willing to accept the social costs that an impersonal, socially unconscious market system has been incurring. The curious thing is that the market mechanism, of itself, need not be so costly. The problems seem to arise mainly by the unconscious and/or unconscionable way the system has been abused by some who sought increasing personal fortunes at increasingly larger costs to those who did not happen to be in the same advantageous position or who did not have the same social inheritance.

There is one smart way to undermine the inevitable demand by the public for the government to tame the carnivorous animals of the jungle. Those who may appear to be the animals might show that they are not carnivorous of themselves and that the lion and the lamb can learn to lie down together. Or, to put it in less utopian language, when management and workers recognize that they are members of communities brought together for common goals of profitability rather than combatants in a boxing ring, then the designing and construction of procedures of consultation automatically becomes a primary objective.

Responsiveness to worker dignity and interest also helps generate responsiveness to other constituencies that are challenging corporate autonomy. Workers and managers are both producers and consumers. Their honesty and self-interest will inevitably lead them to address the question of greater quantitative productivity. They will also soon discover that qualitative productivity is the best method to obtain greater consumer loyalty and continued profitability. Managers, in addition, cannot help but learn that the pursuit of product safety and environmental protection are the best policy. They certainly will save themselves and American society the cost of the bureaucracy that will inevitably result from the pressures of the socially conscious. American corporations might even find themselves blessed with a national consumer public that feels renewed loyalty to American producers who, not only will be able to offer better products at more competitive prices, but who clearly have exhibited a sense of common purpose and democratic commitment.

Workplace reforms get some of their legitimacy from the fact that they can serve as part of the movement to restore and/or maintain democracy and individuality in mass society. When men and women spend most of their energetic and creative time within authoritarian and hierarchical work structures, their understanding and appreciation of societal democracy cannot help but be qualified and easily erode. They will either become resigned and extremely cynical about noble espousals of democratic ideology or they will quickly lose any sense of political efficacy they ever had. To the detriment of the democratic processes in American society, most workers feel virtually powerless within the context of public politics. The irony of life is that their state of powerlessness is considerably greater in the workplace. Thus, in the place where the workers should have individual identity and be able to obtain some degree of personal fulfillment, they are apt to find themselves hardly distinguishable from machines, as if they were tools or instruments to be employed by those in command.

If we consider command economies and totalitarian politics totally unacceptable for American society, why should they then be acceptable in the American workplace? It is true that democracy without leadership can be chaotic and rudderless; no one is advocating that. However, in a workplace where the workers are given a chance to participate in the decision making in certain issue areas, management would still be the leader. Everyone in the organization would have little trouble understanding what the purposes of the business were. The areas that would be left for dispute would be those that dealt with the best ways of meeting those purposes and what might be the best definition of justice in the organization.

Very few workers would ever argue that their work assignments entitle them to exactly the same compensation as those who have greater skills and who are willing to give more of their time, energy, and health to the organization. However, they may well contest any authority and position that is claimed on no other basis than that such authority was delegated by those who hold titles of ownership. Modern corporations do not have owners in the traditional meaning of that term. Most holders of corporate stock are merely investors who have placed and who have withdrawn their capital as their considerations of profitability and income security direct them. The claim, therefore, that management represents those who are said to have placed their heart and soul in the organization through the provision of their capital has an increasingly hollow ring. Management can really only claim and prove its legitimacy on the basis of the comprehensive and technical leadership skills that the work organization so desperately needs and that it is contracted to provide. Even the argument that managers are entitled to absolute authority because they have made a commitment to the company has begun to wear somewhat thin. Professional managers tend to be professionals first and managers of particular firms next; they move as the new challenges, better pay, and career improvement direct. No longer do most of their "marriages" to corporations last till death do them part. The actual tenures of workers and of managers is no longer that radically different. Neither should, therefore, claim greater authority because of radical differences in commitment, at least as expressed in the length of their tenure with the firm. If anyone begins to claim greater commitment of energy and hours per day or week, he should then compare the relative ratios between pay and perks.

Those who fear worker participation should remember that pressures for democratization of the workplace are not just being felt by those who live in the capitalistic West. Similar reform pressures are being experienced by managers in Soviet Russia, the countries of Eastern Europe, and the People's Republic of China. It is extremely difficult to want to be a productive and constructive member of any enterprise where one is shrouded in anonymity (even though one may be called by one's first name) and feels so powerless, irrespective of the political-economic system in which one is working.

All these considerations lead to the conclusion that the drive for workplace reform in the United States is becoming increasingly consensus based. It may even have become somewhat unavoidable, considering slackened productivity and more vigorous competition. The experience of American expatriates in Europe may not have been the primary catalyst for such reforms; nevertheless, it has played and will continue to play a part.

Reform is apparently not contained to the American workplace. Although the presence of worker representatives on company boards is less likely to become a widespread practice in the United States—at least within the foreseeable future—it has not been totally absent. Within the span of five weeks in the late spring of 1980, the annual stockholders meeting of two well-known American companies decided to appoint directors who are generally interpreted to have been selected because of their sensitivity to employee interests.

The most celebrated and most maligned case was that of Chrysler Corporation, which decided to nominate Douglas A. Fraser, former assembly worker at Chrysler's DeSoto Division and currently president of the United Auto Workers Union to the company board. It insisted on having Fraser rather than leave the selection of a nominee to UAW's Chrysler Department. In that way, the company leadership could insist that it did not really nominate a worker representative, but that it merely selected a particular person with his own special qualities. In that way, the potential stumbling block and precedent of establishing constituency representation other than the stockholders, was avoided.

Fraser, in his public statements, exercised great care to point out that he would prevent any possibilities of conflict of interest by staying out of all board actions that would deal directly with collective-bargaining strategy. At the same time, he emphasized that he would participate in every item of board business, including the matter of general collective-bargaining strategy, plant closings, production transfers, new technology, product planning, and major investments. In that way, he would clearly represent the workers' interests without representing a workers' institution.

The Rath Packing Company of Waterloo, Iowa, went considerably further than Chrysler did in making Fraser one of its eighteen directors. Rath's company employees were authorized to be represented by ten individuals, which would give them a clear majority of the total board membership of sixteen. In addition, a plan was approved to issue 60 percent of the company's sharply devalued stock through a wage-withholding plan to be extended over a two-year period. Local No. 46 of the United Food and Commercial Workers International Union, AFL-CIO, designated two retired Rath employees, one of whom was the retired general manager of the Waterloo plant. Two were current employees, and six were "outsiders." The latter group included former Senator Dick Clark, a high-school principal, a construction company's executive vice-president, an attorney, and a university professor. Tove Helland Hammer, an assistant professor of organization behavior from Cornell University, was the university professor. Three of the "outsiders" were from Waterloo.

The ratio of employee representation is not the only thing that made the two situations different. The size and dollar value of annual sales of one company is clearly much larger than the other's. There are, at the same time, a number of interesting similarities. Both companies had been running lengthy and very sizable deficits. Very drastic, last-resort measures seemed to be called for. Both companies had also either obtained commitments for or had received actual aid from the federal government. Rath already had a $3-million loan and expected to receive a $4.5-million grant after the employees would have gained control. Some will undoubtedly allege that employee control may, in fact, have been a way to get the grant they needed to modernize the Waterloo plant.

What the trend will be from now on is somewhat difficult to predict. Fraser said that the UAW would present the issue of placing a union representative on the board of another major automobile manufacturer during the 1982 contract-negotiation cycle. Remarks by Peter Bommarito, the leader of the United Rubber Workers, suggest that other companies may be confronted with the issue even before that date. Having already demanded the appointment of a worker-board representative from the General Tire Company in 1973, he certainly did not rule out the issue for firms like Uniroyal and Firestone, both of which have recently experienced dramatic decreases in business. The Communications Workers of America have had board representation "under continuous review," even though it has been mainly a project for the future. Their president, Glenn E. Watts, has been quoted as agreeing with Fraser that "the mushrooming of corporation size and power obliges unions to consider more direct involvement in the corporate decision-making process." The same story in which Watts's statement was contained reported that "a survey of key unionists indicates that the Fraser appointment would set a pattern for similar demands on a broad front."[3] This would particularly be the case if the courts do not interpret the union leader's board membership as presenting a conflict of interests. Equally significant would be workers' reactions to Fraser's conduct as a member of the Chrysler board. Most crucial would be the fate of the Chrysler Corporation. If the firm rises from its ashes, trade unionists would obviously attempt to show how worker involvement does not destroy, but stimulates, distressed corporations.

Were Chrysler to be revitalized and were it possible, even partially, to link Fraser's contributions and improved worker morale to that resurgence, American firms might find themselves experiencing a long-lasting impact of the European experience. That certainly would be the case if corporate managers heeded the words of Arthur Burns and Douglas Soutar, both of whom are significant voices in the American business community. Mr. Soutar, Asarco's vice-president for industrial relations, has projected worker directors to become the "in-thing" in the future. He said that he personally could see some situations where they would be a good thing and described those situations to be cases where companies were in trouble. Soutar's comment is particularly significant because he is known to be a very influential shaper of labor policy for the Business Roundtable, American business's most powerful lobby organization, and for the National Association of Manufacturers. Mr. Burns projected it to be an educational opportunity for labor-union leaders to sit in on board meetings and to study company affairs.[4] That is exactly what German businessmen reported as one of the results of codetermination in their country.

So we have come the whole way. Some Americans went to Europe and experienced what they thought they would never see back home. Meanwhile, back home, movements for work reform, employee rights, labor-management consultation, quality-of-work-life projects, and quality-control circles had begun to emerge in a quiet, trial-and-error pattern. Occasionally, the initiatives came from employers who wanted to prevent the unionization of their employees. At other times, unions and management arrived at the reforms by the process of collective bargaining and consultation. There have also been circumstances in which entrepreneurs were paternalistically or democratically motivated to give their workers dignity and recognition in consideration for their experience and insights. Whatever the motivations have been, an increasing number of American workers are participating in the management of their work. Some day, they and their representatives will undoubtedly be welcome in a larger realm of decision-making opportunities, not to gain control of their company, but to have a chance to share their ideas and hopes.

It will be interesting to see when the suggestion of Louis Brandeis, presented in 1915, will become common practice in the United States. In his testimony to the National Commission on Industrial Relations, he suggested:

The employees must have the opportunity of participating in the decisions as to what shall be their condition and how the business shall be run. They must learn also in sharing that responsibility that they must bear the suffering arising from grave mistakes, just as the employer must. But the right to assist in making the decision, the right of making their own mistakes, if mistakes there must be, is a privilege which should not be denied to labor. We must insist upon labor sharing the responsibilities for the result of the business.[5]

NOTES

1. Richard D. Rosenberg and Eliezer Rosenstein, "Participation and Productivity: An Empirical Study," *Industrial and Labor Relations Review* 33 (April 1980): 355-67.

2. Matt Witt, "Learning Job-Safety and Health from Europe," guest editorial, *The New York Times*, May 7, 1979.

3. *The New York Times*, April 27, 1980.

4. Ibid.

5. Louis D. Brandeis, "The Curse of Bigness," in Daniel J. Boorstin, *The American Primer* (Chicago: University of Chicago Press, 1966), pp. 761-62.

BIBLIOGRAPHY

Albeda, W. "Between Harmony and Conflict: Industrial Democracy in the Netherlands." *Annals of the American Academy of Political and Social Science* 431 (May 1977): 74-82.

_____. "Changing Industrial Relations in the Netherlands." *Industrial Relations* 16 (May 1977): 139-40.

Alutto, J. A. "Typology for Participation in Organizational Decision Making." *Administrative Science Quarterly* 17 (March 1972): 117-25.

Athos, A. G. "Is the Corporation Next to Fall?" *Harvard Business Review* 48 (Jan.-Feb. 1970): 49-61.

Balfour, W. C. *Industrial Relations in the Common Market.* London: Routledge & Kegan Paul, 1972.

Barkin, Solomon, ed. *Worker Militancy and Its Consequences, 1965-1975: New Directions in Western Industrial Relations.* New York: Praeger Publishers, Special Studies, 1975.

Batt, William L., and Weinberg, Edgar. "Labor-Management Cooperation Today." *Harvard Business Review* 56 (Jan.-Feb. 1978): 96-104.

Bendiner, Burton B. "A Labor Response to Multinationals: Coordination of Bargaining Goals." *Monthly Labor Review* 101 (July 1978): 9-13.

Bendix, Reinhard. *Work and Authority in Industry: Ideologies of Management in the Course of Industrialization.* Berkeley: University of California Press, 1974.

Benello, C. George. *The Case for Participatory Democracy: Some Prospects for a Radical Society.* New York: Grossman Publishers, 1971.

Berg, Ivar. *Managers and Work Reform: A Limited Engagement.* New York: The Free Press, 1978.

Bernstein, Paul. *Workplace Democratization: Its Internal Dynamics.* New Brunswick, N.J.: Transaction Books, 1980.

Berry, A. P., ed. *Workers Participation: The European Experience.* Leamington Spa, England: Coventry and District Engineering Employers' Association, 1974.

Bluestone, Irving. "The Union and Improving the Quality of Worklife." *Atlantic Economic Review* 24 (May-June 1974): 32-37.

Bok, Derek C., and Dunlop, John T. *Labor and the American Community.* New York: Simon and Schuster, 1970.

Bomers, G. B. J. *Multinational Corporations and Industrial Relations: A Comparative Study of West Germany and the Netherlands.* Assen, Netherlands: Van Gorcum, 1976.

215

Bonanno, J. Bautz. "Employee Codetermination: Origins in Germany, Present Prac-
    tice in Europe, and Applicability to the United States." *Harvard Journal on
    Legislation* 14 (1977): 947-85.
Bouvard, Margarite. *Labor Movements in the Common Market Countries: The
    Growth of a European Pressure Group.* New York: Praeger Publishers, 1972.
Burns, Tom R., ed. *Work and Power.* London: Sage Publications, 1979.
Bussey, Ellen M. "Relations Between Management and Labor in West Germany."
    Monthly Labor Review 93 (Aug. 1970): 28-34.
Butteriss, Margaret. *Job Enrichment and Employee Participation.* London: Institute
    of Personnel Management, 1971.
Carew, Anthony. *Democracy and Government in European Trade Unions.* London:
    George Allen and Unwin, 1976.
Chruden, Herbert J., and Sherman, Arthur W., Jr. *Personnel Practices of American
    Companies in Europe.* Washington, D.C.: American Management Association,
    1972.
Clegg, H. A. *The System of Industrial Relations in Great Britain.* Totowa, N.J.:
    Rowman and Littlefield, 1972.
Cooper, Cary L. *The Quality of Working Life in Western and Eastern Europe.*
    Westport, Conn.: Greenwood Press, 1979.
Cooper, M. R. "Changing Employee Values: Deepening Discontent?" *Harvard Business
    Review* 57 (Jan.-Feb. 1979): 117-25.
Cox, Robert W. "Labor and Hegemony." *International Organization* 31 (Summer
    1972): 385-424.
Craypo, Charles. "Collective Bargaining in the Conglomerate, Multinational Firm:
    Litton's Shutdown of Royal Typewriter." *Industrial and Labor Relations Review*
    29 (Oct. 1975): 3-25.
Cullingford, E. C. M. *Trade Unions in West Germany.* Boulder, Colo.: Westview
    Press, 1977.
Cuthbert, N. H., and Howlans, K. H. *Company Industrial Relations Policies: The
    Management of Industrial Relations in the 1970s.* London: Longmans, 1973.
Davies, P. I. *Industrial Democracy: The European Experience.* London: Her Majesty's
    Stationery Office, 1976.
Delamotte, Yves. "The 'Reform of the Enterprise' in France." *Annals of the American
    Academy of Political and Social Science* 431 (May 1977): 54-62.
Derber, Milton. *The American Idea of Industrial Democracy.* Urbana: University of
    Illinois Press, 1970.
_____. "Collective Bargaining: The American Approach to Industrial Democracy."
    Annals of the American Academy of Political and Social Science 431 (May
    1977): 83-94.
_____. "Some Further Thoughts on the Historical Study of Industrial Democracy."
    Labor History 14 (Fall 1973): 500-611.
De Schweinitz, Dorothea. *Labor-Management Consultation in the Factory: The
    Experience at Sweden, England and the Federal Republic of Germany.* Hono-
    lulu: University of Hawaii, 1966.
Douty, Harry M. *Labor-Management-Productivity Committees in American Industry.*
    Washington, D.C.: National Commission on Productivity and Work Quality,
    1975.

Dufty, N. F. *Changes in Labour-Management Relations in the Enterprise.* Paris: Organization for Economic Cooperation and Development, 1975.

Dunlop, John T., and Galinson, Walter. *Labor in the Twentieth Century.* New York: Academic Press, 1978.

Dunning, John H. *The Role of American Investment in the British Economy.* London: P.E.P.-Broadsheet 507, February 1969.

Ellenberger, James. "The Realities of Co-Determination." *American Federationist* 10 (Oct. 1977): 15.

European Commission. *Conference of Work Organization, Technical Development and Motivation of the Individual, Working Papers.* Brussels: European Commission, 1974.

_____. *Employees' Participation and Company Structure.* Brussels: European Commission, 1975.

European Economic Commission. *The Protection of Workers in Multinational Companies.* Brussels: European Communities Information, 1976.

_____. *Worker Participation in the European Community.* Brussels: European Communities Information, 1977.

European Trade Union Confederation. *E.T.U.C. Objectives, 1976-1979.* Brussels: ETUC, 1976.

_____. *Supplement to Report on Activities, 1973-1975.* Brussels: ETUC, 1976.

Ewing, David. *Freedom Inside the Organization.* New York: E. P. Dutton, 1977.

_____. "What Business Thinks About Employee Rights." *Harvard Business Review* 55 (Sept.-Oct. 1977): 81-94.

_____. "Who Wants Corporate Democracy?" *Harvard Business Review* 49 (Nov.-Dec. 1971): 12-28.

Fayerweather, John. "Elite Attitudes Toward Multinational Firms: A Study of Britain, France and Canada." *International Studies Quarterly* 16 (Dec. 1972): 422-90.

Fenn, D. H., Jr. "Responding to the Employee Voice." *Harvard Business Review* 50 (May 1972): 83-91.

Flanagan, Robert J., and Weber, Arnold R. *Multinational Corporations and International Labor Relations.* Chicago: University of Chicago Press, 1974.

Foy, Nancy, and Gadon, Herman. *The IBM World.* London: Eyre, Methuen, 1974.

_____. "Worker Participation: Contrasts in Three Countries." *Harvard Business Review* 54 (May-June 1976): 71-83.

Furlong, James. *Labor in the Boardroom: The Peaceful Revolution.* Princeton, N.J.: Dow Jones Books, 1977.

Garson, G. David. "The Codetermination Model of Workers' Participation: Where Is It Leading!" *Sloan Management Review* 18 (Spring 1977): 63-78.

Gennard, John, and Steuer, A. M. "The Industrial Relations of Foreign-Owned Subsidiaries in the United Kingdom." *British Journal of Industrial Relations* 9 (July 1971): 143-59.

Godson, Roy. *The Kremlin and Labor.* New York: Crane, Russak, 1977.

Graham, G. "Labour Participation in Management: A Study of the National Coal Board." *Political Quarterly* 38 (April-June 1967): 184-97.

Greenberg, Edward S. "The Consequences of Worker Participation: A Clarification of the Theoretical Literature." *Social Science Quarterly* 56 (Sept. 1975): 191-209.

Gribbin, J. D. "The Impact of Direct Foreign Investment on the United Kingdom."
    Business Economist 7 (Summer 1975): 51-70.

Guest, Robert H. "Quality of Work Life: Learning from Tarrytown." *Harvard Business
    Review* 57 (July-Aug. 1979): 76-87.

Günter, Hans, ed. *Transnational Industrial Relations.* London: Macmillan-St. Martin's
    Press, 1972.

Hahlo, H. R. *Nationalism and the Multinational Enterprise.* Leiden, Netherlands:
    A. W. Sijthoff, 1973.

Haire, Mason, et al. *Managerial Thinking: An International Study.* New York:
    John Wiley and Sons, 1966.

Hartmann, Heinz. "Codetermination in West Germany." *Industrial Relations* 9 (Feb.
    1970): 137-47.

Heise, Paul A. "The Multinational Corporation and Industrial Relations: The
    American Approach Compared with the European." *Industrial Relations-
    Relations Industrielles* 28, no. 31 (1973): 34-55.

Hellman, Rainier. *The Challenge to U.S. Dominance of the International Corporation.*
    Cambridge, Mass.: Dunellen, 1970.

Herding, Richard. *Job Control and Union Structure: A Study on Plant-Level Industrial
    Conflict in the United States with a Comparative Perspective on West
    Germany.* Rotterdam: Rotterdam University, 1972.

Hodges, Michael. *Multinational Corporations and National Government: A Case
    Study of the United Kingdom's Experience, 1964-1970.* Lexington, Mass.:
    Lexington Books, D. C. Heath, 1974.

Hovels, B. W. M. *Ondernemingsraad en Medezeggenschap.* Nijmegen, Netherlands:
    Sociological Institute of the Catholic University, 1976.

Hu, Y. S. *The Impact of U.S. Investment in Europe: A Case Study of the Automotive
    and Computer Industries.* New York: Praeger Publishers, 1973.

Huddleston, J. "Industrial Democracy." *Parliamentary Affairs* 25 (Summer 1972):
    224-33.

Hunnius, G., ed. *Workers' Control: A Reader on Labor and Social Change.* New York:
    Random House, 1973.

International Labour Office. *Multinational Enterprises and Social Policy.* Geneva:
    International Labour Office, 1973.

International Labour Organisation. *Multinationals in Western Europe: The Industrial
    Relations Experience.* Geneva: ILO, 1975.

_____. *Participation of Workers in Decisions Within Undertakings.* Labour-
    Management Relation Series No. 33. Geneva: ILO, 1969.

_____. *Social and Labour Practices of Multinational Enterprises in the Petroleum
    Industry.* Geneva: ILO, 1977.

_____. *Social and Labour Practices of Some U.S.-Based Multinational Corpo-
    rations in the Metal Trades.* Geneva: ILO, 1977.

_____. *Workers' Participation in Decisions within Undertakings.* Labour-Manage-
    ment Relation Series No. 48. Geneva: ILO, 1976.

International Organization of Employers. *Multinational Enterprises: The Reality of
    Their Social Policies and Practices.* Geneva: International Organization of
    Employers, 1974.

ITT. *European Attitudes to Multinationals.* Brussels: ITT Europe, 1976.

Jenkins, David. *Job Power: Blue and White-Collar Democracy.* New York: Penguin Books, 1973.

Johnstone, Allen W. *U.S. Direct Investment in France.* Cambridge: M.I.T. Press, 1965.

Kamin, Alfred, ed. *Western European Labor and the American Corporation.* Washington, D.C.: Bureau of National Affairs, 1970.

Kanter, Rosabeth Moss. "Work in a New America." *Daedalus* 107 (Winter 1978): 47-78.

Kapoor, A. *The International Enterprise in Transition.* Princeton, N.J.: Darwin Press, 1972.

Kassalow, Everett M. "Conflict and Cooperation in Europe's Industrial Relations." *Industrial Relations* 13 (1974): 156-63.

_____. *Labor Relations in Advanced Industrial Societies: Issues and Problems.* Washington, D.C.: Carnegie Endowment for International Peace, 1980.

_____. *Trade Unions and Industrial Relations.* New York: Random House, 1969.

Kerr, Clark. "The Trade Union Movement and the Redistribution of Power in Postwar Germany." *The Quarterly Journal of Economics* 68 (Nov. 1954): 535-64.

Kolvenbach, Walter. *Employee Councils in European Companies.* Deventer, Netherlands: Kluwer/Metener, 1978.

Kujawa, Duane. *International Labor Relations in the Automobile Industry.* New York: Praeger Publishers, 1971.

_____, ed. *International Labor and the Multinational Enterprise.* New York: Praeger Publishers, 1975.

Levinson, Charles. *International Trade Unionism.* London: George Allen and Unwin, 1972.

Levitan, Sax A., ed. *Blue Collar Workers: A Symposium on Middle America.* New York: McGraw-Hill, 1971.

Lindblom, Charles E. *Politics and Markets: The World's Political Economic Systems.* Basic Books, 1977.

Lisieur, Fred G. *The Scanlon Plan: A Frontier in Labor-Management.* Cambridge: M.I.T. Press, 1958.

_____. "The Scanlon Plan Has Proved Itself Good (examines the principles of an employee participation-in-management incentive system")* Harvard Business Review* 47 (Sept.-Oct. 1969): 109-18.

Macbeath, Innis. *The European Approach to Worker-Management Relationships.* New York: British-North American Committee, 1973.

McGregor, D. *The Human Side of Enterprise.* New York: McGraw-Hill, 1960.

MacKinnon, Neil L., and Roche, William J. "Motivating People with Meaningful Work." *Harvard Business Review* 48 (May-June 1970): 97-110.

Malles, Paul. *Trends in Industrial Relations Systems of Continental Europe.* Ottawa: Task Force on Labour Relations, 1969.

Marcus, Sumner, and Walters, Kenneth D. "Assault on Managerial Autonomy." *Harvard Business Review* 56 (Jan.-Feb. 1978): 57-66.

Markham, Jerry W. "Restrictions on Shared Decision-Making Authority in American Business." *California Western Law Review* 11 (Winter 1975): 217-54.

Martin, Benjamin, and Kassalow, Everett, eds. *Labor Relations in Advanced Industrial Societies: Issues and Problems.* Washington, D.C.: Carnegie Endowment for International Peace, 1980.

Mills, Ted. "Europe's Industrial Democracy: An American Response." *Harvard Business Review* 56 (Nov.-Dec. 1978): 143-52.

Mire, Joseph. "European Worker's Participation in Management." *Monthly Labor Review* 96 (Feb. 1973): 9-15.

_____. "Improving Working Life: The Role of European Unions." *Monthly Labor Review* 97 (Sept. 1974): 3-11.

Mulder, Mauk. "Power Equalization Through Participation?" *Administrative Science Quarterly* 16 (March 1971): 31-38.

Myers, Scott M. *Managing Change.* New York: The National Industrial Conference Board, 1970.

National Center for Productivity and Quality of Working Life. *Directory of Labor-Management Committees,* 2d ed. Washington, D.C.: National Center for Productivity and Quality of Working Life, 1978.

Nichols, Theo. *Ownership, Control and Ideology.* London: George Allen and Unwin, 1969.

Northrup, Herbert R., and Rowan, Richard K. "Multinational Union Activity in the 1976 U.S. Rubber Tire Strike." *Sloan Management Review* 18 (Spring 1977): 17-28.

_____. "Multinational Union Management Consultations: The European Experience." *International Labour Review* 116 (Sept.-Oct. 1977): 153-70.

Organization for Economic Cooperation and Development. *The Development of Industrial Relations Systems: Some Implications of the Japanese Experience.* Paris: OECD, 1977.

_____. *Gaps in Technology.* Paris: Organization for Economic Cooperation and Development, 1970.

_____. *Workers' Participation.* Paris: OECD, 1976.

O'Toole, James. "The Uneven Record of Employee Ownership." *Harvard Business Review* 57 (Nov.-Dec. 1979): 185-97.

Pascale, Richard T. "Personnel Practices and Employee Attitudes: A Study of Japanese- and American-Managed Firms in the United States." *Human Relations* 31, no. 7 (1978): 597-615.

Pateman, Carole. *Participation and Democratic Theory.* New York: Cambridge University Press, 1970.

Paul, William J., Jr. "Job Enrichment Pays Off." *Harvard Business Review* 47 (Jan.-Feb. 1968): 61-78.

Peninou, George, et al. *Multinational Corporations and European Public Opinion.* New York: Praeger Publishers, 1978.

Perlmutter, Amos. "The Tortuous Evolution of the Multinational Corporation." *Columbia Journal of World Business* 4 (Jan.-Feb. 1969): 9-18.

Peterson, Richard B. "Chief Executives' Attitudes: A Cross-Cultural Analysis." *Industrial Relations* 10 (May 1971): 194-210.

Piehl, Ernst. *Multinazionale Konzerne und Internationale Gewerkschaftsbewegung.* Frankfurt: Europäische Verlagsanwalt, 1973.

Rawat, Christine L. *Worker Participation: A Bibliographic Survey.* Petersborough, England: Emerson, Rawat Information Services, 1976.

Ricks, David E., et al. *International Business Blunders.* Columbus, Ohio: Grid, Inc., 1974.

Riegelman, Carol. *Labour-Management Co-Operation in United States War Production.* Montreal: International Labour Office, 1948.

Rifkin, Jeremy. *Own Your Own Job.* New York: Bantam Books, 1977.

Rifkin, Jeremy, and Barber, Randy. *The North Will Rise Again: Pension Politics and Power in the 1980s.* Boston: Beacon Press, 1978.

Robert, C. R. *Geengageerde Bedrijfsstructuur.* The Hague: Nederlandse Vereniging voor Management, 1973.

Roberts, B. C. "Multinational Collective Bargaining: A European Prospect." *British Journal of Industrial Relations* 11 (March 1973): 1-19.

_____. (ed.) *Toward Industrial Democracy: Europe, Japan and the United States.* Montclair, N.J.: Allenheld, Osmun, 1979.

_____. *Trade Union Government and Administration in Great Britain.* London: Bell, 1956.

Roberts, Ivor. "Trade Union Membership Trends in Seven Western European Countries, 1950-1968." *Industrial Relations Journal* 4 (Winter 1973): 43-56.

_____. "The Works Constitution Act and Industrial Relations in West Germany: Implications for the United Kingdom." *British Journal of Industrial Relations* 11 (Nov. 1973): 338-67.

Robinson, John. "Enterprise Level Worker Participation: EEC Models and the Nine's Practices." *European Report*, No. 233, 24 May 1975.

Rodgers, William. *Think: A Biography of the Watsons and I.B.M.* New York: Stein and Day, 1969.

Rosenberg, Richard D., and Rosenstein, Eliezer. "Participation and Productivity: An Empirical Study." *Industrial and Labor Relations Review* 33 (April 1980): 355-67.

Rosner, M., et al. "Worker Participation and Influence in Five Countries." *Industrial Relations* 12 (May 1973): 200-12.

Rowan, Richard K., and Northrup, Herbert. "Multinational Bargaining in Metals and Electrical Industries: Approaches and Prospects." *Journal of Industrial Relations* 17 (March 1975): 1-29.

Rush, Harold M. F. "A Non-Partisan View of Participating Management." *Conference Board Record* 10 (April 1973): 34-39.

Said, Abdul A., and Simmons, Luiz R. *The New Sovereigns: Multinational Corporations as World Powers.* Englewood Cliffs, N.J.: Prentice-Hall, 1975.

Scase, Richard. *Social Democracy in Capitalist Society: Working-Class Politics in Britain and Sweden.* London: Rowan and Littlefield, 1977.

Schiller, Bernt. "Industrial Democracy in Scandinavia." *Annals of the American Academy of Political and Social Science* 431 (May 1977): 69-73.

Schrank, Robert. *Ten Thousand Working Days.* Cambridge: M.I.T. Press, 1978.

Schregle, Johannes. "Co-Determination in the Federal Republic of Germany: A Comparative View." *International Labour Review* 117 (Jan.-Feb. 1978): 81-97.

_____. "Labour Relations in Western Europe: Some Topical Issues." *International Labour Review* 109 (Jan. 1974): 1-22.

_____. "Workers' Participation in Decisions Within Undertakings." *International Labour Review* 113 (Jan.-Feb. 1976): 1-15.

Seider, Maynard S. "American Big Business Ideology: A Content Analysis of

Executive Speeches." *American Sociological Review* 39 (Dec. 1974): 802-15.

Servan-Schreiber, J.-J. *The American Challenge.* New York: Atheneum, 1968.

Sharman, Ben A. "Multinational Corporations and the International Metal Workers Federation." *Labor Law Journal* 24 (Aug. 1973): 453-90.

Spiro, Herbert J. "Co-Determination in Germany." *American Political Science Review* 48 (Dec. 1954): 1114-27.

_____. *The Politics of German Co-Determination.* Cambridge: Harvard University Press, 1958.

Strauss, George. "Workers Participation: A Critical View." *Industrial Relations* 9 (Feb. 1970): 197-214.

Sturmthal, Adolf. *Comparative Labor Movements.* Belmont, Calif.: Wadsworth, 1972.

_____. "Conflict and Cooperation in Europe." *Industrial Relations* 13 (May 1974): 156-63.

_____. *The International Labor Movement in Transition.* Urbana: University of Illinois Press, 1973.

_____. "Unions and Industrial Democracy." *The Annals of the American Academy of Political and Social Science* 431 (May 1977): 12-21.

_____. *Workers' Councils.* Cambridge: Harvard University Press, 1964.

Taylor, Frederick W. *Scientific Management.* New York: Harper and Brothers, 1947.

Thomson, A. W. J. *Labor in the Twentieth Century.* New York: Academic Press, 1978.

_____. "New Focus on Industrial Democracy in Britain." *The Annals of the American Academy of Political and Social Science* 431 (May 1977): 32-43.

Tugendhat, Christopher. *The Multinationals.* London: Eyre and Spottiswoode, 1971.

United Kingdom Royal Commission on Trade Unions and Employers Associations. *Donovan Report* (The Report of the Royal Commission on Trade Unions and Employer Associations, 1965-1968). London: Her Majesty's Stationery Office, 1968.

United Nations Department of Economic and Social Affairs. *Multinational Corporations in World Development.* New York: Praeger Publishers, 1974.

U.S. Chamber of Commerce. *Host Countries and Multinational Corporations.* Washington, D.C.: United States Chamber of Commerce, 1975.

U.S., Department of Commerce. *Report to Congress on Foreign Direct Investment in the U.S.* Washington, D.C.: Government Printing Office, 1976.

U.S., Department of Health, Education, and Welfare. *Report of the Special Task Force on Work in America.* Cambridge: M.I.T. Press, 1973.

U.S., Federal Mediation and Conciliation Service. *Labor Management Committee: Planning for Progress.* Washington, D.C.: Government Printing Office, 1978.

U.S., Congress, Senate, Finance Committee. *Implications of Multinational Firms for World Trade and Investment and for U.S. Trade and Labor.* Washington, D.C.: Government Printing Office, Feb. 1973.

_____. Subcommittee on International Trade. *The Multinational Corporation and the World Economy.* Washington, D.C.: Government Printing Office, Feb. 26, 1973.

Unterman, Lee D. *The Future of the United States Multinational Corporation.* Charlottesville, Va.: Virginia University School of Law (Virginia Legal Studies), 1975.

Vanek, Jaroslaw, "Decentralization Under Workers' Management: A Theoretical Appraisal." *American Economic Review* 59 (1969): 1006-14.

_____. *The Participatory Economy: An Evolutionary Hypothesis and a Strategy for Development.* Ithaca, N.Y.: Cornell University Press, 1971.

Vogel, David. "The Corporation as Government: Challenges and Dilemmas." *Polity* 8 (Fall 1975): 4-37.

_____. "Why Businessmen Distrust Their State: The Political Consciousness of American Corporate Executives." *British Journal of Political Science* 8 (Jan. 1978): 45-78.

Vogel, David, and Silk, Leonard. *Ethics and Profits.* New York: Simon and Schuster, 1976.

Von Beyme, Klaus. *Challenge to Power: Trade Unions and Industrial Relations in Capitalist Countries.* London: Sage Publications, 1980.

Walker, Kenneth. "Toward the Participatory Enterprise: A European Trend." *The Annals of the American Academy of Political and Social Science* 431 (May 1977): 1-11.

Walton, Richard. "Work Innovations in the United States." *Harvard Business Review* 57 (July-Aug. 1979): 88-98.

Watson, Thomas, Jr. *A Business and Its Beliefs: The Ideas That Helped Build I.B.M.* New York: McGraw-Hill, 1963.

Ways, Max. "The American Kind of Worker Participation." *Fortune* 94 (Oct. 1976): 168-82.

Westenholz, Ann. "Workers' Participation in Denmark." *Industrial Relations* 18 (Fall 1979): 376-80.

Wiedemann, Herbert. "Codetermination by Workers in German Enterprises." *American Journal of Comparative Law* 28 (Winter 1980): 79-92.

Wilkins, Mira. *The Emergence of Multinational Enterprise.* Cambridge: Harvard University Press, 1974.

_____. *The Maturing of the Multinational Enterprise.* Cambridge: Harvard University Press, 1974.

Williams, Ervin, ed. *Participative Management: Concepts, Theory, and Implementation.* Atlanta: School of Business Administration, Georgia State University, 1976.

Wilpert, Bernhard, et al. *Workers' Participation in an Internationalized Economy.* Kent, Ohio: Comparative Administration Research Institute, Kent State University, 1978.

_____. *Labor Relations in the Netherlands.* Ithaca, N.Y.: Cornell University Press, 1969.

Windmuller, John P. "Industrial Democracy and Industrial Relations." *The Annals of the American Academy of Political and Social Science* 431 (May 1977): 22-31.

Young, Stephen, and Hood, Neil. "Multinational and Host Governments: Lessons from the Case of Chrysler, United Kingdom." *Columbia Journal of World Business* 12 (Summer 1977): 97-134.

ABOUT THE AUTHOR

TON DEVOS is Professor of Political Science at Trinity University in San Antonio, Texas. He is the author of *Introduction to Politics*.